JIM JARMUSCH

INTERVIEWS

CONVERSATIONS WITH FILMMAKERS SERIES
PETER BRUNETTE, GENERAL EDITOR

Courtesy of New Line Cinema Corp.

JIM
JARMUSCH

INTERVIEWS

EDITED BY LUDVIG HERTZBERG

UNIVERSITY PRESS OF MISSISSIPPI / JACKSON

www.upress.state.ms.us

Copyright © 2001 by University Press of Mississippi
All rights reserved
Manufactured in the United States of America

09 08 07 06 05 04 03 02 01   4 3 2 1

♾

Library of Congress Cataloging-in-Publication Data

Jim Jarmusch : interviews / edited by Ludvig Hertzberg.
     p. cm.—(Conversations with filmmakers series)
   Includes index.
   ISBN 1-57806-378-7 (alk. paper)—ISBN 1-57806-379-5 (pbk. : alk. paper)
   1. Jarmusch, Jim, 1953– —Interviews. 2. Motion picture producers and
directors—United States—Interviews. I. Hertzberg, Ludvig. II. Series.

PN1998.3.J33 A5 2001
791.43'0233'092—dc21   2001024069

British Library Cataloging-in-Publication Data available

CONTENTS

INTRODUCTION

IN THE PRESS RELEASE notes for *Stranger Than Paradise,* the film that first brought him substantial notice, Jim Jarmusch half-mockingly described his film as "a semi-neorealist black-comedy in the style of an imaginary Eastern-European film director obsessed with Ozu, and familiar with the 1950s American television show *The Honeymooners.*" In many ways, the statement is characteristic of Jarmusch, perhaps the most gifted and invigorating of the American independent directors of the last two decades. As the interviews that follow also reveal, he has always been fascinated with mixing culturally very different ingredients to form something uncategorizably new, to transcend the boundaries between high and low, to offer a fresh look at America, and the familiar, by incorporating the point of view of a stranger, while always maintaining a sense of humor in—and about—his craft.

"I still consider myself," Jarmusch told Jonathan Rosenbaum in a 1994 discussion, "as kind of a fake film director. Because I started making films with my friends, basically, and writing things with them in mind. And I have kind of continued that procedure. . . ." Filmmaking, for Jarmusch, has never had much to do with how it is conventionally conceived, either in terms of production or aesthetics. Instead, he has taken a road less traveled by, and that, indeed, has made all the difference. From the time of his first feature-length film, *Permanent Vacation,* which he finished while still in film school, to the recently released *Ghost Dog: The Way of the Samurai,* interviewers have been curious about the Way, as it were, responsible for the offbeat, deadpan quality which sets his films apart. Tirelessly, Jarmusch speaks of how he conceives his films "from the inside out," how he starts with an actor in mind, how he draws from the collection of random notes that he is constantly jotting down, and how he lets the story and mood of the film evolve from that. Also, he is always eager to acknowledge his debt to filmmakers and artists in other areas whom he has been influenced by or has borrowed from, just as he never fails to stress the important role played by the cast and crew in shaping and co-creating the films he directs.

Whenever he is asked to theorize about the style, themes, or philosophy of his films, however, Jarmusch's responses are much more reserved; "I'm the worst person to analyze [my] stuff and I hate looking back at it," he told Rosenbaum two years later, in an interview also included here. Likewise, in a recent conversation with Chris Campion, Jarmusch says of the sense that there is a deeper connection between *Dead Man* and *Ghost Dog* that he would rather not attempt to analyze it himself: "Better to leave that up to someone smarter than myself who can explain it to me sometime," he says, only half in jest. He insists that he does not remember his earlier films very well, as he has a hard time watching them once he is done with them. And furthermore, he often points out that he is not very fond of sharing his views on his films because he regards other people's different interpretations of them to be at least as valuable as his own and is afraid that his own reflections would only impose.

Interviewers eager to have Jarmusch reflect on his life and career find themselves in a tough spot. Over and over, he notes that he is not a very self-analytical person, and claims, furthermore, that none of his films are auto-biographical in any significant sense. He speaks about growing up in Akron, Ohio, about the inspiration he drew from the New York punk rock scene, about his prolonged semester in Paris where he was supposed to study literature but ended up spending most of his time watching films at the Cinéma-thèque, and about his experiences in film school and what he learned as an assistant to Nicholas Ray. However, being anything but self-centered, he is usually quick to turn such questions about himself into an opportunity to share his enthusiasm about other artists, to express his gratitude to people who have helped him along the way, or to tell very amusing anecdotes. Characteristically, when he talks to Danny Plotnick in 1994 about the option of giving lectures, the idea of sharing his views on filmmaking or explaining his aesthetics does not even enter his mind: "I think I would throw together a bunch of disconnected things. Talk a little bit about films I liked or experiences I've had or anecdotes that aren't related to film at all or maybe read a couple poems that I like."

Throughout his career, Jarmusch has exhibited and maintained an extraordinary degree of integrity in his work and in his relation to the generally profit greedy movie business around him. Since he is one of the front figures of independent cinema, the subject of financing versus complete creative control is a theme that naturally crops up in many of the interviews. Indeed, one of the biggest frustrations in Jarmusch's career seems to have been not being able to raise funds for an idea for a film he had after *Mystery Train*. Secretively, he repeatedly refers to the circumstances surrounding this as "too complicated" to go into, and notes that that was why he embarked on a totally different, unplanned project, *Night on Earth*. As he told Plotnick, "I got very frustrated and ended up writing *Night on Earth* very fast—in about eight days." Like *Ghost Dog*'s main character, Jarmusch has always stayed loyal to his code, regardless of what this has ultimately cost him. His aesthetic preferences seem to have stayed pretty much intact over the years, with some subtle exceptions. He seems, for instance, to have become more flexible in his zeal for "pure" and "minimal" structures and in the skepticism about camera movement and non-diegetic music which he expressed in some of the earlier interviews. Of course, this shift is also mirrored in the films themselves, especially from *Dead Man* onward.

"When Jarmusch answers questions," Jane Shapiro wrote in her 1986 *Village Voice* interview, "he usually begins by hesitating, then making a few false starts, casting about for some words; then swings into a long fluent exposition: in summation, repeats his thesis; then stops. A calm appropriate-seeming silence falls. He waits for the next question, and he can wait in purposeful serenity quite a while." But talking to her about the situation of being interviewed, Jarmusch says, "I *don't* feel articulate. In the films, the stuff I write, the dialogue is so minimal and often there's—well, *always*—there's some kind of communication problem between people. I love language, and I love listening to the way people talk, the way they *elide* things, and the way people are *inarticulate* I like. But my ideas aren't—I don't feel comfortable just talking. Also, I don't like to talk very personally, I feel like it's psychoanalytic. There's a place for that and it's not really in publicity for something. And it's hard to distinguish, too, if something is just publicity, or if you're *actually talking to someone*, or if you're talking to *the press*, or if you're talking to *people who are going to read this?* That confuses me. I'm very confused by that."

Read consecutively, the interviews included here chronicle the career and sensibility of a thoroughly independent mind. Jim Jarmusch comes across throughout as a very kind and attentive person with a warm sense of humor and an ever-glowing affection and dedication for his art, and for all the small and marginalized—the sad and beautiful—aspects of the world.

In conformity with the policy of the University Press of Mississippi in regard to its interview series, the interviews collected in this book have not been edited in any significant way. While this may result in some repetition in Jarmusch's remarks, it offers more integrity for the scholarly reader. More importantly, these repetitions, marks of the director's personality and lasting vision, are themselves never less than revealing. In two cases I was offered and decided to take the opportunity to include interviews in their entirety, rather than in the abridged edits in which they were originally published, since in both cases much of significant interest was originally excluded. I have also decided to include two interviews which have been translated back into English, and I hasten to remind the reader of the second-hand nature of the conversations as they appear here. There is an overriding risk that the translations may often differ from the original conversations in details and language, though it is my hope that there is a correspondance at least in spirit and essence.

In assembling this work, I have received invaluable help from a great number of people. I am especially grateful for the assistance offered by Jonathan Rosenbaum, Gerald Peary, Vreni Hockenjos, Larry Da Silveira, Megan Farrell, Stefanie Koseff, Rachel Dengiz as well as all the authors and editors I have corresponded with in preparation for this book. At the University Press of Mississippi, Anne Stascavage, Seetha Srinivasan, and Walter Biggins have also been wonderfully cooperative. Thanks, finally, to my parents and, of course, Ulrika.

CHRONOLOGY

1953   Born 22 January in Akron, Ohio.

1972   Enrolls in the School of Journalism at Northwestern University.

1973   Transfers to Columbia University, New York City, to study English and American literature.

1974–75   Spends his final semester at Columbia abroad, in Paris, France, where he spends most of his time at the Cinémathèque.

1976–79   Enrolls in the Graduate Film School at New York University, where he studies for four years. The fourth year he doubles as Nicholas Ray's assistant during his time as teacher at the department. During this period Jarmusch is also a member of a New Wave band called the Del-Byzanteens.

1979   Starts working on *Permanent Vacation,* his first full-length film, with money from a grant intended to pay for his tuition. Unhappy with this fact, the school does not award him a degree (until years later). The film wins a prize at the Mannheim Film Festival in Germany and gets some recognition in Europe.

1982   Shoots *Stranger Than Paradise,* a half hour film, on unexposed film material left over from Wim Winders's film, *The State of Things.*

1984   Releases the full-length version of *Stranger Than Paradise,* which wins the Camera d'Or at the Cannes Film Festival.

1986   Releases *Down by Law,* which, among other things, introduces Italian comedian Roberto Benigni to the rest of the world.
Embarks on his on-going short film project *Coffee and Cigarettes.*

1989   *Mystery Train* is released.

1991   *Night on Earth* is released.

1993   The third installment of the *Coffee and Cigarettes* series (*Somewhere in California*) wins the prize as best short film at the Cannes Film Festival.

1995   *Dead Man* is released.

1996   Shoots the music film *Year of the Horse* with Neil Young and Crazy Horse, which is released the following year.

1999   *Ghost Dog: The Way of the Samurai* premieres at the Cannes Film Festival.

FILMOGRAPHY

1980
PERMANENT VACATION
Production Company: Cinesthesia Productions
Producer/Director/Writer/Editor: **Jarmusch**
Cinematography: Tom DiCillo
Music: **Jarmusch** and John Lurie
Cast: Chris Parker (Aloysious "Allie" Parker), Leila Gastil (Leiha), Maria
Duval (Latin girl), Ruth Bolton (mother), Richard Boes (war veteran), John
Lurie (sax player), Eric Mitchell (car fence), Sara Driver (nurse), Frankie Fai-
son (man in lobby)
77 minutes / Color

1982
STRANGER THAN PARADISE
This short became the first part (*The New World*) of the feature film released
in 1984 under the same title.
30 minutes

1984
STRANGER THAN PARADISE
Production Company: Cinesthesia Productions, Grokenberger Film-Produk-
tion, with the co-operation of ZDF, Kleine Fernsehspiel, Christoph Holch
Producer: Sara Driver
Director: **Jarmusch**

Screenplay: **Jarmusch,** Part One (New World) based on an idea by **Jarmusch** and John Lurie
Editor: **Jarmusch,** Melody London
Cinematography: Tom DiCillo
Music: John Lurie, "Music for Two Violas" by Aaron Picht, song; "I Put a Spell on You" by and performed by Screamin' Jay Hawkins
Cast: John Lurie (Bela "Willie" Molnar), Eszter Balint (Eva), Richard Edson (Eddie), Cecillia Stark (Aunt Lottie), Danny Rosen (Billy), Rammellzee (man with money), Tom DiCillo (airline agent), Sara Driver (girl with hat)
89 minutes / B&W

1986
DOWN BY LAW
Production Company: Island Pictures, Black Snake, Grokenberger Film-Produktion
Producer: Alan Kleinberg
Director/Writer: **Jarmusch**
Editor: Melody London
Cinematography: Robby Müller
Music: John Lurie
Cast: Tom Waits (Zack), John Lurie (Jack Romano), Roberto Benigni (Roberto), Nicoletta Braschi (Nicoletta), Ellen Barken (Laurette), Billie Neal (Bobbie)
107 minutes / B&W

1986
COFFEE AND CIGARETTES
Production Company: Black Snake
Producer: Jim Stark
Director: **Jarmusch**
Screenplay: **Jarmusch,** Roberto Benigni, and Steven Wright
Editor: Melody London
Cinematography: Tom DiCillo
Cast: Roberto Benigni (Bob) and Steven Wright (Steven)
6 minutes / B&W

1989
MYSTERY TRAIN

Production Company: Mystery Train, Inc. for JVC
Producer: Jim Stark
Director/Writer: **Jarmusch**
Editor: Melody London
Cinematography: Robby Müller
Music: John Lurie
Cast: FAR FROM YOKOHAMA: Masatoshi Nagase (Jun), Youki Kudoh (Mitzuko), Screamin' Jay Hawkins (night clerk), Cinqué Lee (bellboy), Rufus Thomas (man in station); A GHOST: Nicoletta Braschi (Luisa), Elizabeth Bracco (Dee Dee), Tom Noonan (man in diner), Stephen Jones (the Ghost), Sara Driver (airport clerk), Richard Boes (second man in diner), Jim Stark (pallbearer); LOST IN SPACE: Joe Strummer (Johnny), Rick Aviles (Will Robinson), Steve Buscemi (Charlie), Tom Waits (radio DJ)
110 minutes / Color

1989
COFFEE AND CIGARETTES (MEMPHIS VERSION)
Production Company: Black Snake
Producers: Rudd Simmons and Jim Stark
Director: **Jarmusch**
Screenplay: **Jarmusch**, Cinqué Lee, Joie Lee, and Steve Buscemi
Editor: Melody London
Cinematography: Robby Müller
Cast: Cinqué Lee, Joie Lee, Steve Buscemi
8 minutes / B&W

1991
NIGHT ON EARTH
Production Company: Locus Solus in association with Victor Company/Victor Musical Industries/Pyramide/Le Studio Canal Plus/Pandora Film/Channel 4
Producer: **Jarmusch**
Director/Writer: **Jarmusch**
Editor: Jay Rabinowitz
Cinematography: Frederick Elmes
Music: Tom Waits
Cast: Winona Ryder (Corky), Gena Rowlands (Victora Snelling), Giancarlo

Esposito (YoYo), Armin Mueller-Stahl (Helmut Grokenberger), Rosie Perez (Angela), Isaach de Bankolé (driver), Béatrice Dalle (blind woman), Roberto Benigni (Gino), Paolo Bonacelli (priest), Matti Pellonpää (Mika), Kari Väänänen, Sakari Kuosmanen, Tomi Salmela (men)
129 minutes / Color

1993
COFFEE AND CIGARETTES (SOMEWHERE IN CALIFORNIA)
Production Company: Cinesthesia Productions
Producers: Demetra J. MacBride and Birgit Staudt
Director: **Jarmusch**
Screenplay: **Jarmusch**, Iggy Pop, and Tom Waits
Editors: Terry Katz and **Jarmusch**
Cinematography: Frederick Elmes
Cast: Iggy Pop and Tom Waits (as themselves)
12 minutes / B&W

1995
DEAD MAN
Production Companies: 12-Gauge Productions, Pandora Film with the support of FFA Berlin Filmboard/Berlin-Brandenburg/Filmstiftung NRW
Producer: Demetra J. MacBride
Director/Writer: **Jarmusch**
Editor: Jay Rabinowitz
Cinematography: Robby Müller
Music: Neil Young
Production Design: Bob Ziembicki
Costumes: Marit Allen
Cast: Johnny Depp (William Blake), Gary Farmer (Nobody), Robert Mitchum (John Dickinson), Milli Avital (Thel Russell), John Hurt (John Scholfield), Crispin Glover (train fireman), Gibby Haines (man with gun in alley), Gabriel Byrne (Charlie Dickinson), Lance Henriksen (Cole Wilson), Iggy Pop (Salvatore "Sally" Jenko), Billy Bob Thornton (Big George Drakoulious)
120 minutes / B&W

1997
YEAR OF THE HORSE
Production Company: Shakey Pictures
Producer: L. A. Johnson
Director: **Jarmusch**
Editor: Jay Rabinowitz
Cinematography: L. A. Johnson and **Jarmusch**
107 minutes / Color

1999
GHOST DOG: THE WAY OF THE SAMURAI
Production Companies: JVC, Le Studio Canal + and Bac Films present in
association with Pandora Film, ARD-Degeto Film a Plywood production
Producers: Richard Guay and **Jarmusch**
Director/Writer: **Jarmusch**
Editor: Jay Rabinowitz
Cinematography: Robby Müller
Music: RZA
Cast: Forest Whitaker (Ghost Dog), John Tormey (Louie Bonacelli), Isaach de
Bankolé (Raymond), Camille Winbush (Pearline), Cliff Gorman (Sonny Val-
erio), Henry Silva (Ray Vargo), Tricia Vessey (Louise Vargo), Victor Argo
(Vinny), Gene Ruffini (Old Consigliere), Richard Portnow (Handsome Frank)
116 minutes / Color

JIM JARMUSCH

INTERVIEWS

Conversations with Jim Jarmusch

RALPH EUE AND WOLFGANG STUKENBROCK/1980

THE TEXT IS COMPILED from interviews that Ralph Eue and Wolfgang Stukenbrock did with Jim Jarmusch on October 10, 1980, during the 29th Filmwoche in Mannheim, and on February 22, 1981, during the 11th International Forum for Young Film in Berlin. Translated [into German] by Ralph Eue.

You have said that the actor who plays Aloysious Parker served as an inspiration for you [for Permanent Vacation]. *How did you work together, and in what way did you turn his real life into the story of the film?*
The story was inspired by how Chris actually lives his life. He has no commitments; in real life he doesn't have a place of his own either, he stays with different friends, and he does not have a job. He is not a professional criminal, but in order to get money he might commit some petty crimes just as long as nobody gets hurt. He would never assault anyone. He might sell drugs, or borrow money from a lot of people without hardly ever paying them back. Basically, he is a drifter.

He is a very intelligent person, but he is not interested in school. He dropped out of school when he was mine. He was in some reform schools and juvenile prisons. He is very, very smart.

His ability to interact with people, to talk to strangers, to make them feel comfortable, is in reality much stronger than you can tell from the film.

Published as "Gespräche mit Jim Jarmusch" in *Filmkritik*, Vol. 25:10, No. 298, October 1981, pp. 453–60. Reprinted by permission. Translated from the German by Vreni Hockenjos.

When I was setting out to do the film, I imagined that he would be more flexible. But preparing the shots with him, setting up the scenes, having to take care of the other actors, of locations, connections—all that made it difficult to render him as spontaneous as he actually is.

Are the things that Allie experiences based on real events?
It is not a documentary—everyone is acting. About half of the things that happen to him in the film actually occurred to him; and the other half I made up for him. I thought up situations and placed him in them.

It is not a documentary, and neither is it a realistic film with a critical or romantic touch—it is something else. I would like to know something more about the way in which you turned the reality into a kind of film which at this moment I cannot name.
I am not sure about that myself. I think the thing is that people like him do not have a center in their life. In other words: his life is a kind of rebellion, but not a focused rebellion, not really politically motivated. He does not have any firm convictions, neither in the film nor in reality. He meets people, but he knows from the outset that he will move on and meet some other people. That is something the structure of the film attempts to imitate or express.

It is obvious that Allie is not anything like a "rude boy," on the contrary he is cautious and sensitive. In other films—I call them "Concrete and Neon" films—the heroes gradually succumb to their rotten circumstances until they are no more than symptoms of them.
I think a lot of people get it wrong when it's depicted in the way you just described it—it's always about violence and brutality, and the characters who are thrown into this dangerous world become ruthless themselves. There is nothing of that in *Permanent Vacation.* I want to point out that I have very consciously kept violence and sex, and anything else that is used for the sake of sensation, out of the film. Not because I don't like that in films, but because I want people to pay more attention to the spiritual realm where Allie is living in his mind.

His character is not active, he is passive. Even his plans to go away are an expression of that. The car he steals comes to him almost like a gift—he had no plans whatsoever to do that. It's important that he is passive rather than active, because I wanted people to observe him and his situation. The audience should not be up against what he is up against. I wanted that distance always to be there.

It's a curious passivity. One point is that he's never quite at one with the atmosphere around him. I don't think he is unconcerned with or defenseless against what the world around him is doing to him. Indeed, he is very strong himself. He is, rather, very much himself. He is only passive when it comes to relationships with other people.

He has simply rejected certain aspects of daily life. In most films you'll have confrontations or external things which trigger a certain reaction. I, on the other hand, was interested in the little things and in connecting them. Take the saxophone player by the window early in the morning. Then he hears a joke about a saxophone player, and later he meets the saxophone player from that morning again. Or: he talks to this guy about this car—and then he sees that same car from the roof top, and you don't know whether it's really what he sees or just a recurring image. Or: A guy tells him a joke about a man who went to Paris and then at the end of the film he goes to Paris himself for no special reason and when he does he meets a guy who has just arrived from Paris.

It is more about accidental connections that move the audience than about dramatic action, such as being chased by the police or having an argument with your girlfriend or stuff like that.

Here in Germany, we have a type of film which deals with social problems, parents, school, work, and so on. First it seems like one of those films tells the story, for instance, of a young kid, but then the only thing they focus on is the social frame of problems, and the kid disappears more and more from the film, and in the end everything is just about the social institutions trying to find a way for him.

The question is how to treat social problems. A lot of people criticize my film politically; they say it's an art film, it's harmless, and does not take a clear stand. But whenever I watch a film—even if I almost completely agree with its political aims—I will still lose my interest as soon as I notice that the conclusions are self-evident, because then there is nothing left to discover.

Something I found very strange was that you have a story that takes place today, and then there is an atmosphere which is perhaps contemporary, but is not really

up to date. I mean, he reads Lautréamont; he likes Charlie Parker; he plays an Earl
Bostic record on the old record player. I ask myself what, and how much, all that
can actually mean to a young guy like him today.
Chris is also, in real life, fascinated by this jazz era, by Earl Bostic and all that
stuff from the late forties and fifties. It took place before he was born, he
wasn't there. He was born in the mid sixties so he missed out on the whole
Beat movement of the fifties in the U.S. It is important to him because it
belongs to a time prior to his birth.

I think that is part of it. You are fascinated with a period to which you
don't have direct access. You are influenced by it because you would have
liked to be there. You missed out on a piece of culture and that is exactly
why it becomes important to you.

Charlie Parker, for instance, means a lot to Chris; his graffiti tag is
"Chan"—that was Charlie Parker's pseudonym when he did recordings with
record companies while contracted elsewhere; he took a pseudonym so he
would not be sued.

Why is there not also some contemporary music that he likes in the film?
I kept it out intentionally; I didn't want the film to be seen as belonging to
this or that New York or London scene—that shouldn't matter. That would
have been like inviting the public to an audience with the present by pro-
claiming "This film portrays the new wave lifestyle."

That's not what I wanted to express; in other words: Lautréamont lived a
life that can be brought into contact with the ideas of the new wave—but
still there is no direct link.

I didn't want to make a rock'n'roll film. That is why we also emphasized
the way Chris looks: as if from the fifties, like Gene Vincent. And to under-
line this even more, I chose Earl Bostic as the only found, non-original music
in the film. I wanted him to dance in the bop style of the fifties and not to
some "new wave" or "no wave" rock'n'roll.

Of course I hope that people who are into what is called new wave can
also get something out of *Permanent Vacation,* but at the same time I don't
want the film to be labeled "new wave" by anyone. I have avoided any ico-
nography that might point in that direction.

I have heard that the music in the film is gamelan music. I found it hard to accept
the contradiction between this ritual music, which I associate with peace and medi-
tation, and the constant intensive white noise of New York City.

I chose Javanese gamelan music which is slower than Balinese gamelan music; I slowed it down even more on the tape and reworked it a little bit electronically: I added some echo and filtered out certain frequencies in some parts.

To me, there is no contradiction between this meditative music and the sound of New York. When you live in New York, you get used to the constant noise; it's around even at night. I recently went away from New York to the countryside over the weekend, and the silence there made me nervous. I had difficulties falling asleep, because there weren't any noises.

I felt the same contradiction in the images as in the sound. This drifter, Allie, embodies someone very edgy and restless—once he even says: "Sometimes I think I should live fast and die young"; but the images are the exact opposite; the camera never attempts to imitate this hectic life, instead it is calm, observant and pays focused attention to Allie's actions in a very contemplative fashion.
I found I needed to use a camera style that is very static, almost like in Japanese films, where the camera very often is motionless. Had I decided to use more lavish camera movements it would have ruined what goes on between the people within the shot, and it would have distracted the viewers' attention.

A moving camera forces the eyes of the viewer to move along with the image, it imprisons your gaze. But my film has nothing to do with such arbitrary movements—it's about observing, about watching the hero in an almost voyeuristic fashion.

And if the camera moves after all, it is always a very calm, never a violent movement. The cuts are never fast either, they are gradual and pensive. It is the style of a contemplative camera. People should observe the characters and the locations and not notice the camera too much. I think the locations say enough by themselves without the camera having to point it out to you: "Look here, look there!"

When I force myself to pay attention to the editing of a film, I often feel like I'm bothering with something not worth doing. However, in Permanent Vacation *I noticed cuts at several occasions that I found meaningful; the encounters are not just depicted—what's taking place there is also expressed in the cutting and set-up.*
It is really beautiful when he meets that Spanish singing girl and his two sentences "Are you alright?" and "What are you singing?" determine the basic mood

of that scene, while camera movements, the camera settings and editing turn it into
a melody. The way Allie approaches the girl—he doesn't push himself on her, but
he accepts her anxiety and her hysterical breakdowns—he is not greedy for sensa-
tions, and this corresponds to the way the camera relates to the whole situation.
That scene is edited a little less traditionally than the others. The camera was
supposed to observe, but not from Allie's point of view—subjective camera
is used very rarely in the film: when he comes back into the room and the
girl is gone, we see what he sees.

The basic idea of the scene with the Spanish girl was that he hears something without knowing what it is; in other words: the camera shouldn't see
anything before he can see it. The camera shows her at the very moment
that he sees her, only from a different angle and from a little closer up. And
then we see him, but she doesn't notice him until he starts talking; and while
he is talking we watch her reaction. After that the camera leaps back to show
both of them. Then she tells him to get lost and the camera goes even further
back to show the entire location.

The whole point is that you observe and experience things the way he
does; but at the same time you are separated from him and you observe
him—you don't watch the things through his eyes, but the way they occur
to him as they take place.

I got the impression that you brought the editing in line with the mood of this brief
encounter. It's not your intention to label the event as particularly crazy or weird,
instead you make the tensions within it visible.
All the people he meets in the film are without jobs; they live in the street
and are in the same situation that he is. They aren't his enemies. He wouldn't
understand people who walk around in suits carrying briefcases, he'd find
them alien. He might be mean to them, as to the girls with the car; they have
a car, they have pretty clothes, and they have an apartment in one of the
nicer neighborhoods; you can sense that simply from the way they look and
act.

But he feels a connection with the Spanish girl. She's not totally alien to
him. It's not like "Oh, you're crazy, you're weird, you're not like me," but
more like "You don't belong here, neither of us belongs here—perhaps I'll
find out something about myself if I figure out a little bit about you; maybe
we've got something in common." That's more important than the fact that
she's crazy and that they can't talk to each other, because he doesn't know

Spanish and she's too upset to speak any English. They are both misfits, homeless; they don't belong in the normal social structure, they don't have jobs, they don't have any money, they are not useful members of society. He responds to people like her with understanding and not with aloofness.

Did Chris accept the role of Allie as being him?
Very much. I asked him what he wanted to be called, and he sought out the name Aloysious himself; he thought it was a funny name, and he wanted his character to have a funny and unusual name.

Sometimes it was quite difficult to get him to act in front of the camera, sometimes it was difficult even just to get him in front of the camera. Sometimes we couldn't find him at all, once for two whole days—and we had only scheduled fourteen days of shooting. Sometimes he was difficult to get hold of; we could then find him sleeping in the apartment of somebody he hardly knew. Every now and then I had to play private detective in order to track him down.

But he pretty much accepted the character as himself. And he actually had plans to go to Paris when we were done shooting—not necessarily because of the film, but because he felt he wanted to go someplace, and he somehow got stuck with the idea of Paris—maybe because of the film, maybe because of his French friends or some other people.

What about the color? It is always bluish—was that some kind of mistake or an intended effect?
I shot on reversal instead of negative film, because I like the quality; and besides, I could get the material really cheap from a friend who makes his living by selling film material which he buys from TV stations, sometimes legally, sometimes illegally.

I shot on 7240, also called Video News Film, which has a bluish tint. My cinematographer said that we could shoot on negative and then filter to get same effect. But we thought, why should we do that when this is what we want; so we intentionally made this choice in order to get the color quality. And since the film has to do with being isolated, and, also, New York seems to be a kind of ghost town, the blue color somehow enhances that feeling. I would deliberate very carefully before using this material again—it would have to fit the story and idea of the film.

I only know a few films by Nicholas Ray. His name appears in the end credits, and you say that the film was sort of dedicated to him. Can you tell me something about how he influenced you, and about your relation to his films and to him as a person?

I admired him long before I got to know him. His films were very important to me. And then when I met him and was able to work with him and got to know him better—I cannot express how much I learned from him as a human being.

Nick told me that the working title for almost all his films was "I'm a Stranger Here Myself." In *Johnny Guitar*, Sterling Hayden says this line to somebody in a bar. And there's this documentary about Nick—not a very good one—which is called *I'm a Stranger Here Myself*. That's the theme of all his films, people who don't understand the laws that are supposed to govern them.

I admire the way he managed to walk on a very thin edge: making big budget films in Hollywood on the one hand and bringing something subversive into each one of them on the other hand. He was very cunning, because I don't suppose that his producers had a clue about what he was actually up to, and this may even be true of his actors.

Do your admire his film The Savage Innocents *the most, or why do you quote it in your film?*

I have about ten favorite Nick Ray films. Only a few of his films are poor, and that was, I guess, because he was someone who took risks. And if you take a risk and fail the result is terrible, but if you succeed it is marvelous; and I believe he always risked everything.

I wish Nick was still alive. I would be curious to hear what he would think about my film. When I was writing the script, I showed it to him frequently. He used to say stuff like: "Let this boy be chased by the police, the police always gotta chase him. He's running away from the police, and finally he escapes on board that ship, he wants to get off the ship again when all of a sudden this girl appears, she pulls a gun and kills him." That's the kind of ideas he had, they would have made a wild Nick Ray film, and I liked them, too, though I never would have used any of them because they were too much his style. He influenced me more through the way he worked with actors. A lot of that went into the film, though that isn't all too obvious right away.

The last shots—when he stands at the harbor waiting for the boat—remind me of photo album snapshots or polaroid pictures.
Do you mean the quality or the color?

Both. I got the impression that the images were treated to have such an effect; they are more artificial than the rest of the film.
The only thing that is different is the quality of light. It was cloudy and the light was more diffuse. Had it been a sunny day, we would have shot anyway. I like that you got that impression—nobody has mentioned that likeness to polaroids before—because one thing that isn't too obvious in the film is: if you pay attention to the voice over at the beginning and the end of the film, it's clear that the film takes place in the past, since the voice over is narrated from the future, or rather, from the present.

I wanted the film on one level to be something he remembers: the dissolves were meant to indicate that. The series of empty rooms dissolves into the past in the last shot. In other words: the room is now empty, but then the dissolve fills it with the girl, the bed, the record player—they appear out of the nothing which is the beginning, as in a flashback. But I did not want to emphasize that too strongly, it was supposed to be sort of dream-like.

Why is it that he leaves New York by boat and not by plane? That is such an old-fashioned way to travel.
It is a change of pace for Allie: once in the film he says that he wants to live fast and die young, but he goes away at a very leisurely rate.
He had to take the boat, because travelling by boat or train you have more time to let your mind wander and let the past pass by. And I wanted him to take the boat because of the notion that the two continents are separated by an ocean. I wanted to suggest that he has to cross an ocean to get to the other side: if he had flown it would just have meant covering a certain distance, whether over land or water or whatever.

Jim Jarmusch

HARLAN JACOBSON/1984

AKRON'S MOST FAMOUS SON, other than the Goodyear Blimp, is Jim Jarmusch, whose *Stranger Than Paradise* refashions the image of the American landscape. It's Cleveland where God sat when he made Lake Erie. It's *Guernica* without the terror, a rusting industrial theme-park, where we are the mice left after the giants have died, and existence is a hipster's hustle.

More than a story of aliens and alienation, *Stranger Than paradise* is about the decline of standards. Jarmusch's three characters—Eva, Willie, and Eddie—are doing a hodge-podge *Wizard of Oz* return to the American dream. The road is endless, and the same, everywhere the same. No yellow bricks, nobody home at the controls, just Dumb Luck armed with a wicked humor. This is life as lived by Ralph Kramden, Ed Norton, and Alice transplanted to the eighties, where TV is still the eye that binds.

Jarmusch's second film (the first, *Permanent Vacation*, is an 80-minute pre-amble about drifting), *Stranger Than Paradise* is a black-and-white three-parter that begins with Eva (Eszter Balint) dropping down from Budapest into the New York lives of Willie (Richard Lurie) and Eddie (Richard Edson), a couple of Damon Runyon updates in shades and squashed fedoras. This is the New World, and the joke is on her. The streets are beat, the place is shot, and the culture satirizes itself: "Quality You Can Trust" reads the sign on the bombed-out gas station; "U.S. Out of Everywhere" (something only popped

Published in *Film Comment*, Vol. 21, No. 1, January/February 1985, pp. 54, 60–62. Reprinted by permission.

bubbles can accomplish) screams the graffiti. In the backstory, Budapest was probably in color.

Eva's introduction to Willie was all there was of *Stranger* originally—30 minutes of footage squeezed from 40 minutes of leftover stock donated by Wim Wenders after *State of Things*. Like Eva, Jarmusch came into cash—the paltry $120,000 needed for parts two and three. But this is old news. Still hot, *Strangers* unfolds Jarmusch's new talent in a series of *tableaux vivant* into which his three selves shatter and settle. Ohio, you see, is not a state of mind, after all. It's a state of being—*Just* like the other 49.

You're the hottest name in town now. Are you getting calls from the executives?
Yeah, I am actually, but uh I'm not really interested in doing that right now.

Why?
Because I want to have complete control over my work and I want to make small steps. I don't want to jump into something over my head. I don't want to work with a union crew or have someone telling me how to cut my film or who's going to be cast in it. And also because I have the opportunity to make my next one or two projects with European coproductions which give me part or, hopefully, half ownership in my own film. So it just makes a lot more sense to me to keep it under control and make steps as I go, instead of jumping into some kind of studio production which is not interesting to me now.

Can you identify what influenced the making of Stranger Than Paradise?
I have a lot of influences. Anything that moves me influences me somehow. I take from European and Japanese films and also from America: The characters are really American. There's something very American about the film and yet formally, it's not traditional at all, it's very untraditional. That comes from the way I write, which is backwards: Rather than finding a story that I want to tell and then adding the details, I collect the details and then try to construct a puzzle or story. I have a theme and a kind of mood and the characters but not a plotline that runs straight through. I think that's partly why the narrative takes the form that it does. My first film *(Permanent Vacation)* was similar—and the two things that I am writing now I'm writing in the same way.

The idea of first having the plot scares me. This is more exciting for me, there's something in the process. The story starts to tell itself to me, rather than me formulating it.

When I looked at the film, I thought, That's what this country really looks like—not like Bucks County, Pennsylvania—but like Akron (where Jarmusch grew up).
Yeah, I have a real fondness for those post-industrial landscapes. There's something really sad but really beautiful about them. I don't know if it's just nostalgia for growing up in Akron, but it is America to me much more than big cities, or clean forests, or anything like that. It's extremely ugly, but I also find it very beautiful somehow.

The joke in the film is that in coming here, Eva (Eszter Balint) experienced this incredible decline in standards and values; life in Budapest was a lot nicer.
Yeah. I mean it as a reverse on what we're told about the quality of life in Eastern Europe: gray, depressing, industrial. Eva's coming to the new world to start a new life. She has a sense of adventure, but when she gets here she finds this even tone to every place she goes in the country. Very bleak and very depressing. I think that works a lot in favor of her sense of humor in the film. The contrast makes the humor work, I think. Even though the film wasn't intended to be funny.

Both Willie and Eddie were very different male characters than we're used to seeing. Where did you get them?
Well, John Lurie and I were discussing a story (that the first part of the film eventually evolved into) and our first criterion was not to be like other New York films that are being shown in Europe and being called New Wave—whatever that means. We wanted characters not associated with any kind of music or fashion scene. And although they're working class, they're not really involved in a working class milieu. Their values are not the same. They're more like gamblers and drinkers. They're not really workers. But they're in that milieu. They're the kind of characters who might meet at the racetrack somewhere rather than any place fashionable.

Yeah, they go out to Cleveland with six hundred and they spend . . .
Fifty.
  That's a minor theme—the way money works for them. It's something

that you get by stealing, cheating, lying, crime, or by chance. It's not something that you invest your daily schedule or create the structure of your whole life around. Something that you get as you need it. That will probably be a theme in every film I make. Because I'm not really interested in characters obsessed with some kind of ambition. That kind of American dream thing is just not really interesting.

People in Akron believe in it. When you lived there, did you fit in?
No. I was sort of um, I don't know, withdrawn. Especially in high school, I never felt part . . . that's when everyone is forming social groups and none of them seemed to have anything to do with me. I didn't feel that I had anything in common with them really. So, I was pretty much outside of things.

You used Eva, as an alien, to parade your vision of this country. Did either your leaving Akron or returning to it find its way into this picture?
Yeah, but the film is about all of the characters, not just her. All three of them are really outsiders. The view we get of America from all of them is very much outside of the expected one. It's about people who are outside. And I guess that concern must come from my own experiences of feeling that way. But it's also an approach to doing stories that are not about ambition.

What about ambition don't you like?
Well, I don't like the idea of fashioning your life around money, or lifestyle. It seems just too predictable. There are so many other ways of living. There are people who aren't aspiring to be fashion photographers.
    I've been getting scripts from Hollywood that I've been reading just out of curiosity. Some I've refused by their descriptions on the phone. But I've read maybe ten of them and every single script is concerned with ambition and rise. If there is any class consciousness in the stories, it's always someone rising to the top.

Were you a working class kid?
No, I'm middle class. My father originally worked, when I lived in Akron, for Goodrich. And then he worked for various small businesses and stuff. He has a law degree but he's never really used that. He's just been a small businessman.

So when he was at Goodrich he was. . . .
He was in personnel.

And it was a working class town.
Yeah, pretty much.

Is that one reason you were an outsider, because kids identified you as being better off than they were?
I don't really think so. I don't think it's that, I think it's more of what was interesting or important to me didn't seem to be what was cool to be interested in or what was supposed to be important. I think it's more that than class. I lived a lot in Cuyahoga Falls, a suburb of Akron, where I went to high school. It's homogeneous middle, lower-middle, and working class—500,000 people and there's no blacks and no Jews in the whole city, you know. It's kind of a ridiculous place. There was no tension, because people weren't aware of any kind of class divisions, really. You know, everyone aspired to have certain things—two cars, their own house, a color TV,—but that was about it.

Why didn't you buy in?
Well, first of all I hate the idea. I mean, I worked in factories too to pay for my education and stuff, but uh, I don't know, I just can't stand the idea of working for other people or having a boss. I never got along, or I was never able to hold jobs for very long because I just didn't like the setup. You know, your time being limited.
There's a film by Elio Petri, *The Working Class Goes to Heaven* [1971], in which the guy, Gian Maria Volonté, is a factory worker who flips out and goes home and starts smashing everything in his house. And while he's doing it, he's talking about how many hours of his life it took to buy this TV, or that stereo amplifier, or this vase. "Twenty two hours." Smash. It's really beautiful. That's sort of how I feel. I'd rather have no money at all than to schedule my whole life around acquiring it.
That's why I don't really have a desire to work in Hollywood, even though now I have the opportunity—which a lot of people spend their whole lives waiting for and don't get. It feels a little strange to have people offering me a lot of money, but to direct things that are like, you know, *Porky's* remakes. My only aspiration is to be able to keep working, to be able to pay my rent,

and not have to worry about money. That's really my biggest ambition. It's sort of a contradiction, in a way.

Does that bother your family?
What? The idea that I didn't have their ambitions? Yeah. Certainly my father it bothered a lot. Because he wanted me to go to law school, or enter business, or something like that. And it caused a lot of problems, a real separation between my father and me. But for some reason now, I think because my father is older, he accepts things much more easily than he used to. And he's proud that the film is doing well. So he's not that unhappy. But I think he would be a lot happier if I was a lawyer and didn't live in this way.

Has he been to visit?
He's never been in my apartment, but he did come to New York for the film festival to see the film.

And how did he react?
Well, I haven't really spoken to them about the film, specifically. My father saw my first film, *Permanent Vacation,* and said he thought that there was a reel missing somehow, that there wasn't a story there. He said, "I don't think I saw the whole thing, did I?" And I said, "Yeah, that's it." And he said, "Well, I think something's missing from the story." They seemed to like this film [*Paradise*]. They seem to understand it more. It was more precise and more of a story for them.

How did they react both to New York and your image of it on film?
My father hates New York. He doesn't even like to come here. It just drives him nuts. He's born and raised in Cleveland. He was really happy that we were going to shoot there. Because of the limitations in time and budget we were considering shooting in Long Island City, which could have read Cleveland. But I felt really strongly for some reason in letting the actual place infiltrate the actors and the whole crew somehow. And my father liked that a lot that we shot in Cleveland. In fact, my parents let us use their house—we had the crew in sleeping bags on the floor, and in the living room, and everything. They really liked it. My father helped us a lot. My mother did too. They were real proud while we were making the film, even though they had

no idea what it was going to be or what would ever happen with it; they were really supportive and excited by the activity.

While I was watching the film it hit me that it's a lot like The Honeymooners. *Willie and Eddie reminded me of Ed Norton and Ralph Kramden. Was that accidental?*
Yeah. It is. Really, it is. They live in the same kind of conditions, but it was not really conscious on my part. I never even thought about *The Honeymooners* until after I was done shooting and Sara (Driver, whom Jarmusch lives with) was cutting the film and kept making jokes about it. And then I started finding all the connections, too: the way *The Honeymooners* was always shot from the same angle. I know they cut to another camera. It's always two camera setups, but it's always that same angel, the bleak apartment, they don't have a refrigerator. Sometimes their water doesn't come on. Things like that.

Is there something more "honest" about that America than the affluent one?
Well, I think it's more honest, but I think it's very abstracted in the film: What we choose to show is reduced. And I think it's more honest because it is a view of America that exists, that is more real for more people than the glossy TV view is. But in anything you do in a film, as soon as you make selections, you're manipulating the audience's sense of what's real and what's not. That's the whole idea of a film, so, you know, it's two-sided.

The form of this film as a narrative is so minimal it almost tricks you. It has elements like a traditional plot and it has three sections, but those sections don't do . . . what you would expect: introduce the characters, then some kind of conflict, and then a resolution. Instead, the narrative is very minimal. If you stop the film at any point and ask the audience what was going to happen next, they would have no idea. They wouldn't really be thinking about it, but would be more concerned with the characters and what's happening to them.

Okay, so what's Willie going to do in Budapest?
I don't know. He's going to try to get out of there as soon as possible. He doesn't even have his coat with him.

So he ends up being Eva, but without the "benefit" of connections.
Yeah. He's been working for ten years to dissociate himself from his past—to

be sent back is her joke on him, since he was so mean to her. But there are moments when you feel his emotions and you know he feels close to her. Well, that's Karma: He gets it back by being sent back.

Richard Edson didn't get as much press attention as did John Lurie, but his Eddie was a great character.
Well, I think the character of Willie is a little more complex than Eddie, but I like Eddie very much because he's very warm. It's the first time that Richard acted and I'm really proud of the character that we created together and proud of Richard's ability to—who's not trained as an actor, who's not an actor—to suppress elements of his own personality which did not fit Eddie's. That's really the essence of working toward a good performance.

How is Eddie out of sync with Edson?
Well, you can't just push him around, he's not someone who does what you tell him. He's pretty tough and pretty firm in the decisions he makes. He's just not a pushover. He's just not like that. But Eddie is very much like that. He just sort of goes along. He really cares for Willie to the point of going along with what Willie says, even when Willie's mean to him. It's not as important to him as Willie's other qualities that he respects.

There's a truth in their relationship, in the often unacknowledged leadership of one partner in a friendship over the other.
I don't know if that's always the case but there's something about Willie that . . . Eddie accepts Willie's character as being that way. That's just kind of the way they are.

Have you ever been Eddie?
No. I don't think I have really.

Willie?
Probably in some instances, but definitely not Eddie, because I'm pretty independent and have always been. My close friends feel equal to me in their decision making and self-respect. I've not really been in the position of having friends imitate me. There's something really warm about Eddie, there's something really kind about him, that I like a lot. I really like that character.

Have you ever been Eva?

I think I've been her more. I think I'm closer to that character. She's the one who . . . I don't know, I'm not actually any of the characters. There's a part of all of them in me, you know. And that's part of the story of this film too. Eva becomes a catalyst for the men. I mean, they make decisions based on her presence. Very loosely, but Eva instigates the decisions they make, directly or indirectly. And that's sort of another subtheme in the film. There's something about women—at least women in my life—they have been more capable of making decisions than most men. And I've learned more, especially emotionally, from women than from men. That has nothing to do with role models or anything like that; I'm pretty masculine in my interests and in my reactions to things, but at the same time, I think I've learned a lot more, I've found more wisdom from women than from men.

There is no paradise, is there?

No. Not really. I don't believe in putting a carrot in front of a mule. I think you have to face what is around you.

Florida, which is supposed to be this retirement paradise, is just a different vegetation and a slightly different landscape from Cleveland. That's something that I feel when I travel around, there's a certain continuous tone in America, especially if you don't have a lot of money. All the motels look alike within a certain price range. Although landscapes change, you're still going to the same 7-11 store. It's really that idea of the American dream that I'm not really interested in. And for that reason and for these characters, there is no paradise. It's just something that you imagine or that you construct around yourself to feel more comfortable or secure. But it's just not the reality of things.

I like these characters; their acceptance of things they way they are is important to me. They're not—they are alienated but they're not itching to improve their living conditions. They're just looking for a change, a different card game or something.

Jim Jarmusch

P E T E R B E L S I T O / 1 9 8 5

LIKE MANY PEOPLE, I have been a film junkie from an early age, and although I have witnessed thousands of films in movie houses and on television, there have been damned few that have lodged in my conscious mind as having portrayed the essence of their time without resorting to some fashion cliche. They were archetypes of a sort. *Easy Rider, Midnight Cowboy,* and *Eraserhead* jump to mind. For me, *Stranger Than Paradise* was such a film. In its sixty-seven shots, separated by blackouts, *Stranger* traces the arrival of Eva (played by Eszter Balint) in America from Budapest, Hungary, and her subsequent unwanted appearance into the life of her cousin Willie (played by John Lurie of Lounge Lizards fame) and his sidekick Eddie (Richard Edson). Together they traipse across a bleak, industrial America in a "neorealistic black comedy [made], in the style of an imaginary East European director obsessed with Ozu and *The Honeymooners.*" That self-described "East European director" is in reality Akronbred independent filmmaker/screenwriter Jim Jarmusch, who assembled *Stranger* for the paltry (by Hollywood standards) sum of $120,000. Aside from its oddball integrity, and cool, unhurried narrative style, the startling quality of *Stranger Than Paradise* is its inexpensiveness when one considers that this "little indie" film won the Camera d'Or at the Cannes Film Festival, and has garnered international distribution and critical accolades. The prospect of such unprecedented acclaim was never anticipated by the deep-voiced New York-based filmmaker, who says

---

Published in Peter Belsito (ed.), *Notes from the Pop Underground* (The Last Gasp of San Fransisco, 1985), pp. 56–71. Reprinted by permission.

that it has become a disruptive influence in his life as he concentrates on his next project. But it was the making of *Stranger Than Paradise*, Jarmusch's history, and his overnight fame that we discussed in our interview.

Where did you live when you first arrived in New York?

JJ: Well, I lived on the Upper West Side and I lived for a little while in Spanish Harlem, like Amsterdam Avenue and 103rd Street. I went to school there [Columbia] and my last year of school I went to Paris to study for a semester and ended up staying for a year. I was able to get a job there delivering paintings in a delivery truck from an American gallery.

Great job, I guess.

JJ: It sounds like it, but it was really low pay. And the guy I worked with formerly drove a beer truck in America—it was kinda funny.

What kind of paintings did you deliver?

JJ: We delivered modern European paintings mostly, some American paintings, too—to private collectors or other galleries. One time we delivered a painting by an Eastern European artist. It was about—I don't know—about a hundred pieces of heavy brown paper stacked up on each other. It was a huge painting and pieces were ripped out so he'd paint on different surfaces and tear holes in it, and we laid it down behind the truck and ran over it by accident, and it had tire tracks on the painting, then we delivered it to the private collector who didn't even notice anything different. That was typical of our expertise in handling art. But I stayed there, and that's where I really started becoming interested in film, because at the time the Cinémathèque was still run by Henri Langlois. He died, but he ran the French Cinémathèque since the forties.

Who is he? I don't know him.

JJ: He founded the French Cinémathèque, which is the largest film archive in the world. Since he died, a lot of the prints can't be located because he had them hidden in certain places, and only he knew where they were. But he was pretty amazing because he was able to—throughout the occupation of Paris during the war, he was able to hide and preserve a lot of films that the Nazis wanted to destroy or wanted the copies returned to Germany— things like that.

So you saw a lot of these films?

J J :   Yeah. That's where I first saw a lot of films that I had only read about before, especially European films or Japanese films.

Can you name a few of those films?

J J :   Well, films by Vertov, Vigo, films by Bresson, short films by Raúl Ruiz. I don't know—you probably don't know most of these people.

I'm not aware of them. They're more art filmmakers?

J J :   Well, no, I don't know. I mean, in Europe it's not quite so easily divided between commercial cinema and art films. I mean, even classic films by Renoir and things like that I hadn't really seen before. Films by Jacques Rivette I'd never seen before. Even American films—like I saw a retrospective of Sam Fuller's films there. I had only seen his films on TV late at night. So it sort of opened up cinema for me. And while I was studying—see, when I went to Columbia in New York, I really wanted to be a writer. I studied literature because I wanted to be a writer. And while I was in Paris, and when I came back from Paris, after seeing all those films, my writing became more cinematic and more visual.

What do you mean by that?

J J :   I was writing in forms I was making up that were short, structural narrative pieces, like short stories, but very short and minimalized. I don't know if it's prose-poetry, or narrative, you know, fiction—something in between. I started—I don't know if you know *The Last Words of Dutch Schultz* by William Burroughs, which is a screenplay, but it's something that could never—

Didn't Schultz mumble some obscure words, uh—

J J :   Well, when Dutch Schultz was dying he babbled on and on and with a lot of like free association stuff. Burroughs was interested in that and wrote a whole sound text around it in loosely the form of a screenplay, but a screenplay that could never really be made into a film—a sort of fake screenplay. But that's just an example; my writing started imitating certain elements of screenplays or camera directions and things without actually being scripts, just sort of incorporating that into it. And then I came back to the States and I had a grant to write and read my writing at some of the universities on the East Coast.

When was this?

J J : '75. And at that time I applied to go to NYU Graduate Film School, though I didn't have the money to go there, and I'd never made a film. I just did it to see what would happen. And I did get in, and I got financial aid.

What did you submit to get in?

J J : Writing and some still photographs.

So they accepted you on the basis of that without having made a film?

J J : Yeah, they did. Which I never expected.

That's pretty cool.

J J : Yeah. And then I was able to get a scholarship and financial aid, so I was able to go there. The director of the school was László Benedek, who directed *The Wild One* with Marlon Brando and Lee Marvin. And then I studied there for two years and then Nicholas Ray came there—was brought there by Laszlo Benedek to teach—and I was asked to be his teaching assistant. Actually, it's a three-year program at NYU, and I had completed two years and was going there to tell Laszlo Benedek that I wasn't coming back, because I didn't have the money and because I didn't really think it was worthwhile to continue going there. But Nick Ray was in his office and I met Nick and I talked to him for a long time and then László said, "I can help you get financial assistance, and Nick would like you to be his teaching assistant." So I came back for another semester and worked as Nicholas Ray's teaching assistant. And then it gets complicated. I was writing my first film at the time, *Permanent Vacation,* and showing Nick different versions of the script and he was telling me to put more action into the film. Instead, every time he'd tell me that, I'd go home and take more action out of the script and make it even more passive in a way. Just because I didn't want to imitate him. I think he respected the fact that I did that. But we became good friends, and he was dying of cancer and he was trying to make a last film before he died, which eventually was a collaboration with Wim Wenders called *Nick's Movie* or *Lightning Over Water.* Nick asked me to be a production assistant, to assist him on that film.

What exactly does a production assistant do?

J J : Just go get coffee, take care of Nick's false teeth, you know, things like that.

But it was basically your first encounter with big-time filmmaking?

J J : Yeah, but it was a European type of production—smaller crew, more intimate in a way. And I was the only person that Nick brought to work on the film. Everyone else was crew that Wim brought.

And they had all worked together before?

J J : Yeah, most of them had.

Why is it that Europeans seem to keep the same crews together all the time? It's more like a troupe or something.

J J : Yeah, I think the European way is almost the opposite way of working in Hollywood where you go out and hire people just on the basis of what union they're in. And people in Europe work with a much smaller crew and therefore they tend to keep working with the same people. Like Wim, for example—almost all of his films have been shot by Robby Müller—the same cinematographer. That film, however, was shot by somebody else—by Eddie Lachman. But it's just a different way of thinking about film, and having more control, whereas in the Hollywood studio system, usually a director is hired and his place is only to work as the director. He's not really involved in casting or editing usually. In Europe, the director pretty much has direct control over it.

He's more of a filmmaker.

J J : Yeah. It's less compartmentalized. So then Nick died in '79—June—like two days later we started shooting my first film, *Permanent Vacation,* which was a really low-budget film. We shot it in ten days in 16mm for about $15,000.

How did you raise the money for that?

J J : Well, some of the money was my tuition money I was supposed to pay to NYU to complete my studies. I made the film instead so I never actually got a degree from them.

So what was the shooting of Permanent Vacation *like?*

J J : Oh, it was pretty hectic. It was partly based on the main actor who was not an actor—Chris Parker. The film is in part based on him personally. It was kind of loose and was shot very quickly. I don't know. I haven't seen the film for like three years and I don't really want to see it again just because—I don't know—the last time I saw it, it struck me as a little pretentious in parts and was painful to watch, although I still like the atmosphere and certain kind of attitude the film has.

Do you think Permanent Vacation *will be shown, now that you've had success with* Stranger Than Paradise?

J J :   Yeah, it seems to be getting some bookings now, mostly at very small cinemas and some universities and stuff. But the bookings have picked up a lot since *Stranger.* I've been too busy to deal with it, but now I have someone working with me to book it and also to book a film that I was the director of photography on that Sara Driver directed called *You Are Not I.* That's a film based on a Paul Bowles story. He's an American writer who lives in Tangiers.

What's that story about?

J J :   It's about schizophrenia, really. It's about a woman who gets out of a mental hospital because there's a very large car accident right nearby and in all the confusion she just sort of wanders through the gate and is taken for a shock victim from the accident. She's then sent back to her sister's house even though she's supposed to still be institutionalized. And then her sister—it's funny and kind of disturbing at the same time—her sister tries to figure out why she's been brought back. It's complicated because the story comes from the narrative inside the head of the woman who escapes from the institution, so it's very unclear as to what's really happening as opposed to what are just thoughts being projected. And in the end, at least in her narrative, there is a role reversal where, through some kind of persistence which becomes almost magical, she sends her sister back to the hospital and takes her sister's place. But it's complicated to explain succinctly.

What other early projects did you work on?

J J :   I worked on a film that Howard Brookner made called *Burroughs,* a documentary on William Burroughs. I did the sound recording. Howard and I, for the first few months of the film, were just a two-man crew, with Howard shooting and me doing the sound. We spent time in Colorado filming *Burroughs,* and in New York and other places. I also did the sound recording on *Underground U.S.A.,* a film by Eric Mitchell. It's a film shot in '79 that has Jackie Curtis and Patti Astor, Rene Ricard and Eric Mitchell, too.

Were you living in the East Village by then?
JJ: Yeah, I was.

So when you went to NYU, you moved in down there?
JJ: Well, actually before that. I moved downtown, I guess, in like '75 and then I started going to NYU in '76.

So you got there when the rents were still cheap, huh?
JJ: Yeah. Just before the big increase in rents.

How much did the East Village scene influence your work?
JJ: Well, it influenced me a lot initially simply because in the late '70s, starting in like '76 or so, there was a really important spirit, especially in the music scene, because the spirit was that you didn't have to be a virtuoso musician to form a rock band. Instead, the spirit of the music was more important than any kind of technical expertise on the instrument, which of course was—in New York—first Patti Smith and Television and the Heartbreakers, the Ramones, Mink de Ville, Blondie, Talking Heads—all those bands. And that influenced a lot of people in other forms as well. The first films of Amos Poe were important. Painters like Jean-Michel Basquiat sort of came out of that scene too, in a way, although he comes more from a graffiti street scene. But those things were sort of happening at the same time.

Side by side, more or less.
JJ: Yeah. So there was a lot of excitement because you'd go to CBGB's or Max's (which still existed then), later the Mudd Club, and there was a really good spirit of exchanging ideas which now is completely gone. But at that time it was a really strong kind of, I don't know, energy that was going on.

I sense a disillusionment in your voice when you say "now it's completely gone."
JJ: Well, everyone seems to have pulled their ideas back and there's no real scene anymore, there's no real exchange of energy, there are no places to go where people are really enthusiastic about new ideas. Instead, people are more, well, I guess more careful, more cautious with their ideas and not as free to exchange them.

Why is that?

J J :   I don't know. Partly because of what happened in the music scene. Record companies came and took these bands, you know, to a higher, more commercial level and more accessible to more people. Some of them survived that, like Talking Heads. Others, you know, didn't survive at all, or changed drastically, like Blondie. Well, Blondie really sort of followed the path that they were starting on. They were more interesting as a sort of crude, Punk surf-rock band. But I'm not really sure. Also, the scene became more a spectator scene than one of participants, whereas initially it seemed like everybody at CBGB's was doing something, everyone wanted to make films or paintings or had a band or something. And now it's just not the same thing.

More tourists were showing up?

J J :   Yeah, more people that were spectators rather than people who were interested in creating something.

It went from being a neighborhood scene to being what?

J J :   Well, eventually it became international if you take Talking Heads or something as an example. And that's not necessarily bad. I'm not saying that's bad—it just happened. Maybe it's good that that happened, otherwise it would have just remained an underground scene and nobody would have gotten out of it. I don't really know. It's just a little disturbing that the energy exchange doesn't really exist anymore.

Was there a sense of historical scene-making in the East Village at that time? Did people feel like they were making history?

J J :   Well, I think it varies. Some people were conscious of that and other people weren't really thinking about the consequences or what context to put their ideas into, just the fact that they had the ideas and they wanted to express them. But I'm sure some people thought of Television as like the Grateful Dead of the '80s—I don't really know. But Television is an example of a band that didn't survive all that.

They were one of my favorite bands out of the whole scene, though.

J J :   Yeah, me too. Them and the Voidoids.

What kind of people were you meeting at this time, just in terms of influences?

J J :   Well, people from bands mostly. Well, I started to meet filmmakers, too. Through that scene I met Amos Poe and Eric Mitchell and Beth B. and

Scott B., Charlie Ahearn, James Nares, Bette Gordon and, you know, also a lot of different musicians.

Was there an active exchange of film ideas between that group of people?
J J :   Yeah, there was a real hope of the possibility of making films. It wasn't like dreams of going to Hollywood or anything like that. It was just a really strong desire and a really strong sense that it was possible to make films, without much money and without really any expertise. And that was important. Amos Poe's film *The Foreigner* I felt was really kind of important for the spirit at that time. I haven't seen it recently, I don't even know how it holds up, but I know I really liked it when I first saw it in I guess '78.

What was the club scene like at that time?
J J :   Well, the club thing was always sort of shifting. First it was CBGB's and also Max's to some degree, and for a brief time there was a club called Mother's—I think it was on 23rd Street. And then the Mudd Club seemed more like the center of things because CBGB's got a certain kind of name and so a lot of people were going there from out of town and it wasn't really as easy to talk to your friends there. And then the Mudd Club became important in that way, and there was a club called Tier 3 which was good for awhile, too. And then clubs just started opening up and closing left and right, like The Rock Lounge and Interfuron, which was the original Danceteria, I guess. Peppermint Lounge reopened in midtown before it moved downtown. There were just a lot of different clubs opening and closing all the time. So it kinda got dissipated by that, by confusion. There was no real center anymore or it would shift from month to month and gradually the thing just seemed to disappear in a way, for me. I mean, maybe other people don't feel that.

How did you first encounter each of Stranger Than Paradise's *major players? I guess we could start with John Lurie.*
J J :   Well, John I met like seven years ago and I think I first met him at the Mudd Club and then ran into him on the street a few times. One night he had gotten ripped off by some people and we were on East 5th Street and sat down and talked for like four or five hours. I don't even remember about what. And ever since then we've been friends. When I first met him it was before he had started the Lounge Lizards.

What was he doing when you first met him?

JJ: He had done some performance pieces at Squat Theatre and some other places and was just starting a band at that time. I remember when they were first starting the band they were thinking about calling it the Rotating Power Tools, which I liked a lot, but there was another band called the Power Tools so they changed it and it eventually became the Lounge Lizards.

Did he know Eszter through Squat Theatre?

JJ: Yeah, he knew Eszter through Squat Theatre.

What's her history?

JJ: Well, Eszter has been in Squat Theatre I think since she was nine or ten years old. She was born in Budapest. They performed a lot in Europe—in Rotterdam, in Paris, in Germany—and then they moved to New York and they lived in their theatre on 23rd Street, Squat Theatre. Mostly the whole company still lives in that same building.

She started playing a child in I think *Andy Warhol's Last Love* or maybe their other play *Pig, Child, Fire.* So she has since worked consistently with Squat Theatre.

Her father founded Squat Theatre, didn't he?

JJ: Well, yeah, he's the Director, I guess. Stephan Balint.

What kind of theatre do they do?

JJ: Well, it's kind of hard to categorize. I mean, it's called avant-garde theatre, although that's an outmoded term—it doesn't really mean anything anymore. It's hard to explain. Usually their plays begin with a film sequence that then turns into live action on a stage, and they almost always use random occurrences on the street within their performances. The audience faces a large window through which you can see the street and the stage is between that window and the audience so that action occurs on that stage and sometimes outside on the street, so there are always people passing by that have no idea that a play is going on, no idea exactly what's happening, that sometimes get involved or dragged into whatever's actually happening in the play itself. It's hard to describe, but they're really interesting and I always get a lot of ideas watching their stuff.

So you had seen a lot of their work?

J J :   Well, I've only seen two of their plays—*Mr. Dead and Mrs. Free*, which was their last one, and the one before that, *Andy Warhol's Last Love*. They're working on a new one now, and the one before those two I mentioned, *Pig, Child, Fire*, I never saw.

So you had seen her acting at Squat Theatre?

J J :   Yeah, well I met her and also at the same time had seen her at Squat Theatre, first in *Mr. Dead and Mrs. Free*, in a film sequence. And when I first met her I guess she was fourteen. She's nineteen now. And I had written a script after *Permanent Vacation* that I was trying to get produced, and I had written a part for her, but I was never able to get the money together to make it. And then instead, through circumstances, I made *Stranger Than Paradise*. But I had written something already—a different character and story—specifically for Eszter. That was a film that I also had written one of the main characters for John Lurie.

Did Richard Edson meet you through John Lurie?

J J :   Well, no, I don't know if I knew Richard before John knew Richard or what, but I knew Richard really just through music. And I'd seen him perform and when I had written the character of Eddie I talked to a lot of different people about doing that character but always in the back of my mind I had Richard and finally I just decided that my instincts were right and to work with him.

You gave him all the best lines.

J J :   Well, he was amazing to work with because I think he's a really good actor although he had never really acted before. I had that sense that he would be a good actor by watching him perform on stage in various bands. But he worked really hard and developed his own process. He and I, working together, created that character, and Richard was really amazing to work with because he worked really hard and seemed to be really adaptable. I don't know, it was easy for him to find a process to suppress certain qualities of himself that were not the character and at the same time emphasize the qualities of himself that were the character.

That's one of the questions about the movie I wanted to ask you. How much direction did the actors receive and were they shaped or were they primarily playing themselves?

J J :   Well, it's a combination of both. They're certainly not just playing themselves. Again, I worked individually with each actor, to create the character, and what we did was basically what I said before: find what parts of their own personalities fit with the character and what parts didn't, and then work on finding that balance in creating the character. I think good acting is always a collaboration between the director and the actor. It's not my style to just let actors do whatever they want, just be themselves. And yet I also don't want to tell them exactly when to cross the room and what direction to look in. You know, it's a collaboration.

So, first of all you wrote the part and then you worked individually with them in a private session?

J J :   Yeah, we rehearsed a lot. The film was made in two parts. It was first made as a thirty-minute film (which is now the first part of the feature version called *The New World*). That first script came from ideas that John and I had together and some of the scenes specifically he wrote or some of the scenes I wrote or conceived of, and then I wrote the thing into a story, into a script. So John and I started collaborating from the very beginning with his character by really developing the story together around his character for the first part of the film. And then, after that, I wrote the rest of it pretty much by myself, but always improvising in rehearsal with the actors, and changing things and being open to certain ideas that they had which were very important, and a lot of them helped shape the story. But also I had to remain in control of the story myself and make decisions as to what suggestions of theirs fit, and what didn't, and keep a certain control of the film, otherwise the story would have taken much different turns, because a lot of their suggestions didn't fit and a lot of them did.

The story would change as you went along?

J J :   Well, actually the story really didn't change much. Mostly what changed was the dialogue itself. We improvised off my script. The important thing is that an actor appears to be natural and not acting, so if the sentence keeps the same sense but they change the construction or the way they say it, that's what I want.

This may seem a little redundant, but I just want to cover the reasons you chose non-actors to play the leading roles, or all the roles? Except it seemed like the card players might have been actors.

J J : Well, Rockets Redglare, one of the card players—the big guy who has most of the dialogue—is a stand-up comedian and an actor. But mostly the film is non-actors, although now I think of them as actors just because of the process we went through, and their ability to be actors. But I find that people who are trained as actors, in Method acting or certain kinds of Stanislavski techniques, often are very difficult for me to work with because the—I don't know, I have a problem with actors who already have their process down completely. Sometimes I find that they're closed to other methods, and I think that every actor and director and every film is different, and the style of acting is different, and because the individuals are different, there has to be a process between the director and each individual actor to create that character, so there's no way to really teach someone exactly what guidelines to follow. I just don't believe in that. I also find that actors, especially actors who are trained in theatre, almost always tend to get too big in their acting, too over-dramatic. And what I hate about that is that whenever you watch an actor and you're aware of their process as an actor, you've completely lost the sense of the character they're creating, and then it's pointless. So I have a lot of trouble with people like Meryl Streep, for example, who I think is very proficient at the technique she uses but every time I see her in a film I'm always aware of the process she's going through as an actor, and there-fore I lose the character somehow. That is what I'd like to avoid in my future projects. What's most important to me is working with actors and getting really natural performances.

Do you think you will always work with people that you've known beforehand? It won't be some kind of bring-in-the-hired-star deal?

J J : Yeah, I don't think I could do that. If it were the case, I would have to spend a lot of time beforehand getting to know them before I could work with them.

Someone I know brought up the idea that all the characters in Stranger Than Paradise *are aimless and going nowhere and to him it almost seemed like a West-ern was the model for the film. Did Westerns ever play a part in your inspiration?*

J J :   Not specifically, although there's a certain similarity to most Westerns and to Road movies, where people are travelling. Westerns usually have some character that is drifting or aimless. But at the same time I think that most Westerns really, thematically, are about death, and this film is not. So there wasn't anything really conscious about Westerns. Although I would like to make a Western sometime.

Stranger Than Paradise, *as you just mentioned, has no death, it has no sex, and it has the most minimal chase scene possible. Why did you eliminate the three most common themes in American cinema?*

J J :   Well, I wanted to make a story that didn't have to rely on certain things that have become cliché, like character's sexuality, like certain over-blown action scenes, or overly dramatic scenes. I'm not really interested in that. For example, in one of two scripts I'm working on now, the sexuality of the characters is really important. It's a love story. But in this story, that just seemed out of place to me, and those things are often handled as clichés. The whole idea of this film was to avoid certain clichés while incorporating other clichés, details like the TV dinner, things like that—cheap hotel rooms. But in the way they're incorporated into the story—they're not used just as gags, you know.

I don't like the kind of ambition in American films, and these characters don't have ambition really and are also not intellectual characters, so it's not an existential film. They're not constantly questioning their existence or questioning the state of the world around them. Instead they have a kind of acceptance of it. Instead they move through the world of the film in a kind of random, aimless way, like looking for the next card game or something, rather than interpreting things as philosophical symbols or anything. So that relates to the reason why there isn't the violence and sex and certain ex- pected things in the film. The whole idea of the film was not really to give the audience anything that they would be expecting. And the form of the narrative itself works that way, too. If you stop the film at any point the audience wouldn't have any idea what was gonna happen next, or really be that aware or that conscious of the narrative itself. Instead they're more in- terested in smaller details, and situations, and characters. The sense of humor works in the film that way, too. It works from details, not from big gags or jokes, verbal or visual. Instead it's humor of small details.

Why did you use the blackouts?

J J : Because each scene is a single shot and leaving that image in the memory of the audience for a moment before going on to the next one was something really important to me. I didn't want to cut it picture to picture. It also solved a certain problem of cinema language for me which is, How do you indicate the lapsing of time in a film? Usually it's done with a dissolve or fade or you cut to another place and then come back and you have a sense of time, but by using those black spaces I could jump, in terms of the narrative, to ten minutes later on the same day, or two days later, or to one year later, which happens at one point, without even having to indicate that. (Although we indicate it when it's one year later.)

Did the length of the blackouts vary?

J J : They get shorter toward the end as the pace of the story picks up a little bit. That was something done very carefully. It took a long time to make those decisions and you wouldn't even know it unless you had a stopwatch, but I think the rhythm influences the story a lot. It's something that took a long time to decide. We decided each one individually.

Why was there so much emphasis on industrial ugliness?

J J : Well, I guess for two reasons. One, that I grew up in Akron and the Midwest has a very industrial kind of landscape which somehow is personally important to me. I don't know why. There's something sad and beautiful about it. And I just respond to it. But also because one aspect of the story is that Eva is coming from Central Europe where—you know, in America we have a certain image that we're given of what life is supposed to be like in Central Europe, and I wanted to reverse that, and apply it to America.

Is there a particular character trait of yours that comes across in the story?

J J : Well, I don't know, I'm interested in stories that are about people that are outside of things, as I said before, that are not obsessed with ambition or climbing to the top.

Would you say that the people in the film are a sort of caricature of yourself?

J J : Well, I wouldn't say it's a caricature, I would say that it's a part of myself that comes through in what I'm interested in, in terms of the story and characters. It's not specifically autobiographical. I think the most important personal things in the film are very small things, just things I think that other people relate to as well—the idea that Willie has trouble accepting Eva until she's gone, and only then does he realize she's like him. It's really one of the most important themes in the film, that you really don't know what you want to say to other people often until it's too late to tell them. And I think I identify with aspects of each character certainly, especially with Willie and maybe most especially with Eva. But it's hard for me to say in what way the film is very personal, because I devised the form of the film, and there are personal characteristics of just the way that it's presented and shot and cut and things, and then the writing itself contains aspects of me. But it's hard to be specific because it's not particularly autobiographical.

Has the success of the film surprised you?

JJ: Yeah, it surprised me a lot because I still think of the film as an underground film that somehow crossed over and got this fairly wide distribution—in a slow way, but real distribution—in the States, and also it's doing extremely well in Europe. So I thought that the film would be like a cult film in Europe, and in the States it would be very difficult to see.

You didn't think it would be in major theatres for weeks and weeks, huh?

JJ: No. So I've been very surprised and very happy by it, but at the same time I don't believe in thinking too much about the audience when you're making a film because when you do that you get into—whether you know it or not—a subconscious kind of sense of marketing, or like "who is the audience and what should we play to?" which to me defuses anything that is really original or strong. So I believe in not really thinking too much about what the audience will think. So I had no idea, when we finished the film, what would happen. So I was very surprised. And at the same time, because it was so well received, especially by critics, I'm really prepared for my next film to be really chewed up and pulled apart by the critics. I'm preparing myself for that, but psychologically at the same time I don't want to think about the audience or what will happen with the film I do next.

I felt that Stranger Than Paradise *was to 1984 what* Eraserhead *was to 1978 or '79. Not necessarily in terms of the content or even the way the film was made, but just in terms of the general feeling of the time and the popular underground.*

JJ: Well, I think there's a relation to *Eraserhead* in the fact that *Eraserhead* was an independent film that became very widely known over a kind of slow process of releasing the film. Both films, along with other films, have made important steps for independent film directors, or anyone working in film independently, to kind of step back and think twice before they think that the only way to work is to try to get some kind of studio deal in Hollywood. I think both films made a certain step in that direction. As far as aesthetically and stuff like that, I think they're pretty different.

Has the success of the film changed your life much, at this point?
JJ: It changed my life in that now I have to find a new rhythm of working, because I got a little too much attention for my own good as far as my own working schedule. I don't think it's affected my ego or anything. It's made me feel good that now for my next two projects there's not really a problem of getting the money because they're both fairly small. It's changed so that I don't have to fight and work for two years just to convince somebody to give me the money.

Will you work on the same money scale again?
JJ: No, it's going up, but my next film will be a half-million dollar film instead of being two million or something.

What's it going to be?
JJ: Well, I don't really want to talk about it because I'm writing two and I'm not quite sure which I will do next. One is kind of like *Stranger* in that it's funny and sad, but it's a love story between two seventeen-, eighteen-year olds, who are petty criminals. It's kind of a road movie, but it's much more emotional and passionate than *Stranger,* and it's more delicate because the sexuality of the characters is very important.

Is it set in America?
JJ: Yeah. And then I'm writing another one, too, for two main male characters.

Will that be Edson and Lurie?
JJ: No, it'll be John and someone else, but I shouldn't say yet because I'm not sure that the other person wants to do it. It's somebody who's known as a musician and a little bit as an actor.

Do you have any idea how much Stranger *has grossed at this point?*

J J :   In the States? Over a million, but I still haven't gotten a cent for the movie. We have gotten a part of our advance from Goldwyn, but it all went to pay back the cost of the film.

What, the prints and all that?

J J :   Well, just the budget of the film itself. Because the producer put money in and he has to be reimbursed first. So we did get money from them but so far that all went to my producer, Otto Grokenberger, in Germany. We will get some money but we just haven't yet. But it's grossed over a million in the States and it's doing really, really well in Europe so it's probably, all over Europe, grossed another half million, maybe more.

So there's an outside chance that you may be able to finance your own film on the same kind of a budget.

J J :   Well, if I made a film of this small budget I probably could.

As a filmmaker, when you go into a deal to make a film like Stranger Than Paradise, *what kind of percentage do you actually get?*

J J :   Well, the way I'm working—which is why I don't want to work in Hollywood—is that I want to own my own film and have 50% of any kind of revenues from the film.

That's pretty unusual in Hollywood.

J J :   Yeah, that's completely unusual. I don't think that ever *ever* happens in Hollywood. And it's even somewhat rare in European productions. Usually a director gets like 30%. But I want to own half of my film, I want to own the film copyright itself and I want to make all the decisions myself. I don't want anyone else having any control over casting or editing or anything. And I want to own 50%, so I have a producer that is able to do that with me and we want to work together and sort of make small steps together instead of jumping off the ledge.

So you're not dealing with a very greedy producer.

J J :   No, but he's very smart and he's been very satisfied with this film.

How and when will a film like yours actually pay off?

J J :   Well, I think it takes about a year from a film opening to see money. But it's such a small film that it's already made its money back. But then there are all these costs. For example, the distributor's costs in the States alone is gonna be like, I don't know, $300,000 or half a million dollars. So they have to get that money back before we see profits after the advance. I think it takes a couple of years.

Stranger Than Paradise *was partly financed by German television. What is it about the German TV industry that would finance a film like yours?*
J J :   Well, German TV is run partly by the state and the general quality of TV is at a much higher level there and they take more chances, showing what in America would be considered experimental or avant-garde. A lot of European directors get money from German television.

Can you give me some examples?
J J :   Well, that's how what's called New German Cinema really started— getting money from TV—Fassbinder, Herzog, Wenders, Schlöndorff, all those people originally got money from German television. So it's supported a lot of German filmmakers, and it's recently supported a lot of independent American films like *Stranger Than Paradise, Wild Style* by Charlie Ahearn, Alexander Rockwell's films, Bette Gordon's film, I think. So it's helped American independents. Mark Rappaport got a lot of financing for his films through German television. Right now it's a lot harder because the Germans are sort of pulling back and are forced to give more money to young German directors and less to foreigners.

Would you say that the fact that German television was involved with it had something to do with the European feel of the film?
J J :   No, not at all. I would have made the film the same no matter where the money came from.

Would you agree with me that it has a European feel to it?
J J :   Well, I think the film takes influences from both sides. I mean, the characters are really American even though in the story itself they come from Central Europe—two of them. But formally the film is very non-American and much more influenced by European cinema, and also Japanese cinema, so it's very non-American in terms of style and form. But that's not because any money came from Europe, but because I've gotten a lot more inspiration

and energy from European films in the last twenty years than anything in Hollywood.

So it doesn't really have anything to do with the fact that it would be seen first in Europe?
JJ: No. I never thought about that at all.

So, for example, Cannes wasn't consciously in your mind while developing the film?
JJ: No, not at all. I didn't even want to have the film finished in time for Cannes, but my producer convinced me that it was possible to get it done. We just worked harder. So I did and it was accepted for Cannes, but it wasn't anything calculated at all. I didn't even know that there was a possibility of having it in Cannes until I was half-way through the editing process.

Did you attend the festival yourself?
JJ: Yeah, I did.

What was that experience like?
JJ: It was pretty weird and exhausting because, I don't know, it's a lot of people impressing each other with how much money they have and it's very theatrical in one sense, and on another level there are a lot of really amazing people from European cinema and American cinema, too, who show up there. So it was interesting and fascinating but I was there for like ten days or so and that was about eight days too many for me. But it was interesting. It was pretty jive in a way—Cannes.

What is your personal relationship with Wim Wenders at this point?
JJ: Well, I met him through Nick and it took me a long time to get to know Wim because he's pretty guarded. But now I've known him for six years so I know him pretty well, you know. He's a friend so I keep in touch with him and always see him if we're in the same city at the same time. I like him a lot as a person, but it took a long time to get to know him because I'm a little shy and he's fairly guarded.

Why do you think that is?
JJ: Well, just his personality. I think he's careful because he's a public figure and he's learned to be careful about his personality. But just in his nature

he's a very observant person and often doesn't talk until he knows what he wants to say. He's not that loquacious—he doesn't just babble.

Originally he gave you the stock to do the film with?
J J : Yeah, his company did in New York—Gray City Films. They had some stock left over from *The State of Things*, a film he made in Portugal and Los Angeles.

Was the stock a gift or in form of a payment?
J J : It was initially a gift and then a co-production—we produced the first part of the film together, my company and his company, Gray City. His producer, Chris Severnick, actually gave me the stock but Wim offered it, too. But then, to produce the feature version of the film—Wim's company wasn't prepared to do that because they were raising money for *Paris, Texas* and for another movie by Chris Petit filmed in Germany. So they weren't able to do that, and I had to go elsewhere to find a producer for the feature version.

What did Paul Bartel have to do with Stranger?
J J : In order for me to become involved with a new producer after Wim's company had co-produced the first part of the film I had to pay them back for the money they had spent on the first part of the film, legally, otherwise no producer could get involved. I had no money. So Paul just really liked the first part of the film—he actually wanted to try to produce it as a feature, too, but he wasn't able to come up with enough money either. So he loaned me the money, as a friend, to pay them back, for no percentage, no interest, nothing. He loaned me $15,000 just like that, and as a result I'm giving him points in the film—I'm not even sure he's aware of it yet. But really he served as a kind of associate producer, and without his help I have no idea how I could have continued with the film.

How did you come to meet him?
J J : I met him in Germany, oddly enough. In Hof, at a small film festival in Germany, and he was there showing *Eating Raoul* and saw the first part of the film. Then he read my script and he just was really excited, and he said that he had spent so much time fighting to work independently that now, since he had a little money from *Eating Raoul*, he wanted to turn around and help someone else.

What's he done besides Eating Raoul?

J J :   Well, he has two new films right now. One is called *Not For Publication* and another one called *Lust in the Dust,* with Tab Hunter and Divine. He made *Death Race 2000* for Roger Corman. He made a film called *Private Parts,* I think, which I've never seen, and he made some other films, too. I think he sort of came up through Roger Corman.

Have you ever been tempted to do some kind of American B-film?

J J :   No, not really. I've gotten a lot of scripts sent to me from Hollywood and a lot of offers and even offers from my own script, but I don't want to get involved with anything where I don't have control over it at this point. So I haven't really been interested in anything that's been offered.

How do you feel about the kind of instant celebrity status you've attained in terms of people all of a sudden wanting to do projects with you? What do you think of that?

J J :   Well, it's a mixed blessing because I have met some really amazing people that I would like to work with, but that's a very small percentage. Most of the things I've gotten have just been a pain in the ass to me, like sending the script back or calling them and saying, "No, thank you," and all these agents calling up have been a pain in the ass too because I don't really need an agent at the moment, and yet they're all swooping down on me. And I don't really want to be marketed as a hired director. I want to make my own films.

What do you think of America as a place?

J J :   Well, I love America as a country itself and the landscapes and, for the most part, people that I meet just out on the road somewhere. But as far as the government and the recent attitudes of the American public, I find them appalling. I really love a lot of things about America, but at the same time I feel like I'm a stranger in terms of general sense of economic and political direction that people even my age have in America—that's really disturbing to me.

Who? Yuppies?

J J :   Yeah, Yuppies and the fact that, you know, if someone had told me ten years ago that Ronald Reagan would be our President I would have fallen on the floor laughing. So it's kind of hard for me to believe that it's come to this. But at the same time I've always been relatively cynical, and I stopped being politically active in '72, so I don't know. I also feel like New York is not part of America. It's sort of like a free port—it doesn't really have that much to do with America.

Do you ever see yourself making a film critical of American government, or making a political film?

J J :   Well, see, I don't think something that's explicitly ideological serves any kind of even subversive purpose anymore in America, because if you make a political statement that is completely direct then you're only reinforcing opinions of people who would agree with you anyway, and the people that don't agree with you won't agree with you—you're not changing anybody's way of thinking. So I feel that I would never make something that was directly political or ideological, yet at the same time I think that the two films I've made and the things I plan to make are—I don't know how to put it—it's not blatantly presented, it's something that hopefully changes the way people think about their own lifestyles or their own values, that would cause them to think about their lives and maybe make some changes in things, or at least in what they value. But I don't think that in the States at this time—you know, anything you *do* that is very specifically against the government is used for their own purposes, which is why I don't think terrorism works anymore in America or in Europe, because it's so easily turned around and made a tool of the state against any kind of activity that's critical. So it's pretty cynical but I don't have much faith in specific ideological propaganda.

What do you think about the reviews of Stranger *since the reaction by critics and audiences has been so overwhelmingly positive?*

J J :   Well, it's weird. At certain points I became almost embarrassed that certain critics that I didn't respect liked my film, and I wondered if I had done something wrong. But at the same time, generally I'm really happy that it got a good response, because I don't feel like I directed the film toward any specific audience.

You weren't directing it toward the post-Punk art crowd?

J J :   No. In fact, the reason John and I even got the idea for this film, for the character of Willie, was because we wanted to make a character and a story that no one would say is New Wave. Because my first film and all the other new New York films—recent underground narrative films—have been labelled New Wave films, and the whole idea behind *Stranger* was to make characters that weren't associated with any specific fashion trend.

Do you think that idea worked?

JJ: No, because people always try to find a handle or some way of categorizing the work anyway. I think it worked on a certain level. It did avoid any specific reference whatsoever to any kind of scene, which was important. But, you know, I think the tone of the film or the content of the film itself does attract a certain kind of younger audience, just in the kind of attitudes the characters have. But it wasn't really conscious, it's just an attitude that the people making the film—myself, the actors, and everyone else—had. So it's in our work. But it wasn't calculated to just appeal to that specific audience.

Before I went to the film a friend of mine, who liked the film, tried to decrease my expectations, because I had heard a lot of the hype surrounding the film. He basically knocked my expectations down so I almost thought I was going to see a bad film that had gotten a lot of hype, and I was pleasantly surprised.

JJ: *[laughing]* Oh, that's good. I like that. That's good. I was a little worried just recently in Paris because there was so much press on the film that it made me feel like the audience is not gonna go and feel like they're discovering something. They're gonna go and feel like they've been told to go, which I think is really dangerous for this kind of film. But it's working really well in Paris so I guess I don't know if I'm wrong or not.

What are the other films that we hear in Stranger Than Paradise? *There's a science fiction film—*

JJ: We hear *Forbidden Planet*, which is a science fiction film. The only other things we hear are part of a Super Bowl game and a cartoon which is a Fleischer *Betty Boop* cartoon.

What about the Kung Fu film?

JJ: I don't know the name of it. It's actually a sound collage of two different films that I taped off TV.

I thought that was the most humorous scene. My eyes just kept running up and down the row of characters and I couldn't stop laughing.

J J :   Yeah. What I like about the way the film is shot is that it doesn't give you—you know, normally in a film they give you a close-up to tell you "this is dramatic," or over-the-shoulder shots while people are talking so you watch only the person speaking, and what I like about the form of this film for this specific story is that the audience is given more freedom than usual to choose what they want to watch. Often a character who's not saying anything but is listening to another character speak is more interesting or important somehow in the story than the character speaking. And in this case you have your choice of what to watch. I think that's why that scene works in the movie theatre. You don't see anything but them sitting there, so you end up watching their reactions to the film, to each other, and it seems to work on that level.

Were there any scenes that didn't get used?

J J :   Yeah, there are a few scenes cut out of the first part that weren't used—a really great scene which was going to be the introduction to the character Willie, where he's outside with a guy who's selling fruit, a fruit vendor, and he's trying to make a bet with the guy whether they can throw certain fruits over nearby rooftops. And the fruit vendor is annoyed, saying, "Come on, you wanna buy fruit or don't you? I don't wanna throw my fruit over the roof." And finally Willie convinces the guy, then they start throwing fruit over the rooftops, and making bets. But that scene got cut because I felt it didn't fit in terms of the chronological sequence of things. It was too early to give that much information about Willie. I wanted Willie to be discovered more by Eva. I liked that scene very much, but I took it out. There was another scene of Eva at the train station after she leaves and is on her way to Cleveland—that I cut out. It was beautifully shot but didn't really say much about the story. There were a few other things cut out, but mostly we used everything.

How was the soundtrack composed? Was it done afterwards?

J J :   It was done afterwards. He [Lurie] wrote the music for the first part while I was editing the first part of the film, and then he came in and placed the music with me. I had certain ideas of where it should go. For the second part he composed the music pretty much for specific places. He had a crude video of a rough cut of the film so he could compose at home, and make general placements for each piece of the music he wrote.

Did he perform the music?
J J :   He didn't perform because it's a string quartet and viola duets. It was performed by people John found. They don't always work together—he sort of assembled them.

There was an allusion in a Village Voice *interview with John that he was jealous of all the attention that you were getting for the film. Has the success of the film affected your relationship with him?*
J J :   Yeah, it's made it stronger I think. We fought a lot during the filming because John is not used to giving authority up to other people. Especially in his music, he's always in complete control. For the Lounge Lizards he writes and arranges everything. And he also had made some of his own Super 8 films, and since we had initially collaborated on the writing of the first part of the film to some degree, and then the second part of the film I wrote pretty much myself, there was a lot of—we had some problems between us while filming that made things very difficult and tense. And yet somehow I think it helped things. It also made John and me ultimately closer I think, and more aware of each other and more respectful of each other—I hope anyway [laughs]. But it's very emotional working closely with actors. I think it's better that things come out. If it's bad energy or good energy it's more important that it's dealt with than what kind of energy it is, and I think we learned a lot from it.

What was the most difficult point in the filming?
J J :   Well, it was difficult in Cleveland because it was so cold. We shot that scene by the lake with a wind-chill factor of thirty below.

I thought I caught Edson smiling at the camera there.
J J :   Yeah, he does that.

As if to say, "When are we gonna get outta here?"
J J :   Well, what's funny is when those shots—I did three takes of that scene by the lake and when I yelled, "Cut!", when we saw the uncut rushes of the film, the actors just literally fly out of the frame and run to the car when I

say, "Cut!" because it was so cold. But the most difficult part was the filming in Florida, because the whole crew and cast were living in that same motel and there were only four rooms in the motel. So we were like, you know, three people to a room, no privacy for the actors. We didn't really have cars to just drive away when we needed to. That was the most intense part.

Were there ever any personal flare-ups that disrupted the flow of making the film or did everybody behave well?
J J :   No, there were a lot of them, but they never disrupted things. They just made it difficult. They just had to be dealt with and we had to continue working, and I was kind of a slave driver because I had to get it shot and there wasn't a lot of time and there wasn't a lot of money, and our whole schedule was already completely made so we knew what we were shooting each day. Those things made it very tense, but they never stopped us.

Did you have to remain in character as the director the entire time? What I mean is, did you sort of have to lapse as Jim the person?
J J :   Well, I think that working with actors and with the crew, it's your own personality and their personalities, and in the connection between them is the way you find to work together. They're always intertwined with me, although I'm capable of becoming fairly fascistic about certain points. Somebody's gotta have a vision about what's going on, and keep things going on time, so I'm pretty single-minded while working and the main thing is to get the film done in the best possible way. But my personality is always involved in any decision I make.

The Jim Jarmusch Interview

CASSANDRA STARK/1985

CASSANDRA STARK: *How long have you been making films?*
JIM JARMUSCH: My first feature, *Permanent Vacation,* was shot in '79. Before that I only made a few student films at NYU graduate film school.

cs: *What were your student films like?*
jj: Only one of them did I finish. It was a very structural kind of narrative film. It was shown at the Museum of Modern Art once, but I never showed it again. Another one I made called *Cinesthesia* was shown at the Times Square Show, in 1981, I think. I don't know, they weren't really completely realized films. I wouldn't want to show them again. The one that was shown at the Museum of Modern Art was all cut to some music by Henry Cowell—a piece of his percussion music from 1934.

cs: *Can you tell me about* Permanent Vacation?
jj: It's a film I made based on the main actor, or partly on his life—this friend of mine, Chris Parker. We just abstracted—we took a lot of things that happened to me and just kind of accumulated scenes and made a story out of them. It's a very loose narrative about a kid who just sort of wanders around. He doesn't go to school. He's sixteen. He doesn't live at home. He doesn't have a job. He just drifts around the city and encounters other sort of marginal people.

Published in *The Underground Film Bulletin,* No. 4, September 1985, pp. 12–21. Reprinted by permission.

c s : *It did really well, right?*

J J : Not here. In Europe it got a kind of cult following. It did pretty well in Germany and in Holland and in Paris.

c s : *Why do you think that is—in Europe—not here?*

J J : I think there is a lot less of a distinction between underground films and commercial films in Europe because countries are smaller. TV is much different there; it's not so all pervasive. People are just more open to different kinds of things whereas here, it's really divided, or it was at that time, between commercial cinema and underground cinema.

c s : *And if you fall into the realm of "underground" you're bound not to have any success at all here?*

J J : Basically, yeah, although I'm not so sure underground films even exist anymore. The main problem is just distributors and whether they think it's commercial or not. I think that *Stranger Than Paradise* is basically an underground film that crossed over and got picked up for distribution here so it was able to be seen by a wider audience, but it wasn't my intention to make a commercial film. John Waters said in an interview a year ago that underground cinema doesn't exist anymore, because it's just—it's a game of distribution and not—it's not really based on aesthetics anyway. It's just what the market decides can be marketed, and I think that's true. I think it's changed a lot.

c s : *Maybe "underground" needs to be redefined, at least from the seventies. What was going on in the seventies? I guess you weren't involved in the Super 8 of the seventies, were you?*

J J : I wasn't really, although a lot of my friends were people who founded New Cinema and I was briefly in some of those movies—Eric Mitchell, James Nares, Michael McClard, Becky Johnson. That was really, I think, the most interesting thing in the seventies. And also, Amos Poe's films—especially *The Foreigner,* which to me was a really important film because when I first saw it, it was before I made *Permanent Vacation* and when I saw that he made a feature film for like $6,000, I knew that I could make a film too. I still like *The Foreigner* a lot, too. I think it's his best film.

c s :   *Are you aware at all of the Super 8 underground that's going on now?*
J J :   Well, I like Manuel DeLanda's films. I see those when I can, and, you know, I didn't see Nick Zedd's recent stuff. I saw his feature films.

c s :   *Which one?*
J J :   *They Eat Scum,* and . . .

c s :   Geek Maggot Bingo?
J J :   Yeah.

c s :   *What did you think of those?*
J J :   I think they're interesting. I think they're important. It's not my aesthetic. I feel kind of personally distanced from certain kind of provocateur, camp style, you know, which I respect: I respect that aesthetic, but it's not mine. I think I'm more concerned with form and stuff than those kind of films.

c s :   *Form as the process?*
J J :   Well, the structure of a film. How it's designed. I'm real interested in design on all levels—the art direction, the way the shots are done, the way the scenes are cut together, movement within the scenes. Personally, since I guess my own personal life is often chaotic, I try to find some kind of precision in my work. But I don't ever use a storyboard. I like things to happen as a film is being made, and I like to allow improvisation, but at the same time, I like to rehearse a lot with the actor. I believe really strongly in acting as a craft, and working with actors, and not just using personalities and saying "OK, camera's rolling. Do whatever you want." And they start screaming, you know?

c s :   *Really? I thought everyone in* Stranger Than Paradise—*they seemed kind of type cast. They didn't seem like they were actors.*
J J :   Well, they were not really actors. Well, they're actors of varying degrees but they worked very hard rehearsing the film and developing a character. I don't think they're playing themselves.

c s :   *It appeared that way . . .*
J J :   I think that good acting is finding parts of yourself that are also parts of the character and emphasizing those aspects and suppressing parts of your-

self that aren't in the character. I think all of the actors did that. Certainly, Richard Edson, for example, is not that kind of person. In the film he plays Eddie, and Willie, who John Lurie plays, is always pushing him around which is not the way Richard is.

c s :   *How did you finance* Permanent Vacation *when you were at NYU? Was that a school grant?*

J J :   Yeah. It's kind of a complicated story. I made it as a thesis film for my school, but I got some money from my school to pay my tuition as a kind of scholarship and instead of paying that to the school, I got the money paid to me, and therefore was able to make the film with that money that I was supposed to pay tuition for, so I never got a degree from school, 'cause they really didn't want people to make feature length films. And I thought, well, what's the point of being here and paying this money if I end up with some little ten-minute film, and that's not what I want to do. I mean, there's nothing wrong with ten-minute films, but I wanted to make a longer film.

c s :   *Did you ever pay back your school loans?*

J J :   Ahhm, gee. Who's gonna read this? I'm working on it. Ha. I'm working on it. I haven't paid them back completely, no.

c s :   *How did you finance* Stranger Than Paradise?

J J :   I first made the first part of it as a short film which was financed by my company, Cinesthesia, which was money I got from selling *Permanent Vacation* to German TV. So I put that money in the first part of the film, and Wim Wenders's company, Grey City in New York, put in the other two-thirds of it for the first part. And then, for the feature, it was financed by German TV, ZDF, and by my producer, Otto Grokenberger, who's a young German producer from Munich. He's gonna be the Executive Producer of my next film.

c s :   *What's that going to be?*

J J :   It's a film that I'm going to shoot in Louisiana, mostly in New Orleans, in November and December. The main actors are John Lurie, Tom Waits, and an Italian actor named Roberto Benigni. It starts off as a kind of a sinister film but ends up being a comedy. Like *Stranger,* it's not a real genre. It doesn't quite fit in to being just a crime film, or just a comedy. I'm interested in kind of, subtle comedies.

c s : *What's your association with Wim Wenders? I've heard yours and his name mentioned together a few times.*

J J : He's a friend of mine. I met him through Nick Ray and then they made a film together, *Lightning Over Water,* which I worked on, and I met Wim at that time and since then, he was very supportive, trying to help me find money for my projects, some of which never happened, and then helping me with the first part of *Stranger.* Sometimes in the press they say that I'm like his protégé, or that my film's imitative of him, which really makes me furious because I feel like I have a very distinct style and yet I like his stuff a lot.

c s : *So you were inspired by him but not influence, too . . .*

J J : Well, I've been influenced by anyone whose films I liked; by Godard, Antonioni, Wenders, Ozu, Bresson, Dreyer. Of course, I'm influenced by things that move me, but when people say that my work is imitative of his, I think, it's just these idiots in the press that have to relate everything to something else. They can't see anything as in its own right. It's got to be influenced by this or by that, and that comes from the whole way that movies are thought of in the United States. Everything refers back to something else. I got a script, after *Stranger* was successful, from Hollywood they wanted me to direct, and they said they'd pay me a quarter of a million dollars to make a teenage sex comedy. The letter said "We know that this script reads a little like *Risky Business,* but, take our word for it, after the re-write it will read much more like *The Graduate."* You know, it's just like, fuck it, you know. They always have to refer to something else. Nothing stands on its own.

c s : *So you turned it down, right?*

J J : Of course. I want to make my own films. But that's just an example. I was offered a lot of schlock like that. And they always think in those terms—of remakes. It's upsetting. But it's kind of funny, too.

c s : *When you were planning* Stranger Than Paradise, *was your intention to shoot something in a way that was not representative of most films?*

J J : No. It wasn't in our minds to be rebellious or anything formally. It was just to do something we thought was interesting and get away from this kind of horrible TV editing and language of TV and Spielberg-type editing. I hope it's gonna happen. I hope that younger filmmakers start just disregarding all this special effects bullshit and try to make simple films that are about real people's lives or about something real in some way. I don't mean in style, but just something that's honest.

c s :   *But then, where would surrealist film fit in?*
j j :   Surrealism was a literary form. It comes from the influence of dreams and very ordinary, normal things that somehow you see in a different light. Surrealism is really, especially as a literary form, important to me as an influence, but it's a past period.

c s :   *There do seem to be people that are interested in revealing more of the subconscious on film. Are you familiar with* El Topo?
j j :   Yeah.

c s :   *What did you think of it?*
j j :   I hated it.

c s :   *Why?*
j j :   I thought it was heavy handed. I thought it was kind of pretentious and overdone.

c s :   *So is pretentious not to be desired?*
j j :   Not by me, because people are too conscious of what is fashionable, which doesn't mean anything. And anything that is fashionable is already from the past because it takes the media—they are always several years behind anyway. I don't trust anything that is trendy or fashionable. John Lurie and I—when we first started *Stranger*, before I started writing it, said, "We gotta make a film where the characters are not like new-wave type characters, just because everyone was labeling my first film, and Amos Poe's films, and Eric Mitchell's, and Michael Oblowitz's, and Bette Gordon's, . . . and Nick Zedd's—they were all saying, "These are new wave films from New York." We just wanted to make something that was not gonna be labeled "new wave." It still has been, anyway.

c s :   *When I was watching it, I kept feeling like I was in the fifties, especially with the male characters.*

JJ: We didn't want you to know exactly when it takes place. It takes place in the present. We wanted to make it kind of subtle. My new film I want to do the same thing with. I don't want it to be specifically dated that "this takes place in 1960 or '50 or '70, but yet it has things that could suggest that it was in any of those periods even though, in fact, it takes place in the present.

CS: *Where did you get Aunt Lottie?*
JJ: Cecilia Stark. My lawyer's grandmother. Jim Stark, who was my lawyer. I was auditioning actresses and he said, "You should meet my grandmother in Cleveland," so I went and met her and just really loved her. But she died recently.

CS: *Your publicist said you were involved in being a cameraman on some big company film.*
JJ: No. It's a film by Sara Driver who was the line producer of *Stranger Than Paradise* and the production manager of *Permanent Vacation* who made a film called *You Are Not I* . . . which I shot. She's making a new film called *The Year of the Dog,* which is being shot in a couple weeks. I'm gonna be the director of photography. Well, actually, I'll be more like the operator because Frank Prinzi is gonna be the lighting director, so he and I will work together on the image. I just finished a video for Talking Heads, too, which is out in Europe. They have two singles from their new album. The American single David Byrne directed the video for and I directed and wrote the video for the European single. I had a lot of other offers to do other videos and I didn't want to do them. I just am not interested in rock videos. I don't like them as a form. I think the whole idea of them is fucked up.

CS: *Tom Verlaine and Patti Smith predicted that. They said that it would be a really bad thing to mix television and music.*
JJ: Yeah. Well, they were right. It's funny, I haven't seen any videos by Tom Verlaine.

CS: *I don't think he'll do any. At least I hope not.*
JJ: What's great about music, especially pop music, is hearing it and having some connection with it, like what's happening in your life at that time, and then you hear it ten years later and you remember. It cues your memory

of something. When you have these videos and they give you these stupid images to go with it, then you're a slave to those images. Every time you hear that song, then you think, "This is horrible—"

c s : *Even if you try to make one, you have gotta choose either to be a slave to the music and then cut up the images in a way that would follow the music or vice versa. It seems like it never comes together. When it does, it's a real rare thing.*
j j : There aren't too many I like. I love this one from Art of Noise, "Close to the Edge." Generally, I really don't like them at all. I'm surprised somebody hasn't assassinated Hall and Oats with those stupid fucking videos they make.

c s : *MTV is really pathetic.*
j j : I never watch it. I heard New Order just did a new video that Jonathan Demme directed. It's supposed to be eight minutes or eleven minutes long, or something.

c s : *Before, you named some of the people in film that you admired. Who were they again?*
j j : I like Antonioni's films a lot, and Godard's a lot. I like Jean Eustache and Jacques Rivette, but especially Jean Eustache. He killed himself a couple years ago. His most known film here is called *The Mother and the Whore*, which is, I think, one of the greatest films ever made.

c s : *What was that film about?*
j j : It's a film with Jean Pierre Lerou and Bernadotte Lafond, who's a great, great actress, who's the woman he lives with who's older than him, but he's very uncertain about his responsibility to her and to being in love with someone. He's asking another girl to marry him who won't, and then in the meantime, he meets another girl who he spends a lot of time with who's younger than him and he keeps going back and forth between the two women. Throughout the whole thing, Lerou just talks constantly about his own emotions to them and you just get this running commentary on someone's emotional insecurities and indecisiveness. You hate him and yet you really, like, understand him, but you can't forgive him and yet, you can. It's just a really amazing film.

C S :   *It doesn't get boring?*

J J :   No. It's a beautiful film. I like really classical people like Bresson and Carl Dreyer and Ozu and Mizoguchi. Also, I love Jack Smith's films, and I like some of Warhol's "Warhol" films like *Nude Restaurant—Lonesome Cowboys, Blow Job.* He made hundreds of them.

C S :   *Is Burroughs one of your favorite writers?*

J J :   I don't know if he's one of my favorite writers. He's certainly someone I respect a lot . . . for his process of thinking more than the final results, often. He's very amazing. I worked on a film about him called *Burroughs,* a documentary by Howard Brookner.

C S :   *Who else do you like in literature?*

J J :   I love J. G. Ballard. I love Marguerite Duras. One of my favorite writers is somebody not known; a friend of mine, Luc Sante. He wrote a series of what he calls "fast novels" that are one-page narrative things.

C S :   *What struck you most about New York when you came here for the first time?*

J J :   Just the idea that, especially in Akron, Ohio, anything that was unusual or abnormal—even a superficial thing like the way people looked—was like a big deal and you were made to feel funny about that and in New York, no matter how weird you look or act, you can walk down the street and in ten minutes you're gonna see somebody a hundred times weirder, which made me feel really happy. Also the idea that there's so many mixtures of cultures in Manhattan, I like really a lot. There are a lot of things I hate about New York, but there's no other city that makes me feel like anything is possible. I like Berlin a lot, too because it's kind of similar, but I still like New York, better than Paris or Rome or London. Certainly better than LA, that's for sure. LA is a big pagan town. Heh!

C S :   *I've never been anywhere. But that's good. I guess I don't have to go anywhere now. What advice can you give to someone such as myself?*

J J :   I dunno. I feel really, like, not responsible for advice because I'm, just—I think people learn as they go.

C S :   *Do you think school is very important?*

J J :   I think film school is good for technical things. Making films is hard technical. I think it's important to know how to use the equipment. I do believe that in order to break rules, you have to know what they are. At the same time, aesthetically, I don't think film schools are worth—they're worth absolutely zero.

c s : *Film schools don't seem to encourage you at all to study things that might lead to what your film is going to be about.*
J J : Exactly.

c s : *You wind up having all these technically OK people out there making films about nothing 'cause they haven't studied anything.*
J J : I don't like film schools as a concept. I don't like institutions, but there's always some person you meet there or somebody that becomes important. Being in school is like any other experience—95% of it is wasting your time; but the 5% that isn't, is really important. I met good people that I still work with from school.

c s : *When I was young, it was a terrible thing. I vomited and cried every single day from kindergarten to third grade.*
J J : Really!?!

c s : *Yes. It was really terrible. I wouldn't want to send my kids. I wouldn't want to put them through that.*
J J : I don't think I would either.

c s : *Is there anything else you'd want to say?*
J J : I think there is a good spirit of people right now, in films, of just ignoring Hollywood, or all the given methods of producing films. I think it's really important to stay outside of that if your ideas are going to be changed if you don't stay outside of it. I don't like the distinction between 35mm film and a Super 8 film. I mean, a film is a film and if there's good ideas in it, that's what's important. It's just a matter of distribution then—y'know, "How many people can see it?" I just hope people stay true to their ideas and keep doing things they believe in. But then, there are so many traps out there—people wanting to be famous or rich or whatever that don't mean anything. You just have to think of what you want to do and do it, and people will help you or not help you, but they won't stop you if you really want to do it. That's why I like New York too, because it makes you think you can do whatever you want. It's hard to, but you can. If you pretend, then you can do it.

Stranger in Paradise

JANE SHAPIRO/1986

AT THE FIRST NEW YORK screening of Jim Jarmusch's new film
Down By Law, viewing the movie in Art Deco lounge chairs we repeatedly
experienced the caress of expensive velour, while Paul Simon sat upon a fold-
ing seat in the back. Cognoscenti were here. The publicity woman (Susan) is
a mere child in leather sneakers. In the elegantly rendered production notes,
the director described his movie's style as "neo-beat-noir-comedy." Aggressive hipsters (polished boots and oiled hair) had filled the elevator, saying
few and arcane hipster things, opening their mouths around postmodernist
gum as they smacked at the buttons to make themselves rise in the building.

Soon this moment in the middle of the dead summer will have given way
to September 19th and *Down By Law* will appear in a coveted position, opening the New York Film Festival, and then the famously unambitious Jim Jarmusch, age thirty-three, late of Akron, so recently a youth in Paris goggling
at the *nouvelle vague,* will suddenly have arrived in America to receive even
more frequent and pressing offers from Hollywood than he did after his tiny
$150,000 black-and-white movie *Stranger Than Paradise* appeared at the festi-
val two years ago to deep if not wide acclaim: ever more lavish offers to direct
Porky's. Stranger was a precisely formal movie, composed of long single takes
punctuated by blackouts, musically rhythmic, elegant, disaffected, and full
of Jarmusch's insistent niceness; and so cool and minimal it seemed to be
watching you about as often as you were watching it.

Published in *The Village Voice*, 16 September 1986. Copyright © by Jane Shapiro. First appeared in *The Village Voice*. Reprinted by permission of Melanie Jackson Agency, L.L.C.

Pauline Kael said it was full of "bombed-out listlessness," and that "there's no terror under or around what we see—the desolation is a gag."

What do you think of this? I ask Jim. Jim is sitting on the couch in an apartment I borrowed, looking sympathetic with the apartment's gray-black cats in his customary gray-black ensemble, smoking cigarettes and doing something he hates, because *Down by Law* he decided needs some "support": having an interview. I look at his silvery white hair which started turning when he was fourteen. I look at his pointy-toed boot with the chain reaching from under the arch of the foot to encircle the leather ankle. He refused *Vanity Fair* and *Esquire,* but I got him. When he walked in, I told him, I was just sleeping and I dreamed the young cult filmmaker Jim Jarmusch came with twenty vicious punkers and they flowed into the apartment and they were being mean and pinching me and putting joints out on the cat and one of them ate all my money and wouldn't spit it back up! and Jarmusch said, "Oh. Um. You dreamed that?" as if it were like Freud's dream of the erudite nursling, a known, named dream. I thought that answer was wonderful. Now I am reading to him:

". . . Those blackouts have something of the effect of Beckett's pauses: they make us look more intently, as Beckett makes us listen more intently— because we know we're in an artist's control. But Jarmusch's world of lowlifers in a wintry stupor is comic-strip Beckett." You remember that review?

Politely: "No. But I stopped reading them after awhile."

Oh, you don't—?

"Well, I did for awhile, but then *Stranger* just got too much stuff, and I don't think I ever read hers. Yeah, I don't think I read that. But what did she mean by that?"

I say, I was going to ask what you thought.

"Did she expect terror? Or did—see, out of context—"

Hey, maybe I have the whole review! You want to see it? I laugh at his amazed, bored face, chuckling alone like Dr. Ruth. Susan the publicity woman told me, You have to draw him out but he's a real sweetie.

"I don't care," Jarmusch says. "Sure."

Jim Jarmusch, serenely: "Well, I would take that comment about a comic-strip Beckett to be a . . . compliment." Naturally, to be compared to Beckett however glancingly must be quite exciting. (Earlier I said, She compares you to Beckett and he said absently but pleasantly, That's nice.)

"Because," he says, "I like comics a lot.

"I think structurally the film *is* like a comic strip, and I think comic strips are a great form! And in Europe, y'know, they're *amazing artists*. In France the comic strip artist is like a rock star! He's a celebrity, he's: *heroic*. But here"—sadly—"we don't even know who they are.

"But that has nothing to do with Pauline Kael's, with her, uh—" Jarmusch chuckles. "I don't know what she meant!"

On the tape is: click click click clickclickclickclick, a mouth tidily clicking, and a doleful voice says: "Cat."

I am on the phone. "Hmp," he says. Click click. "C'mere." And to me as I hang up, "I *like the color,* of this cat." (Deep silvery blackish gray.) Softly: "Such a beautiful color." He watches the cat walk past him twice. "Charcoal," he says to it going by.

Jarmusch inhales smoke, then blows out: "Well, maybe Pauline Kael was expecting, or wanted, something, y'know, meaningful, or more obviously existential, or something, in the film—I don't know."

I say I think she usually likes sensation; a thrill, what she calls "trashiness," an appeal to the nerve endings, or—

New young filmmaker Jarmusch looks glum. Glumly he says, "Yeah. Those were all the things we tried to remove."

Down by Law, the Jarmusch movie to be released next week, is another gentle, funny, rhythmic, cartoony, black-and-white film about the disheveled and disaffected, this time set in a luminous imagined New Orleans, shot by cinematographer Robby Müller in Jarmusch's typical long slow takes, and what is "removed" from this one—some of what is missing—are point-of-view shots and quick cuts and, Jarmusch thinks, the concomitant ordinary instructions to the viewer: where to look. He says that the long takes, which are so very different from the prevailing "image-fetishistic, information-crazy" style in movies and television and rock videos, have the effect of changing the way you think about what you're watching, because you're not told what to look at and you have the right to choose.

I tell him, another effect of the long takes, for me, is that I got to hear words, which fast cutting intercepts. And I felt that as in the theater there were pauses and I could have the pauses.

Patiently: "Yeah. Well. The pauses are—y'know. The pauses to me are more important, really, often, than the words. Often the *calm moment* when people aren't saying anything is much more important than the dialogue. Because" as he often finds himself putting it—"it's true in life."

Well, that may be, but this is a typical Jarmusch construct of the sort that will naturally be uneasily received by most people immersed in the business of making movies. And then the question is how long you go on having people cry *Oh please* let us finance your picture! and you trotting around saying, Well, pauses are more crucial than dialogue, and Comic strips are a *great art form,* and It's how it is in life. I tell Jim I am interviewing him right before he becomes famous. Jarmusch says what he always says, who cares, I'm not interested in a career and I'm not interested in ambition, I'm a brat this way and I just wanta make movies exactly the way I want.

Oh, what a little type of an artist. Susan, his own publicist, nice intelligent young publicist, already talks about him as if he were an expensive pet prone to shivers. When he showed his script for *Down by Law* to some distribution companies, potential backers, he says they said, Well, that is not a full-length movie. That might be a sketch for a movie or a script for a short movie, but it is not a feature film, and they *brought in an expert,* guy from USC who said, A real screenplay is one minute per page, so your picture is only 59 minutes long, that is not a screenplay.

Jim almost said (but did not say), *Well, then get your movies made by the fucking guy from USC.*

Susan tells me, "He just wants to get the photographs out of the way first. Because he doesn't particularly like photographs. Then his frame of mind will be better."

Susan says, "I'm not even going to the shoot. It got to be really a scene with the photographer. I don't want to go into it but—I got a message on my machine that it would just be better if they did it alone."

I asked Susan how much time I'd have in which to talk with Jarmusch.

Susan: "You can feel it out. See if he's getting antsy."

Jim Jarmusch lives with filmmaker Sara Driver in a ragged and minimal setting, up seven flights in a remarkably lackluster building at a margin between Little Italy and the Bowery, a place that like a Jarmusch movie *calls into question* commonly held ideas of *American hospitality,* this idea of *furniture,* where he gets home after work like any suburban corporate guy and crouches on the floor to read the mail. He hangs out at a bar whose clientele seems to comprise artists, ranch hands, and little kids, where the floor tilts and the decor runs to a large photograph of Frank Sinatra near his peak and signs reminding the putative customers not to loiter. Jim affects all-black clothes and sunglasses edged with a gold strip that runs across his face like one fine gold eyebrow; rides a motorcycle, gets exercised detailing the time-honored argument that Mickey Spillane is the equal of Cervantes, sweats and sheds salt tears doing perorations in defense of popular culture. Was only thirteen years ago a sprout at Columbia University thinking he would be a writer, composing "little kind of seminarrative abstract pieces," taking very seriously "post-post-structural fiction and the deconstructed narrative and all that stuff"; doing these wonderful compelling writing exercises, translating poems into English from languages, other languages he didn't understand at all. Some days go by and he forgets to eat. If you ask him how he learned to make movies—who have been his "influences"—he will look deeply embarrassed, but then like somebody at the podium he will immediately begin to worry that he might leave someone out.

"Man, that's—" Anxious sigh, peers around pleadingly.

Or whose work you're especially passionate about?

"Hhhh, that's something I can never really answer. Because *so many people,* film, or painters, or architects, or, y'know: literature . . ."

Okay, Antonioni, all of whose movies Jarmusch screened before making *Down by Law,* because "Antonioni is so elegant in the way he can let the scene *go past its normal length,* or the *shot* even, and the *whole weight* of the scene changes, the essence, I mean he's just one example."

"Nick Ray, obviously." (Nicholas Ray literally taught him filmmaking; and that "if each scene is there the movie will be there.")

Also: the famous, accomplished Robby Müller, *Down by Law's* cinematographer; seems like a sixteenth-century Dutch interior painter born into the wrong time. Jarmusch's grandmother, ninety-four now out in Akron, with her library books of Matisse plates and her leather-bound volumes of Proust. In Japan this year Kurosawa offered him a beautiful unsolicited testimonial about the elegant and musical shooting and editing in *Stranger,* and by messenger sent him a book, *very very moving,* and those paragraphs were the only two paragraphs about the movie that Jarmusch got translated from Japanese. There in Japan he met Toru Takemitsu and went to Ozu's grave. Only later, years after living as a twenty-one-year-old new film buff damp from the shell on the Rue des Ursulines in Paris, did he discover it was the historic street where *Un Chien Andalou* was first ever shown in the universe.

The *nouvelle vague!* Godard. Jacques Rivette. Jean Eustache.

Dziga Vertov, the Soviet filmmaker, who does use fast cuts.

"Raúl Ruiz. His films don't really get shown here. Amazing.

"The Italians, the neorealists, also the early Fellini films, and Pasolini, and Bertolucci, and—I just saw Bertolucci's brother's film, Giuseppe Bertolucci, which is called *Berlinguer I Love You*, which is a *great* film!

"And the great European directors who worked in Hollywood. Fritz Lang, his Hollywood stuff as well as his German. And Douglas Sirk, and Edgar Ulmer. Jacques Tourneur! I mean"—Jarmusch looks overwhelmed—"*I don't know!* The earlier French directors, Jean Vigo is one! But there's so many people, then I'm gonna start talking about Kurt Schwitters and—then I'm gonna start talking about, y'know, Rimbaud and Baudelaire, and—!"

He laughs a sudden propulsive mortified laugh, and stops. He looks at his lap, snorts smoke. He growls: *"William Blake."*

Jim Jarmusch is on the roof of his building in the summer afternoon sun, getting away up where there is completely nothing because the phone might ring downstairs and a distraction could occur. He sits upon a ledge and holds still for me to clip on his mike, and I clip it onto his shirt with tender fingers as he is talking about Susan, sighing out smoke: "Yeah, I don't know why she doesn't just take care of these things. She gets so *flustered.* She doesn't give me *any forewarning.*"

On the other hand—this is a habit, stating the other position—"I'm difficult too. She just had *all these people* wanting me to do things, and I—I just didn't want to do those things." He refused to have his photograph taken at an expensive Cajun restaurant: *a place I would never go.*

Sirens floating up from the street and airplanes roaring up here. Jim looks around to see what comes to hand. *"Should I get a chair? I guess I could—* bring up a . . . chair." (Downstairs in the apartment he said, "I guess I could look for a . . . drink," and came back awhile later saying, "There isn't anything.")

No problem, I say, and settle onto the tarpaper which immediately beams heat up through my trousers, my shoe in actual tar. Jim tentative in his black duds, me eying him with approval. This is our second meeting. We are talking about art.

About black and white: "Most people who were going to get involved said Yeah, we'll do it if it's in color, because we can't sell it to video otherwise. And that's just a constraint they manufactured in their own minds; that made me *more adamant* to make it in black and white! I had an argument recently with one of the few guys I respect that do rock videos, and he was haranguing me about black and white being *passé,* and that it was trendy *because* it's passé, and—I don't buy that; that's like saying everything you do has to be new. Which is of course nonsense. Narrative movies are not a new form, and road movies go back to Homer! Even the Dadaists . . ."

About directing the actors in *Down by Law:* "It was a delicate thing for them. It was hard for them. They were always demanding to have more individual traits that would make them seem different from each other. Which I kind of—in a way, I was kind of—I tricked them to some degree, by humoring them but not really wanting them to seem that distinct from each other.

"And I don't want John Lurie or Tom Waits, in this case, to think about the entire progression of his character. And that's also why the film was shot out of continuity. I don't want to say I was deceptive to them, but there are certain things that actors have to be concerned with and other things they shouldn't."

About a late scene in *Down by Law:* "Robby created that beautiful light to *make it* have that feeling of when you've just woken up and you're talking with people you like and you're having breakfast. And also because Nicoletta—because she's Italian—she's making it pleasant: the eggs are in little egg cups, and she's bringing the espresso over from the machine.

"And I love the dancing scene too. I'd like to have dancing in every movie. There's no sex in the movie and to me that scene is the sensual moment, to me that's better than: y'know. And I love that song, I just love to watch Roberto and Nicoletta moving together. She is *so illuminated on screen.*"

When Jarmusch answers questions he usually begins by hesitating, then making a few false starts, casting about for some words; then swings into a long fluent exposition; in summation, repeats his thesis; then stops. A calm appropriate-seeming silence falls. He waits for the next question, and he can wait in purposeful serenity quite a while.

Jim says, "*I don't* feel articulate. In the films, the stuff I write, the dialogue is so minimal and often there's—well, *always*—there's some kind of communication problem between people. I love language, and I love listening to the way people talk, the way they *elide* things, and the way people are *inarticulate* I like.

"But my ideas aren't—I don't feel comfortable just talking.

"Also, I don't like to talk very personally, I feel like it's psychoanalytic. There's a place for that and it's not really in publicity for something.

"And it's hard to distinguish too, if something is just publicity, or if you're *actually talking to someone,* or if you're talking to *the press,* or if you're talking to *people who are going to read this?* That confuses me. I'm very confused by that.

"So the only solution for me is to: not do it!" Pained laugh.

Jarmusch's face clouds up behind his gold shades. With roars of airplanes flying through the hot sky rendering him almost inaudible, Jim tells me:

"But I did another interview yesterday, straight kind of interview and I was not"—guiltily—"open like that. Y'know they asked me some things and I gave them answers that I had decided were answers I wanted to give."

Right, I say, leaning his way in the heat and din.

"Which is something I also did to you yesterday, when you asked me were there scenes in the film I wasn't satisfied with."

You said it wouldn't be in the movie if you didn't like it.

"Yeah. I did. I said that." Jim says: "Which is really not the truth!"

Right, I say.

"And, y'know, if we'd had more time—I mean, there are always excuses but—*they're a lot of things I'm not happy with in the film.* It's dishonest to say, 'Oh, everything's fine, I think everything's good!' It's a good dumb little story and it has good characters, and some really great moments of perform-ances, and it's flawed and kind of lopsided and—

"Y'now, I said to that other person, 'Oh yeah, it's fine! Oh yeah, I'm really happy with it.'

"Y'know?"

Well, yes I do.

They would set out on these vacations. His father would *load* the car, and *get* behind the wheel, and they would start driving together south through the alien state of Florida on the road between motels with the heat steadily rising. Which you can chuckle about from the current vantage point: "those horrible trips."

I say, don't you have nostalgic affection for that? I think of those motels with such fondness, those kinds of strange poignant American scenes.

"Yeah, but—it was still a series of identical motels, y'know. It just always seemed that everything looked the same to me."

On the other hand, before this he had seen *The Fly* and James Bond mov-ies and *The Night of the Hunter* with the thrilling evil Robert Mitchum with "love" and "hate" tattooed on his fingers, and then at a drive-in in Florida with his mother and sister, while his father was back at the motel *probably hiding,* sitting in the car age eight in the dark he got his first idea what movies could be like: saw *Thunder Road.*

"They're bootleggers! And they have these souped-up cars, that, y'know, they worked on the engines, they run the stuff at night, and there are chase scenes with cops, and it's in the swamps somewhere and very rural! I remember getting *really excited* by that! Before that time I didn't know movies could be this dangerous and this seductive.

"And I think Robert Mitchum's son was in it too; I don't know."

But he wouldn't have been, I say.

Jim gazes my way, dreamy, unfocused. "Yeah, how could he be?"

Jim says, "Well, erase that. I don't even—But you're not going to quote me on anything anyway, right?"

I look at him. The tape is quietly grinding, its little wheels turning, four hours into our talk.

"You're not gonna quote things I say, are you?"

I'm not gonna quote you?

"Are you gonna quote me?"

There is a silence, into which I laugh an unhappy laugh. Well, I don't have to quote you on that exact particular thing, but yes, I will be quoting you.

On the roof appears Sara Driver, wearing her black downtown shoes like wrapped leather feet and a fashionable sweatshirt cut to fall off one shoulder and down her arm. (She has a new movie of her own right now with no American distribution yet, and Jim says, Yeah, she's sad but she's tough; she's a warrior.)

Jarmusch: "You gonna go?" Blindly he looks down at me where I am not squatting on top of my bag. "Should we go down there then? Is it—too hot up here?"

Whatever you want, I say, it's hot but it's—

"I don't care either. So let's just stay here. Where you going?"

Sara: "The post office, and then I'm going to buy you a sketch pad."

After she descends, I say she looks so sweet.

"*Yeah.* She's gonna get me a sketch pad 'cause I'm trying to do this—uh." Glancing down past his own nose at the black front of his cowboy shirt. "I shouldn't tell you this with the microphone on."

Right, I say. I won't write it. Tell me. I won't put it in.

Years before Jim Jarmusch met the redoubtable John Lurie and Tom Waits and the brilliant Roberto Benigni and the *illuminated* Nicoletta Braschi and became the simple *orchestrator* of their talents and the *conduit* to pipe them to their audience and the modest *navigator* of *Down by Law*—before he had the experience of loving them, wondering and figuring what these actors needed so he and they could make up a movie in concert, the process much more valuable than the mere product itself; before he was twenty-one in Paris haplessly apprehending *cinema* and driving the art truck with a robust guy from Chicago who had already, with a similiar level of respect for the cargo, driven a similar truck (carried beer); before he was thirteen and suddenly it comes to him the spiritual part of religion is only *marginalia;* before he met Godard while Godard was eating Italian ice cream and of all the 200 complicated things he was wanting to say to Godard he could only bring himself to ask the master, What flavor!—before these things happened, Jim Jarmusch was back in Akron, several years old, walking around, walking around, watching other people go about their days.

His grandmother said someday you'll age, you'll receive my translations of Proust. His grandmother had the scrapbook of photographs showing his interesting mother, before her marriage, as a journalist for the *Akron Beacon Journal,* with Ginger Rogers, with *Roy Rogers,* covering the wedding of Humphrey Bogart and Lauren Bacall, with her little notebook interviewing movie stars. His father was a strong person, struggling with business. His grandfather ran away and all the women in the family know why now and knew why then, his mother knows, his sister knows, his father doesn't know, his little brother doesn't know, and he doesn't know, just another privacy of women which is fine, you can respect it, but even now it's funny, makes you laugh, it's kind of *weird* today still. Fled, or died, or something.

Other people's activities, women's breasts of the '50s, and once in awhile an amazing thing would slide into view: *pink car.* His mother stood in the yard and around her were one plum tree, one quince tree, one pear tree, black walnut with the green skins, catalpa with pods, a single cherry tree. She seemed to love it, loved unusualness, her hair was *so white* you could always see her from far away, and she'd stand out there while guys regularly dropped down from Kent State University dressed in white lab coats (working on trees) all clotting around one given tree and declaring, "It's not a tree, it's a bush." The neighbor who came over and said sotto voce all the time, low intense strangled voice, *"You could make opium from those red poppies, y'know."* These vivid repeated sentences with their resonance and their oblique continuing application: It's not a tree. It's a bush.

This is a surprising thing, to get a million dollars in financial backing in exchange only for English-language rights, get notes from Kurosawa and open the New York Film Festival with the second small black and white movie you own yourself. Although Jim didn't have a good sense early on what was going on, he did get a normal inchoate young person's idea: I will not be remaining in Akron. There was the unknown tree living in the yard and his mother attracted hummingbirds with her hair. He was a kid, he was peripheral, he didn't speak the language.

When Jarmusch went home to see his parents a few weeks ago, he was surprised to discover he hadn't seen them in two years. Got so occupied with the making of films with the compelling motif, We three travelling.

He says, "I like being displaced. I can sleep anywhere.

"But what I like to do is lie down in the early evening, just for half an hour anywhere I am, and listen to all the sounds I can hear. As if I were listening to music. And being attentive to things very far and very present, and when you hear voices and they're speaking a language you don't understand, it's really beautiful. I love that."

I say, I recently realized I love the moment when you first wake up someplace away from home and you don't know where you are yet? Thinking, Am I in a hotel, or am I in—?

Jim says, "It only lasts for such a brief time."

We conclude our interview with a spirited rendition of that ordinary discussion. The state of film today.

Jim: "The public must, I mean people must—they *must not be that stupid,* to not at least suspect they're constantly being condescended to, *shoveled shit,* y'know? I mean, how many teenage-virginity movies can you see without catching on that: *Jeez, I guess dis is a formula!"*

I proclaim, People like formulas, we like things to be the way we expect them to be.

Jim (genuinely inquiring): "Because they've been trained to think that way?"

Unembarrassed, I launch into a lengthy impassioned description, which steadily gains in intensity and speed, of my personal impression of the impoverished lives most people must lead, and *so much television,* and *eating terrible food,* and—

Jarmusch suddenly laughs a snuffly laugh and casts me a look very bright and amused. *"Yeah, life is terrible,"* he says. Grinning: *"Life sucks."*

The morning after that, I was out on a turnpike driving up to Cape Cod, and there were all the big families out next to their loaded cars in the rest area parking lot, many of them so cheerful and calm together as to suggest the Roy Rogers rest stop had been their original destination. I felt like calling Jim to tell him how nice it was out on the road with the families, but when I got to the Cape, Jim called me instead and began by saying, I'm sorry I bothered you, disorienting me with the past tense.

He said, I didn't feel good about the second day we talked. I wasn't very on target in my thinking. I wasn't very articulate. I felt very good about the first day because I felt *finally* somebody's talking about something besides how many takes did you do, how much did it cost. But the second day I felt not concentrated, and I just feel very funny about certain subjects. I just feel I don't want to say publicly certain subjects.

I said, Like which?

He said: Like my living situation, like that one private thing I told you the first day, and that one thing about my family, my views about politics, my views about the Palestinians, my views about having children, about drugs, about what I think about psychotherapy, that whole long thing about what I think about women and men—

I said, but those are all the important things you already told me! That's all the central stuff! If I leave everything out, I don't have a piece.

Jarmusch said, Yeah, well, but to you it's a *piece*. But to me it's . . .

I mean, I wasn't very on. I mean, for example, just for a specific example, you asked me about Mamet and I told you about a great play, but it's not even by Mamet, it's by David Rabe!

I'm just a very private person, and it just makes me nervous that everybody I know in New York will read it. It's just . . . hard for me.

I said pettishly, You won't be able to keep retracting so many important things you've already said with other journalists!

Yeah, I know.

I'll transcribe the tape and see if there's any way I can do it and I'll call you back.

Jim said through the wires in a lugubrious voice, I know I shouldn't be calling you even now.

Anyway, says Jim, it is confusing, striving to *be sincere,* and all this attention paid to *what happened in my life.* I was thinking, I was telling her all this stuff about me, blahblahblahblah, and we're really just talking about dumb little movies. This external hype when it's really just: people doing work. I got a review that said, "Jim Jarmusch is the darling of the intelligentsia in the same way that deaf and blind parents would claim their retarded son to be a prodigy!" And *I was happy.* I was really relieved, and getting that review took a lot of pressure off me.

And his plans are what?

"Oh, I don't know. I have no idea. Prepared to get eaten alive. I don't really give a fuck *what* people *want of me,* or what I'm supposed to do as a *career move* or any of that stuff, really. I don't care. Yeah, ultimately it doesn't really concern me."

You just want to make your movies.

"Yeah, and I'll still be able to."

So here is one small thing it is okay to print: "In *Down by Law* the two women characters are important to me because they define the indecisiveness of those two male characters.

"And—*I don't know, I really like women.* I feel like I've learned so much from women who are my lovers or women I've been really close to, about emotions, and about imagination, and about—just things that, just being around men, never occurred to me. And I can't really be more specific than that.

"But I really—I don't know, women—it's important to me to be around women. I get—when I'm just around men, I get very, I feel kind of . . . *one-sided.* Like I can't—

"I don't know—I just . . ." Hopelessly: *"I can't talk."*

No, you're talking, I say.

He stops and falls silent and looks at me.

I see it's my moment to speak. In a small lilting encouraging voice I hear myself tell Jim Jarmusch: No. It's okay. *You're talking.*

In Between Things

PETER VON BAGH AND MIKA KAURISMÄKI / 1987

PETER VON BAGH: *What is the birth process of your films like?*

JIM JARMUSCH: All three of the films I've made have had pretty much the same birth process, backwards, in a way, compared to the normal process. Instead of first conceiving of and sketching out a story, and then choosing the actors for it, I start by thinking about the characters I'd like to write about, characters I'd like to develop, with certain actors in mind. I have a sense of the atmosphere and the actors I'd like to write for, and then I collect details which are connected to the characters and the atmosphere I have in mind, and in a way I let the story evolve out of other, less specific ideas. It's sort of like those drawings that come into existence when you connect the numbered dots. I don't actually have an idea for a story, but ideas about the characters, and I collect those ideas over perhaps the course of a year and then put them all in front of me, and from that the story emerges. I write the dialogue and story outline very quickly, since because I have started with the characters, writing the dialogue is very easy for me. Subconsciously I hear the characters talk to each other and I can write it down very quickly. But nothing is really fixed beforehand, because then I rehearse with the actors and work with each of them to develop their characters. We improvise at rehearsals and I may get new ideas from the actors, and sometimes even the story changes at that point. While rehearsing I'll rewrite the script but when

Published as "Asioiden välissä" in *Filmihullu* 5-6, pp. 63–66. Reprinted by permission. Translated from the Finnish by Ludvig Hertzberg.

I shoot I won't improvise a lot, simply for financial reasons, I don't have the time for it. We shoot pretty much according to the script at this stage, there's some improvisation, but not a lot.

MIKA KAURISMÄKI: *Did* Stranger Than Paradise *have the same birth process?*

JJ: Yes.

MK: *To me it seems more personal, John Lurie's character, the way he moves, acts, talks, that's closer to you yourself and your way of making films than in* Down by Law.

JJ: I'm not sure if that's true or not. *Stranger Than Paradise* is in no way autobiographical. I don't regard it in that way. I think I can identify with his character, and I can identify with both of the American characters in *Down by Law.* And Roberto, who's the center of the story, is in a way a resurrector of these two people, Jack and Zack. But I don't think of my work as personal in that way. I don't analyze where the characters come from, but they are not intended to be about me. A lot of the inspiration for *Stranger Than Paradise* came from John, since it was based on ideas about his character and the mood of the film that we both had, we talked about them together and then I took those ideas and wrote the script. I wanted to write something for Eszter Balint and Richard Edson who are the other two main characters. But that film was different in the sense that I started it as only a half-hour short film. Only when I was editing that first half hour did I begin to write the rest, everything happened kind of gradually.

PVB: *What did the first short version contain?*

JJ: Just the first third of the film, which in the long version is slightly re-cut, slightly shortened. It was just that first part in New York that ends when the two guys sit in their room drinking beer.

PVB: *It's easy to imagine that you became curious about your characters—there are very few films in which the environment interacts so deeply with the characters, and for this reason you were obviously interested in taking them to Cleveland and to Florida. It's fascinating to see them in these different places when at the same time the tensions between them do not change.*

J J :   It was in a way a very peculiar process. While I was editing the first part I originally wanted them to go to Los Angeles, and I wanted the film to end in the same observatory where certain parts of *Rebel Without a Cause* took place. But then I decided it did not suit them to go so far as to California, it suited them better to go to Florida, which is less mythical, which has fewer associations, or less complex ones. When I was a child my family once drove all the way from Ohio to Florida on vacation, and we didn't have a lot of money so we lived in motels, and all of them, it didn't matter if they were in Tennessee or Georgia or Florida, they all looked exactly the same.

P V B :   *It's interesting that you mentioned Los Angeles as being too mythical a place, because your films are concerned exactly with uncovering myths—you manage to uncover the essential ordinariness of the characters.*
J J :   In a way the most ordinary things are the strangest of all, and things that are bound up with more associations and preconceptions are something else. I'm interested in very mundane things—that's why, for example, I didn't take them all the way to Miami in Florida, even if I could have used very beautiful old hotels and stuff like that visually, but I wanted to leave them in some very mundane place.

   To me, rather, *Down by Law* is almost like a fairy-tale, a more imaginary piece. In *Stranger Than Paradise,* the lighting and shooting is deliberately very down to earth. *Down by Law* is more imaginative, since imagination is a theme in the film, Roberto's ability to imagine things, to live in the imagination. *Stranger Than Paradise* is just about things that happen, seen from a certain perspective at a certain time, there are no different points of view, rather all of them are caught up in the same present.

   Italians are very intuitive, imaginative, emotional. The very landscape of Italy, especially of Tuscany, opens up my imagination, at any rate. It's easy to understand why the Pope's residence, the center of Catholicism, is in Italy, since it is the only place where I have been ready to believe that miracles might happen. And Roberto is a true Tuscan. I met Roberto for the first time through a friend of mine whom I was visiting in Italy. At that time I was already writing John's and Tom Waits's characters, but I didn't have the story yet, and as soon as I met Roberto I started collecting notes for a role for him. He spoke no English before the making of the film, so his struggles with language are real, though at the end I had to try to hold him back, since he learned English so fast, and I sometimes had to lie to him by teaching the wrong way of saying something.

P V B :   *Which American directors have been the closest to you in their relation to their actors, who are your favorites?*

J J :   My favorite is Cassavetes, although the style of his films is perhaps the complete opposite of what I'm trying to achieve. I know that they improvise a lot in front of the camera, but I also know that they rehearse a lot, and Cassavetes works very closely with the actors during rehearsals. In the films of Cassavetes, something happens in the actors which I don't think happens in any other American films—sometimes maybe in the early films of Scorsese, some of the acting is similarly moving, but never to the same degree as in Cassavetes's films. I don't think you can translate Cassavetes, there's something very delicate in the way people speak and act in the films of Cassavetes, and it totally disappears for example if they are dubbed, and I'm not sure you can grasp all the nuances and details if you're not an American yourself. There is something in the presence of the actors which is very American—something very transient—I can't really explain it, but I think the acting is what strikes me the most in his films.

And Nick Ray was of course influential, since he worked directly with me, taught me, tried to teach me how to deal with actors. But Nick was very cunning with his actors, while I'm that way only to a very small extent, I may tell different actors different versions of the significance of the sequence. I'm deceitful towards the actors in that respect, but Nick was so in a manipulative way, which worked very effectively for him—I think *Rebel Without a Cause* is the very best work James Dean ever did, he did other good stuff as well, but never on the same level. I don't think Kazan or the others got the same intensity out of him.

P V B :   *In what Kazan did with James Dean there was probably an element of cliché of the kind that marks many of Kazan's films, and which at the same time is also closely connected with his genius.*

J J :   Kazan also had a certain trust in the melodramatic style. His style was more expressive than routine melodrama, but in a way it is still rooted in melodrama. And Nick Ray came from that school and in a way re-invented that style. But there sure is an element of cliché in Kazan's direction of his actors, and even in his choice of subjects, and it is also his strong side, but he isn't as interesting or creative as Nick Ray was, not as daring. In Kazan's films you expect the emotions to come when they do, but the rhythm in Nick Ray's films can be deceptive in the sense that you aren't prepared for a certain burst of emotions at a certain moment.

M K : *I've noticed that you like Nick Ray and Sam Fuller, Hollywood's most merciless directors, in a realistic sense, both at the same time very pathetic, romantic.*
J J : I'm not sure if you can say that—*They Live by Night,* Nick Ray's first film, was probably one of the most romantic films ever made, but I have trouble with the word "realistic." I don't think Sam Fuller's or Nick Ray's films are very realistic; films aren't realistic in general. And especially Nick Ray's films are in a way like architecture, so heavily constructed, manipulative, and Sam's films too, in a less complex way. Sam's films are more intuitive, Nick's films more intellectual, also emotional. I also like Douglas Sirk a lot.

P V B : *No doubt it's true what you said about Kazan, that his approach to his subjects is clichéd as well. It's easy to imagine how the subject of* Down by Law *would have been handled by some Hollywood director, what twists the story would have been given to make it a completely conventional movie. And then your film turns this pattern around completely, it's much more complex.*
J J : My story is perhaps much simpler.

P V B : *It's both, more complex, and at the same time faithful to the simple basics of life.*
J J : Whenever I see a new commercial American movie, and I figure out how the story is structured, I would like to see those pieces that they left out of the movie, more than those they put in. I'm more interested in the moments in between, people waiting for a cab rather than people in a cab. I'm always more interested in the small, ordinary things, and that's why I guess I have a tendency to write the kind of scenes which would be left out in a more conventional or commercial or transparent style. I'm more interested in a conversation between people playing cards than if they are carefully planning an escape from jail, carve a gun from a soap or get a file in a cake or whatever. To me, the important point is that they escape from jail, not how they escape, for example. When I see a movie in which the plot is very clear, I'm always interested in what happens between those sections.

P V B :   *Those black sections in* Stranger Than Paradise, *they have a peculiar, poetic effect: everything is there. During them you start to reflect, to feel and reflect, which a normal film keeps you from doing.*

J J :   I think very simple structural things in films or songs, or in anything else that moves you, are somehow another way of expressing something. I don't want to sound pretentious, but I think the subject of *Stranger Than Paradise* is people who are about to leave each other without knowing what to say to each other, and as soon as the other person has left they know what they would have wanted to say, but then it's too late. Rhythmically, those black sections give the film a measured breath and give the audience a moment to think, to digest the scene they have just been watching, even if it is so simple that it doesn't have to be digested intellectually—it also means that the audience is robbed of the picture for a moment, which is related to the theme of the film, that something is taken away. I don't think the film would work without those black sections; when I edited the first part one of the co-producers of the film wanted me to take out those "empty spaces," but I said that's just why I needed them, I needed empty spaces between the scenes.

P V B :   *A French saying springs to mind, that to leave is to die a little—that's what is at stake here, and in* Stranger Than Paradise *there are sporadic references to death, which is what makes it so moving.*

J J :   There is a Japanese concept, *ma*, which can't really be translated. It expresses the spaces between all the other things—it's not really possible to translate, but in Japan the significance of it is quite obvious, with certain painters. With Ozu and Mizoguchi as well. This feeling, of what is there between everything else, is also very important to me, it's not just a question of the black sections, but also about how the dialogue is written. My favorite moment in *Stranger Than Paradise* is that ending of the first part, where the two guys sit in the room drinking beer. You know that Eddie wants to say something to Willie about the fact that Eva has left, you can sense it, but he doesn't say anything—and I think this sense that he wants to say something is stronger than if he had actually said something.

P V B :   *In a way you render visible for the first time the out-takes, in which there often is something of deeper significance.*

J J : In *Down by Law,* Roberto is, in many out-takes that I didn't use in the film, much funnier than in the film itself, but they didn't work, they were too funny, I had to try to hold Roberto back all the time—the funniest parts did not fit the style of the film, they would have been too obviously comic, they lacked his character's sensibility. But that is actually a completely different matter.

P V B : *What kind of variation do you have in the number of takes?*
J J : Normally I have about three takes of everything, sometimes I have just one and sometimes six, it depends on the shooting conditions, sometimes it's for technical reasons—but sometimes I know that this is that take, and I don't need to shoot it again. I would, however, never use a video monitor connected to the camera, because then I would not use my intuition and not be concentrated since in the back of my mind I would know that I could watch everything again in a second. Then you aren't concentrating at that moment, and to me that would be awful, because I would feel like I was not directing the actors any more, they'd act for the camera and not for me. To me it would be disastrous since it is through intuition and the fact that you observe what is happening on the set while you shoot that you learn to make a film, to direct actors.

P V B : *And what about sound, what's your philosophy in that regard?*
J J : My sound men are in a tough position because I use many wide shots, and we don't like to use radio microphones, since their sound is a bit flat. We use boom microphones in perspective—in other words, if somebody is in the back and somebody in the foreground of the shot, I don't want their voices to be on the same level. And I try to create that perspective on the set, because if you do it afterwards in the mix it's never the same. This means that the quality of sound in my films will never be the best in the field, but it's always in perspective from the point of shooting, and that's important to me. And that's why I won't allow dubbing of my films—I did allow *Down by Law* to be dubbed into French, but on certain conditions, Roberto would have to dub his own character and the dubbed version could not be shown until half a year after the premiere of the original version, and in Paris the dubbed version could be shown only if the original version was also playing in some other theater.

But it was just an experiment, I don't like dubbing, I don't like the fact that the voice is changed—I understand for example Fellini, he chooses the faces on the one hand and the voices on the other, it's his style, but I'm closer to Jean-Marie Straub's conception of sound, she only uses sound recorded directly on the set. I'm not as strict, I do add sound, but I wouldn't want to record the sound to my films in post production. Some films work when they're dubbed, for those these things have little importance, but since I start my whole idea from certain actors, I don't want their voices to be taken off and others put in their place—how could you for example give Tom Waits another voice? I haven't seen the version dubbed into French yet, and I would not want to were it not for Roberto, it'll be interesting to hear him speak French because he speaks French in the same way as English.

Roberto is very aggressive with language, his comedy in Italy is based on language, he uses it like a weapon, he talks as fast as a machine gun, plays with accents. Because of that, *Down by Law* was something very different for Roberto, and that's what the film is ultimately about, that he is robbed of this basic element of communication. He is also very physical, but language is his strength, and it was very challenging for him to try to function without it, he liked that idea.

Personally I like being in a state of bewilderment, I've now lived in Berlin for three months and I have deliberately not studied any German whatsoever. I enjoy visiting Japan, where I'm not even able to read the street signs—it opens up my imagination, it makes me interpret things the wrong way, I live in a state where in a way I'm dependent on my imagination. About fifteen years ago when I was living for a short while in Paris I once shared an apartment with another American guy, who spoke even less French than me—and I asked him to translate some of Mallarmé's poems into English, and the poetry that he wrote was really beautiful, he interpreted things all wrong, assuming that a tree was a boat and so on. There's something very powerful about translating something you don't understand. And then we read a couple of chapters from the Bible in French, and it was a really wonderful book, when you had to imagine for yourself half of what it said.

I like the state of mind when you don't know for sure whether you misinterpret a culture when you don't know its language. I admire poets more than any other artists; you can't translate their work, it is bound up entirely with the character of their culture and language. Poetry is a very abstract thing, very tribal, because only the poet's own tribe can appreciate the music of their language—it's the opposite of music or silent films, they are universal, and in another way I think they are higher forms. But you can't translate poetry, and that's why I respect poets the most. Problems of language make this planet so beautiful and strange. We all live on the same planet but we can't all talk to each other, and that's also the reason for the sad fact that certain ideological solutions which have been introduced throughout history, like that of Marx and Engels, can never actually work. They only work theoretically, in a way, on a global scale, but we can never break free of that tribal feeling we have. The problems of language are to me the most sad and beautiful thing. That we think of things in different ways because the structures of our languages are different is what makes everything interesting.

P V B : *In every respect your films reflect a love for small, important things, the things that are really the basic fabric of our lives. That's why society is the big joke in your films; few films are as supreme in their relation to society. That's very much of what Nick Ray felt and thought.*

J J : Nick Ray's films are always about outsiders. He of course said that the working title for all his films could have been "I'm a Stranger Here Myself." In America, there's such a concern with ambition. We're so fed up with it, this idea about ambition and success. Sure it's everywhere, but especially in the U.S. It's something I'm not interested in, something I don't like, that all my life I've been taught that I have to achieve a certain stage on some economic scale. Who and what is considered important is also based on this economic way of thinking. I've learned a lot more talking to plumbers or truck drivers than I would have learned from politicians and bankers, who are so transparent. Their ambitions are so transparent, and I don't trust anybody who is in politics, I don't trust their ambition. I'm also cynical. When I was younger I was very political minded, I was very idealistic, and now I feel like we have already spoiled our planet. It's based on greed. We have destroyed so many things—how can people even think about continuing for example the use of nuclear power after Chernobyl. They don't care because they're only concerned with their own lifetime. In a way, everything is so late for this planet that to me the simplest things seem to be the most important ones, like a conversation, or going out for a walk with somebody, or the way a certain cloud drifts by, or the light falling on the leaves of a tree, or smoking a cigarette with somebody. Those things are much more valuable to me than all this gibberish. In a way it's cynical. I wouldn't say I'm a nihilist, but to me this planet is really destroyed, and it's very sad, but still there are some small, beautiful things which may perhaps not be around a hundred years from now.

Asphalt Jungle Jim

MARK MORDUE/1988

M M : *What was it about Robby Müller's style that made you want to use him for* Down by Law?

J J : Well, I'm a big fan of Robby's work. I don't think, though, that he necessarily has a signature. In other words, he's worked with Wim Wenders, he's worked with Peter Bogdanovich *(They All Laughed)*, he's worked with Peter Lilienthal *(The Country Is Calm)*, he's worked with Hans Geissendorfer *(The Glass Cell)*, as well as many other people . . . Barbet Schroeder *(A Question of Chance)*, Peter Handke *(The Left-Handed Woman)* . . . it's difficult to explain . . . he doesn't really light from the outside in like most people. He doesn't think of trying to light the characters at a dramatic moment or line. He lights instead, in a way, from what he interprets the emotional content of a scene to be, discussing it with me—which I found rare and interesting. I learnt a lot from him. In America the tendency has been, especially from Hollywood photographers—at least it was fashionable in the last 10 years—to pre-flash things and soften and mute everything. A kind of backing away from the sharpness of the lens, which I never understood at all. Robby's aesthetic is the opposite to that, I think.

M M : *Did you discuss making* Down by Law *in black-and-white with him, and what is it that attracts you to using it?*

J J : No, I decided on that as I was writing the script. As for the attraction, I think there are some people like Woody Allen, for example, or Scorsese, who

Published in *Cinema Papers*, No. 67, January 1988, pp. 20–24. Reprinted by permission.

make an occasional film in black-and-white and the rest in colour. I'd probably like to do the reverse. I'm planning my next two films—one is in colour
and the other in black-and-white. So for me it's a consideration of how I see
the story in my mind when I'm writing it.

I think black-and-white is very interesting and *more* abstract by being minimal and having less information. It seems like people of my generation and
younger grew up seeing newsreel footage in colour, so we associate colour
with reality. Whereas most older people associate black-and-white with a
kind of reality. But for me it's not as realistic.

And there's that whole period of classic film noir in the late forties that's
very unrealistic. That's a style I love. Not to imitate, but to get lost in.

M M :   *You're in Berlin at the moment. Have you found the environment there helpful for what you're writing?*
J J :   Well yeah. But the film's not to take place here. I just came to get out
of New York for a while. Berlin's a strange city because it's really just an
island in the middle of East Germany. We're not on the border of West Germany, we're *inside* East Germany in a walled-in city—it's a strange atmosphere. But New York is also a kind of island, and it doesn't really have
anything to do with America. I don't know . . . I love New York, it's my
home, but I just needed to get away from the mass environment. I like being
in other cultures too because you misinterpret things and somehow it helps
your imagination. I wrote *Down by Law* when I was in Rome.

M M :   *I was curious about your work process for scripts. You've said in the past
that, to an extent, you almost approached writing backwards, starting off with little
details, impressions or characterisations, and that the story sprang out of them,
rather than starting off with the story first.*
J J :   Yeah. The story is, in a way, secondary to me. And the characters are
most important. And the atmosphere. Then the story suggests itself: the
playing out of all the details I've selected. It's then I tell the story, as opposed
to telling the story, then filling in all the details.

M M :   *From having seen* Stranger Than Paradise *and* Down by Law, *it seems to
me that process is reflected in what happens to the characters too. It's like they
experience a whole lot of events, small details and more significant ones, and by
the end they've come to a story of sorts.*

J J : But that seems more accessible to me. Maybe that's just objective, but it seems more like life. I don't see life as a very structured, big dramatic story—it's more a collection of events that you interpret, depending on chance and your emotional state.

M M : *You don't seem to deal with existentially tormented figures so much as people who accept, perhaps fatalistically, what's happening around them.*
J J : Yeah . . . but that gets complicated. You can find instances of existential thought in these kinds of characters. But at the same time I think of my films as comedies—they're *dark* comedies. I'm interested in the sense of humour and emotional qualities of the characters rather than the existential distancing which seemed to be very fashionable in the cinema of the late seventies.

M M : *Unfortunately that notion of existential distance has also become a tool of reaction. It's led to a kind of ugly fatalism.*
J J : Well, I'm very cynical anyway. And I think we have pretty much destroyed this planet, and I don't really understand it. Certain solutions have been offered throughout history—and thinking—and they've not been able to be applied. So I'm at the point of cynicism where I think that the small things which happen between people are very beautiful . . . the very special things that happen on this planet. And if we experience them as humans, at least we're still here to experience. But in general I don't have a lot of respect for the way governments have treated this planet, my own country in particular.

M M : *In light of your successes and added pressure or interest from major film groups to come over to their side, how do you feel about that whole politics of film?*
J J : Well I've certainly changed since *Stranger Than Paradise* in that I'm not blind to the politics of making a film, in that films cost a lot of money. What I'm interested in is doing my own work, not working with someone else. And therefore it seems like the best way for me to continue is to produce my own stuff, which is how I plan it to be for my next film, with my partner Otto Grokenberger. But I have another film planned after the next one which may require a bigger budget . . . not big by American standards, but maybe $3 million.

With that film, I don't know. I keep my options open. But what I will *not* do is be subject to some producer who should be running an underwear factory telling me how to cut my film or who to cast in it. I'm not about to compromise that stuff. I'd rather be a motorcycle repairman than make some kind of film I don't believe in or feel good about.

At the same time I do want to reach some kind of audience, even though I don't think about the audience very much when structuring the films. I do still get a lot of interest, and there are a lot of possibilities for production, but I'm not ready to compromise to those people and that ends a lot of possibilities immediately. They say they're interested but I don't really trust them.

M M :   *When you say "they," you're obviously talking about Hollywood?*
J J :   I'm talking about people who think of films as packages, and therefore want to control how the package is put together.

M M :   *How alive, then, do you think the American underground, left-of-field, low budget cinema is at the moment?*
J J :   Well I don't think underground films exist anymore. If they do exist it's on the Super 8 format, and therefore underground by format alone because they can't be shown in the conventional cinema. . . . The term independent is relative because you're not independent unless you're independently wealthy and produce films with your money—which no-one in their right mind does. So you're not independent financially.

I don't really know what the state is. I mean, I see interesting directors like Susan Seidelman make a fairly large budget film and I don't see that it has hurt her style or what she wants to do. So it depends on how people want to work. Spike Lee has just made a new film for Columbia Pictures. I know he was in vogue and formerly considered as an underground director. Same for Alex Cox.

So I don't really know of any underground "scene." I just hope these so-called independent directors want to protect their own ideas and are able to make films any way they can, even in the studios. As long as their ideas are protected. We're at an interesting stage right now in that regard—we can *see* what happens to Spike Lee and his new film. I'm real happy when I see a film like *Blue Velvet* doing well in the States commercially at a time when *Top Gun* is the major money-making film. The thing is, if ideas are protected then life is breathed into the American cinema. It's *essential* to protect those ideas in order to breathe with life. I don't know if that will happen or if those ideas will just get compromised.

M M : *In your films you lean towards using people who aren't strictly actors—*
people who come at acting from a skewed perspective, such as musicians.
J J : Well I think that helps because I have an odd sense of constructing a
film, and also of directing. So, for example, the long takes themselves allow
certain actors without a very strong method to be stronger because they're
able to maintain their character over a longer period of time without their
being cut-up every five minutes for the camera positions and repeating the
same things from different angles.

There are a lot of actors who are just actors and are always acting. That's
something that annoys me—when I see an actor's method going on outside
the character, then I'm not involved with the character, I'm involved with
them as an actor. I think that certain people who have, somehow, a broader
sense of performance, like musicians, or Roberto, who is also a comedian, are
sometimes able to bring something to the style of acting or to the character
that actors aren't. It's nothing against actors, because I think some actors are
really great—someone like Ellen Barkin for example. But it's rare. There are
so many bad actors, and the style of acting in American commercial films at
the moment isn't very good at all.

M M : *Well it's television acting, isn't it? Looking at American TV from an Austra-*
lian perspective, seeing what they're supposed to represent, it seems that year by
year the reality and morality become less and less real. It's hard to believe that
audiences can accept them at any level.
J J : Yeah, and it's getting worse and worse. It's very sad to think that American TV audiences are just *mesmerised* by something that is so condescending.
And there's so much of it, especially with cable and video as well. In the
States everyone watches television constantly—they don't read books anymore. That's partly why there's no underground cinema. It's also affected
people politically—things are not polarised anymore. It's all homogenous. A
wash of mediocrity over everything that emanates from television.

M M : *Well television is so physically small and confined—it shouldn't be that*
way, but the ambitions and fantasies are similarly confined. Whereas cinema is
such a large and total experience. Television diminishes the dreams.
J J : That's true. When you see a movie it's very magical, because you're
watching it in a theatre, a darkened room, with other people. Somehow it's
like Plato's Cave. With TV everything's interrupted. Your attention span is

reduced. I like what Godard said once when he was asked about the difference between cinema and television. He replied, "When you watch cinema, you look *up* at the screen. When you watch television, you look *down* at it."

M M :   *Is that sense of something foreign and magical why you seem to be attracted to Europe and/or European characters as a kind of pivot for the dreams of the people around them?*

J J :   Well, not specifically. I think that America is a country that doesn't really have its own culture, and is made up of the various cultural influences of the people who inhabited it. I'm like a mongrel. My family is Czech, German, and Irish. So I'm all mixed up. And American culture is made of those strange mixtures. That's something which *is* very American.

So I'm drawn to European characters because, in a sense, they're the essence of America also. And I'm influenced by the style of film directors from Europe or Japan, in a way, more than I am from Hollywood. So I'm also in the middle of the Atlantic floating around somewhere when it comes to the themes in my films.

It's funny. I feel like I've been exposed to some American directors only through being in Europe. I became interested in Samuel Fuller and Nicholas Ray through Godard and Wim Wenders's writings. So it's kind of a strange circular pattern, coming back to directors in your own country through directors in Europe.

And I hope that some younger American directors, in a way, will move it back again. Reflect those ideas again. Create an interesting circular pattern. Because Godard, in a way, his *misapplication* of American style in terms of *Breathless* and *Alphaville* is very fascinating. It's like a misinterpretation that brings something new.

Mystery Man

LUC SANTE/1989

W ITH THE RELEASE OF *Mystery Train,* his fourth feature film, Jim Jarmusch is almost ready for his own adjective. His lyrical comedies—with their spare look, deadpan dialogue, archetypal American settings and music, and characters who are variously immigrants, tourists, vagrants, and amiable lowlifes—are absolutely distinctive. His eye and ear animate a whole spectrum of marginalized people, places, and situations whose humor, beauty, and pathos might otherwise be overlooked, and they have the power to carry that vision off the screen and out into the world. Maybe "Jarmusch-esque" is a bit of a mouthful, though.

Jarmusch, born and raised in Akron, Ohio, came to New York as an undergrad to attend Columbia, and has lived and worked in the city ever since. For the last decade he has lived in the toughs of Little Italy with filmmaker Sara Driver. At NYU film school he studied under Nicholas Ray, among others (and worked as a production assistant on the Ray–Wim Wenders memento mori *Lightning Over Water*). His senior-thesis project turned into *Permanent Vacation* (1980), which won prizes at the Mannheim and Figueira da Foz festivals and became a long-running cult favorite in Europe. A half-hour featurette called *Stranger Than Paradise,* which he made using 35mm black-and-white stock left over from Wenders's *The State of Things,* attracted so much attention in 1982 that two years later he expanded it into a ninety-minute feature film, which won the Caméra d'Or at Cannes and became a

Originally published in **INTERVIEW**, November 1989. Reprinted courtesy of Brant Publications, Inc.

hit all over the world, including the United States. His third film, *Down By Law* (1986), was also well received; not the least of its many distinctions was that it alerted audiences everywhere to the idiosyncratic talents of the Italian comic actor Roberto Benigni.

Mystery Train, which won the prize for Best Artistic Contribution at Cannes this past May and received its American premiere at the New York Film Festival, is a meditation on nighttime and transience, on rhythm-and-blues and the city of Memphis, that comes camouflaged as a deck of three stories. Like its predecessors, it mixes high and low comedy, sadness and high jinks, and extracts a subtle, limpid beauty from the rawest of materials. It also features a dazzling and motley array of actors: from the Japanese teen star Youki Kudoh to the veteran R&B singers Screamin' Jay Hawkins and Rufus Thomas; from Joe Strummer, who formerly fronted the Clash, to Rick Aviles, who hosted TV's *It's Showtime at the Apollo. Mystery Train* opens this month in major cities, and nationwide in January.

Jarmusch and I go back to early college days, where we formed half of the Columbia Poetry Team (we once read to an audience of three at Harvard's *Advocate* house), and later shared the squalor of a series of group apartments. We are nevertheless still friends. The following conversation took place over two Sunday afternoons distinguished by high humidity.

LUC SANTE: *Did you start wanting to make movies when you were a kid, or did that come later?*

JIM JARMUSCH: It really happened by accident. I wanted to be a writer or a poet or something. After finishing college at Columbia I didn't quite know what to do with myself, and I couldn't really afford to go to graduate school. I went to NYU film school on scholarship because I had always had an interest in still photography. When I was a kid I worked after school for a friend of mine's father who was a semiprofessional part-time photographer and did wedding photos and stuff on weekends. His son and I had beat-up cameras and were always taking pictures, so he hired both of us to work in his darkroom.

LS: *What's the first movie you ever saw?*

JJ: The first one that made an impact on me was in Florida, on vacation—I went to a drive-in with my mother and sister and saw *Thunder Road,* with Robert Mitchum. I think I was seven years old. But I remember all the car chases and roadblocks they crashed through in hopped-up '57 Chevys. It made a real impression on me. It was an exciting and violent and dark criminal world that was on the screen. I've avoided seeing it again, maybe to preserve the abstract haze of my memory.

L S :   *I remember your telling me about this place you used to go to for kids in Akron, an underground-movie house.*

J J :   During normal hours it was a porno theater, and then on Friday or Saturday nights they had what they called under-ground cinema, films nobody else would show. They'd show three-hour programs, starting at midnight, and we'd go every weekend. They'd begin each week with an episode of the Buster Crabbe *Flash Gordon* series, and they'd stick in things by Stan Brakhage and Andy Warhol, along with semi-porno shorts and cartoons. It really opened us up to "noncommercial" cinema.

L S :   *In a place like Akron you probably weren't seeing Godard movies.*

J J :   We didn't know what they were. But we knew a lot of things because of our friends' older brothers. I don't have an older brother, but my friends did, and when they weren't home we'd sneak into their rooms and listen to *Freak Out,* by the Mothers of Invention, and borrow their copies of *Candy* and *Naked Lunch.* We were a little secret club of younger kids trying to pilfer some kind of alternative culture. Otherwise culture for kids in Akron was only rock 'n' roll and cars, which I guess was true all over the country.

Going back to the subject of wanting to make movies, I should mention that when I was in college I went to study in Paris for a semester and ended up staying for a year. In Paris I saw so many films, especially at the Cinémathèque, that I hadn't had a chance to see even in New York. Ironically enough I discovered American films—films by Nick Ray, Sam Fuller, Don Siegel, Preston Sturges . . . I'd seen only a few of them on the late show on TV.

When people ask me whether I consider myself more European or more American in my style, I say sort of facetiously that I see myself in a small boat somewhere in the middle of the Atlantic. For me and a lot of filmmakers of our generation, much of our awareness of the American cinema came, in a strange circular way, through the Nouvelle Vague. I would read what Rivette or Godard or Truffaut or Rohmer wrote about Howard Hawks, for example. I knew Godard's films before I knew Sam Fuller's, and I learned about

Fuller from books, or from references within other films, or from Fuller's acting appearance in a Godard film. The Nouvelle Vague also helped to eliminate the division between high culture and low culture. There shouldn't be a differentiation between Mickey Spillane and Herman Melville—as long as the book affects us. That's something that also comes from rock 'n' roll.

L S : *Ten years ago, when you were making films in school and a lot of people our age were just starting out, there was a rejection of virtuosity going on, in music especially. It was possible to make music without necessarily knowing how to play an instrument. Do you feel you were influenced by that idea at all?*

J J : Definitely. The people who were making films ten years ago in New York—Eric Mitchell, James Nares, Becky Johnston, Amos Poe, Vivienne Dick—all of us were really influenced by that. If it hadn't been for that music scene we probably wouldn't be making films. Rock 'n' roll bands said, "Fuck virtuosity. We have something that we feel, and even if our expression of it is musically amateurish, it doesn't mean that our vision is." That helped me, and other people, to realize that even if we didn't have the budget or the production structure to make films, we could still make them, using Super 8 and 16mm equipment, and scratching funds together.

L S : *Now it seems as though the current has come back the other way—it's not virtuosity so much as a deadening professionalism.*

J J : We're in a new phase of technology where you don't have to know how to play an instrument because you can pre-program it. People orchestrate music instead of composing or performing it. Which is a little bit disturbing to me. I think we're about due for a new reaction against completely computerized music, against high production values. There was recently a retrospective of Cassavetes's films at the Museum of Modern Art, and everybody I know seems to have gone and has been talking about them. I think in a year or two you'll start to see a kind of swing away from production value and back toward the heart of things, which Cassavetes epitomizes. He didn't give a shit if his shots cut together well. What mattered was which take was most true emotionally. Technological advances are fine as long as people think of them as tools and not as ends in themselves.

L S : *Don't you, as an American independent filmmaker, sometimes feel lonely? Independent films seemed to blossom for a while, and then so many distributors went out of business. A lot of people who were making independent movies in New York are now either working in Hollywood or not doing much at all.*

J J :   You have to stick to your guns. Some people see making a successful independent film as their ticket to Hollywood, and if so they should be direct about it. There's nothing wrong with that; I won't criticize them. But there aren't enough people who stick it out and say, "Fuck that, I'm not doing it. I'd rather walk away." That's my attitude, and maybe some people think it's arrogant. But it's true, I'd rather walk away. Life is too short.

Of course I want to continue with my work; I hope to do it for my entire life, however long that is. At the same time I know I wouldn't be able to function in a certain system, so I have to create my own in order to do my work the way I do it, and I hope I'm learning to do it well. If I had some producer telling me, "You've got to have these 'stars' in the film; you've got to use this generic Jan Hammer music. We're going to edit it when you're done; just take a vacation and don't worry about it," I might end up in jail for shooting somebody.

L S :   *Imagine if you'd been around in an earlier era, if you'd been born thirty or forty or fifty years earlier. Would you have been a Hollywood director; or would you have been an avant-garde director, making little movies in semi-clandestine fashion; or would you have pursued some other line of work?*

J J :   If I was interested in the acting-out of stories, I think I would have been drawn to the theater, and then maybe, as in Nick Ray's case, that would have led me to Hollywood. Or I might have been a painter. That's impossible to say. I might have been able to function in the way that Howard Hawks talks about, designing and shooting movies so that they could be cut only in a certain way. There were real strengths to the Hollywood system, and meanwhile people who were sure of themselves, like Hawks, were able to make their films the way they wanted by means of sneaky tactics. There's a story about Sam Fuller making *Shock Corridor.* At that time they would shoot two endings, so that the studio could choose between them. Fuller made sure they could use only his ending by saving the flood scene for the last day of shooting. He flooded all the sets, causing all kinds of lawsuits, so that there was no way they could go back into production.

L S :   *If, somehow, you didn't have to worry about raising money, would you make movies more often? Or do you need a hiatus of a year or two between films as a gestation period?*

JJ: No, I'd make them more often. I could never be as prolific as some people, because I have a slow rhythm, but each film wouldn't take so long. It's like this: I write the film, I go through preproduction and production, I shoot it, and then I'm there for the entire postproduction. I'm there to make decisions about who the film is sold to and to be consulted about how the film is released. I could sell the film off to one company and then let them sell it in Europe to whoever they want, but that would mean my films would be dubbed, shown in shopping malls in Germany for two weeks, and then pulled. If the distributors I wanted got my films every time and I didn't have to go through all the nonsense, I could make films more often. I have four or five ideas for projects right now. I think my rhythm is ideally one film per year, but business slows it down to two years.

LS: *Did you ever have the impulse to make a movie on a larger scale?*
JJ: Like a sci-fi soft-core Western for Coca-Cola Pictures? If I had an idea like that I would go for it, but I don't have those kinds of ideas. You know, would you rather be Victor Hugo or Paul Verlaine? I consider myself a minor poet who writes fairly small poems. I don't try to make epic-scale things.

LS: *I was thinking of John Huston and whatever sort of devil's agreement he had with the industry. On the one hand he'd make little movies, such as* Wise Blood *and* Fat City, *and on the other hand he'd make epics*—Moby Dick, The Bible.
JJ: Fassbinder also wanted to do that, to get grander and grander, but his aesthetic was suited to that. I make films about marginal characters. I'm not sure how to fit marginal characters, which are the most interesting to me, into something grand. As I say that, though, I think, Wow, there are a lot of possibilities. You could set a couple of bums in the middle of World War I. It would be a great movie, just following by small details these traditionally insignificant characters in this huge historical setting. But I'm not really drawn to that. I'd rather make a movie about a guy walking his dog than about the emperor of China.

LS: *What's the worst review you've ever gotten?*
JJ: I think it was some Parisian right-wing newspaper that published one that said: "The French intelligentsia's praise for Jarmusch reminds one of deaf, dumb, and blind parents applauding their retarded child." And it even

went on to say, "Jarmusch is thirty-three years old, the same age as Christ at the time of his death. One can only hope for the same for him."

L S :   *That's unbelievable. It's like physical assault.*
J J :   Yeah, but it's my favorite review.

L S :   *About* Mystery Train: *which came first, the idea of setting a movie in Memphis or the idea of doing a movie with three stories in it?*
J J :   The idea of three stories came first. I began the first story before we even started filming *Down by Law,* but I was thinking of it as a one-act play. The idea of the second story vaguely came from something that happened to Nicoletta Braschi, and the third story came later on.

L S :   *You'd never been to Memphis before you decided to make a movie about it, right?*
J J :   Right. At one point, though, I even thought I should call this movie *Memphis,* and call the last one *[Down by Law] New Orleans,* and make another one called *Kansas City,* following the music. Music leads me to the location somehow, and it also gives me all kinds of excuses to do research. I can search for rare records, and I can study the histories of these cities.

In this case Memphis related because of the ghost story. Initially the first story had nothing to do with Elvis or Memphis; it was just a story of young lovers who argued all the time, and one gradually realized that their arguments were somehow a cohesive element in their relationship. The idea of the ghost came in before all the Elvis-sighting stuff, although I'm sure some people will think it was a conscious attempt to be au courant.

What I like about the idea of Japanese kids in Memphis is, if you think about tourists visiting Italy, the way the Romantic poets went to Italy to visit the remnants of a past culture, and then if you imagine America in the future, when people from the East or wherever visit our culture after the decline of the American empire—which is certainly in progress—all they'll really have to visit will be the homes of rock 'n' roll stars and movie stars. That's all our culture ultimately represents. So going to Memphis is a kind of pilgrimage to the birthplace of a certain part of our culture.

L S :   *Music is always so important in your movies, even when it's used minimally.*
J J :   The pop music or rock 'n' roll in the films is always the music that the characters are listening to. With the exceptions of the title sequences in

Down by Law and *Mystery Train*, I don't use songs specifically as sound track. What I like about pop music is how it affects your emotions through memory. I like it when characters actually select music to listen to—it somehow deepens your understanding of them.

L S :   *How did you direct the Japanese actors? Were you able to direct them in English, or did you work through an interpreter?*

J J :   Youki Kudoh speaks English minimally, but she's a real quick study of languages. Masatoshi Nagase really didn't speak English at all; I'm not sure if he'd ever been outside of Japan, though as a result of the film he lived in New York this summer, studying English. So it was a complicated process. I wrote the script in English, and then a Japanese director named Kazuki Oomori translated my script into Japanese. I worked on the dialogue with the actors and my interpreter, Yoshiko Furusawa. As with all actors, I let them improvise in rehearsal, and then I changed my script according to what made us all feel most comfortable about the language. For me, the creation of a character is always a collaboration with the actor, which also comes from writing with specific actors in mind. In Japanese the process was a little complicated, since I couldn't know exactly what the nuances of the changes were. My interpreter was very helpful in trying to explain those nuances, but I couldn't know precisely how the dialogue was changing. I had to rely on intuition and trust the actors. Then, when the film was shot, I had yet another translator translate the Japanese dialogue back into English, and then I translated that English into my choice of English, and my retranslation is what appears in the subtitles. In the end the subtitles are pretty close to my original script.

When I auditioned actors in Japan I wrote out little sketches for them to improvise from, in which there were a few words of English that I could use as markers to follow the dialogue. I have always wanted to make a great Japanese film, but obvious circumstances prevent that.

L S :   *So you had the film pretty much cast in your head when you were writing the script?*

J J :   I had Youki already in my head while I was writing, I had Nicoletta in my head, and I had Lizzie Bracco as Dee Dee sort of fluttering around in my head. I had Joe Strummer, I had Steve Buscemi, I had Screamin' Jay Hawkins, and I had Cinqué Lee. I had all the actors except for the parts of Jun and Will

Robinson. It's very difficult for me to write a blank character and then go out and try to find the actor.

L S : *I wouldn't have guessed that you didn't have Nagase in mind when you wrote Jun.*

J J : I was just lucky to find him, and Rick Aviles for Will Robinson. I auditioned a lot of people for both those roles. I don't like auditioning. It makes me nervous; it makes them nervous. I have a lot of sympathy for actors and the erratic pattern of their lives. They're always waiting, they don't know what's next, they don't know if they're going to get cut out of the last thing they did. They have to trust the director, they have to trust the editor, they even have to trust the people releasing the film, and then if the film is a flop, even if they did great work their next job is in jeopardy.

L S : *Here's an inevitable question: Why did you decide to make this one in color?*

J J : I wish I could think up something more clever, but the truth is that when I start conceiving a story, imagining it, I have a certain sense of it visually. This one I always thought of as being in color. I spouted off a lot in the past, defending my use of black-and-white, saying that people who use color these days take color for granted because it's worth more in the video and TV markets—and that's all true. They don't pay any attention to what color means. They haven't read Kandinsky's essays on color; they don't study color the way Nick Ray did, or use it deliberately, the way he did in *Rebel Without a Cause* or *Johnny Guitar* or *Party Girl*. It has a lot to do with the story. In this film we paid a lot of attention to color. We had meetings constantly, with little memos, between the art department, the wardrobe department, the photography department, and the prop master. On locations we all worked together to limit the colors to certain values. Red objects are at least subconsciously symbolic, and the choice of which objects are red wasn't random but very intentional. Things don't jump out, they're not pointed to, and yet they have an effect. The spectrum doesn't include orange or bright green or bright blue or bright red or yellow. The palette needed muted tones of browns and greens and blues.

L S : *Back to acting. The three guys in the third story have such disparate acting styles, and yet their interaction is wonderfully harmonious. How did that happen?*

JJ: Something I've learned, that I'm learning, is that there's no such thing as a single procedure to follow, not even from the director's point of view. Each actor has a totally different way of thinking about acting. Steve Buscemi comes from theater and performance. Rick Aviles comes from stand-up comedy on the street and at the Apollo. Joe Strummer comes from rock 'n' roll performance; he doesn't think of himself as an actor. Nicoletta is different from all of them, and Youki is different from Nagase, and Screamin' Jay and Cinqué are very different from each other.

Screamin' Jay wasn't familiar with acting, with the lingo. He's very quick, but it took *me* a couple of days before I found a way of speaking to him on the set. I talked to him as if it were a recording studio. I'd say, "O.K., don't overlap her line, because you're going to bleed through, like one guitar part over another," or "Now we're going to overdub." Strummer came the closest of any actor in the film to using a method, a very classical method, and he arrived at it on his own somehow. He said to me at one point, "When I walk onto the set to shoot a take, I feel like I'm carrying a basket of eggs. Staying in character is like trying to get there without dropping any of the eggs." He always went to a corner and stayed there chain-smoking until we were ready to shoot. Whereas Rick Aviles was all over the place chatting, a ball of energy, and then when the camera came on he was in character.

If I were to cast a film based on commercial considerations, the actors' methods might be closer to one another, but I like the differences. They excite me. That's why I like the neorealists' use of nonactors, or Cassavetes's way of blending them with more experienced actors, who often help pull their performances up to the same level. I'm trying to learn to work that way.

LS: *What directors do you admire these days?*
JJ: I've discovered a great Japanese director named Suzuki, whose films haven't really been shown here. He's kind of a cross between Sam Fuller, Douglas Sirk, and Buñuel, and he made most of his films in the '60s. Raúl Ruiz is certainly original. He makes at least two or three films a year—he just keeps working—and he's completely on his own stylistically, with a very rare kind of vision. Jacques Rivette is like that too. I really look forward to seeing *La Bande des Quatre*. I like Aki Kaurismäki's films a lot. They speak to me somehow, especially *Shadows in Paradise* and *Ariel*. I love Chantal Akerman's film *Toute une Nuit*, although it's not really a recent film. Claire Denis is an interesting director, with a very strong sense of craft, a sense of rhythm, and

a very elegant, minimal style. I actually prefer her documentary, *Man No Run,* about a rock group from Cameroon called Les Têtes Brûlées, to her fiction film *Chocolat.* I loved *Dead Ringers,* by David Cronenberg, and his *Videodrome* was a great film too. I thought *Wings of Desire* was great. I didn't like the ending, and I had some other problems with it, but it looked like no other film I've ever seen. I liked *Do the Right Thing* a lot. My problems with it are very minor, just little details that bother me. The overall effect and intention are very strong and important. In twenty years, when Spike is the minister of culture, I'll be making whitesploitation movies.

L S :   *That's a very international community.*

J J :   It is kind of an international community. If I can find some affinity with Raúl Ruiz, but I can't find an affinity with, say, Brian De Palma, who is supposedly from my culture, then all those lines are disintegrating, which is good. I can feel close to young filmmakers in Tokyo or Rome or Helsinki; they don't have to be from the Lower East Side. And video ultimately is great, because it gives us access to more films. It's still disappointing to see a film alone on a small screen instead of experiencing it in a big space with the lights off and with other people, but on the other hand we can go out and find, for example, Georges Franju's movies on videotape when we want. It reminds me of what Godard said when he was asked what the difference was between cinema and video. He said, "In the cinema you look up at the screen, and with TV you look down at it."

L S :   *Do you feel you have any political role?*

J J :   I have very strong political opinions, but I don't feel that my work is the place for overt political expression. Everything is political, and what I truly detest in cinema is films that take things for granted, films that passively lead you to believe, consciously or not, that capitalism, racism, greed, the concept of success, Christianity, the family as a consumer unit, etc. are just part of the way things are. That, to me, is dangerous. At the same time I think the only films, or works of expression in any form, that are politically effective are those that ask questions and that cause the audience to ask questions. At the very least, my films concern characters who consciously locate themselves outside the zombie mainstream.

A few years ago, when I'd been looking at Rossellini's historical films, I wanted to make a film about Andrew Jackson: the true story of Andrew Jackson, about a guy who commits genocide, who slaughters the Indians in Florida, who starts his law practice in Tennessee by importing hookers over the mountains from Virginia and pimping them off. These are things he actually did, and now he's on our currency and revered as an American hero. People say my films are optimistic, but I have a very deep pessimism that maybe comes from being American. America is about objectifying everything and making it marketable, about greed and profit. I react against that by making films about displaced or marginal characters and the seemingly inconsequential little things they do.

People say there are a limited number of possible stories, and that they've already all been told. I believe this is basically true. There are billions of people, yet their stories all fit into a limited number of plot categories. But what fascinates me is that every single person's perspective on life is individual and different from anyone else's. My interest is in those minor differences of perception and circumstance. That's why I like Balzac. Those differences, and where the edges blur, are the things that excite me most about being alive on this planet. But sadly, ironically, those differences, while defining the beauty of the world, are also the things that may prevent its continuing existence.

L S :   *I understand that you're a member of a cabal called the Sons of Lee Marvin International.*
J J :   That's true. I'm not at liberty to divulge information about the organization, other than to tell you that it does exist. I can identify three other members of the organization: Tom Waits, John Lurie, and Richard Boes.

L S :   *These are all people with long faces.*
J J :   That's one prerequisite for being a member: you have to have a facial structure such that you could be related to, or be a son of, Lee Marvin. There are no women, obviously, in this organization. We have communiqués and secret meetings. Other than that, I can't talk about it.

Shot by Shot: *Mystery Train*

CATHLEEN MCGUIGAN/1990

THE LAST TIME FILMMAKER Jim Jarmusch was in London, he was talking to a friend who makes rock videos. "He was telling me that on his newest videos, these producers and technicians kept asking, 'What's the IPM factor?' 'The what?' he wondered. 'You know, IPM—images per minute. What's the image-per-minute ratio you're going to get in this video?' " Jarmusch grins. "I mean, for me, if you tried to get an IPM breakdown for my films, it would be, like, *four*—four images per minute."

There's no doubt about it: in the age of MTV, when dizzying quick cuts make most movies jump, Jim Jarmusch is the slowest shot in the West. His 1984 sleeper hit, *Stranger Than Paradise*, a laconic comedy in black and white, was so minimalist that watching it was a Zen experience: each scene was a single take, and the camera panned only to follow a character who ambled across a room. Jarmusch's next feature, *Down by Law*, was a little fancier. Though his backers couldn't persuade him to shoot in color ("I already had the film in my head in black and white—and I don't let anybody change my mind"), the camera traveled more, following his trio of convicts on the lam. But he still stuck to a strict code that bucked such movie conventions as close-ups. "When you put a big close-up on the screen, it has a *meaning*," the thirty-six-year-old, writer-director explains. "It's a kind of manipulation that's supposed to signify a *big* moment."

As anyone who's seen a Jarmusch movie knows, he likes *little* moments—

Published in *Premiere* (U.S.), Vol. 3, No. 5, January 1990, pp. 80–83. Reprinted by permission of the author.

attitudes and visual details that create an offbeat universe and showcase the idiosyncrasies of his oddball characters. The essence of his movies is the stuff most moviemakers leave out. "When I watch more mainstream films," he says, "I realize that I drift away and wonder what happened between scenes, the little incidental things. If a guy has an argument with his girlfriend on the phone and then it cuts to him showing up at her house, I'm still back there wondering how he *got* to her house, what was his mood like, did he drive around a while, did he listen to the radio?"

With his latest film, *Mystery Train,* Jarmusch has created his most elaborate series of little moments yet, and his most lavish junk subculture. Made on a budget that's big by Jarmusch standards—$2.8 million—and shot in color, the movie is a series of three stories, each of which takes place on the same night in the same seedy hotel in Memphis.

"I'm not a mainstream kind of guy," explains the lanky Jarmusch as he smokes a Camel Light. "I just don't relate to mainstream movies or music or literature. I like things that are on the extremes, either what's considered trash or what's considered 'artsy,' unfortunately." Jarmusch's powerfully quirky film style comes from the B movies he grew up watching in Akron and especially from the elegant austerity of the foreign filmmakers he admires, such as Max Ophuls and Yasujiro Ozu.

Like *Stranger Than Paradise* and *Down by Law, Mystery Train* looks at American culture partly through foreign eyes. In the first segment of the film, a pair of young Japanese tourists, visiting America's rock 'n' roll shrines, arrive in Memphis by train. "I write characters with specific actors in mind," says Jarmusch, explaining that he wrote the role of the bubbly, innocent Mitzuko specifically for the Japanese actress Youki Kudoh. Later he cast Masatoshi Nagase as her dour boyfriend, Jun. Jarmusch has been to Japan five times, and his films are popular there (*Stranger Than Paradise* won a major Japanese award), but he says he didn't set out to make a movie about Japanese visitors in America. (*Mystery Train* also happens to be the first independent American film fully underwritten by JVC, the Victor Company of Japan.) "It's really more the fact that I travel and meet these people and get an idea for a character for them, and less my intention to go out and make a film about foreigners in America," he says.

He heisted the idea for the first segment from a one-act play he'd written about a young couple who always argue. "At first you think it's something that keeps them apart or that it's tension between them," he says, "but as the play progresses, you realize that it unifies them, that they enjoy it, that it's their way of communicating." As they wander about Memphis's streets and take a hilarious tour of Sun Studio, Mitzuko and Jun continue to argue one key question: Who was the greatest Memphis musician? For her, it's undeniably Elvis; for him, it's Carl Perkins. They play out their debates in Japanese, of course; the film supplies English subtitles. In order to work with the actors, Jarmusch had to have an interpreter on the set in Memphis but claims the language barrier turned out to be "no problem at all."

Jarmusch says he starts thinking about a film visually and collects ideas for maybe a year. "Before I've written anything except notes, I already know how I see it, whether it's color or black and white, or what kind of color," he says. He saw *Mystery Train* in color but wanted a cool palette—"There are no yellows or oranges"—with just a few jolts of red, such as the big red suitcase the Japanese lug around. For each film, he devises a set of "oblique strategies," a term he lifted from musician Brian Eno: a code of constraints to guide the shooting.

Some of his unconventional methods drove the original script supervisor on *Mystery Train* so nuts that she left the production. "We paid no attention to the rules of screen direction," says Jarmusch. "The first thing you learn in film school is that there's an imaginary line across the set, and the camera's not supposed to cross it." Contrary to established procedure, Jarmusch gleefully crosses the line on a number of occasions.

Here are some of Jarmusch's dos and don'ts of moviemaking:

Don't storyboard every shot of the movie. "If I have to follow a map, I'm not on an exploration anymore."

Don't cover each scene with the traditional master shot, medium shot, close-up, close-up. "I like the camera to stay far enough away from the characters. It gives a certain rhythm that allows the audience to choose the details they want to observe."

Forget the rest of the rule book. If a character walks out of the frame to the left, who says that in the next shot, he has to enter the frame from the right?

An early passage in the film shows off the economy and formality of Jarmusch's style. Mitzuko and Jun have been wandering around Memphis without a place to stay. After hanging out near a statue of Elvis, they set out in search of lodging. The sequence starts with a static shot of a street; then they enter the frame, and the camera begins to follow them. Jarmusch couldn't get the dolly tracks he needed, so he put the camera on the tailgate of a station wagon, and eight crew members pushed the car. "It's a hell of a weight to stop dead within three inches of a mark," he says.

Mitzuko spots the red-neon-lit Arcade hotel down the street. "We break the rule, cross the line, and see them from the other side in a medium two-shot, and then we cut back again to the other side as they walk toward the hotel. Then we cut to inside the hotel, a kind of establishing shot of the lobby."

In the lobby scene, Jarmusch introduces two of his great supporting characters: R&B singer Screamin' Jay Hawkins, who plays the night clerk in a screamin' red jacket, and Cinqué Lee, Spike's younger brother, who plays the bellhop, complete with pillbox cap. The two Japanese kids come in and register, and the bellhop takes them upstairs.

The scene cuts to a grotesquely wallpapered hotel room with a big portrait of Elvis hanging over the bed. After a scene in which Mitzuko tips the bellhop with a Japanese plum that she's pulled from the neatly crammed suitcase ("I told my property manager that I wanted it to be packed so that it looked like the inside of a transistor radio," the director says), the camera cuts to the two kids sitting on the hotel-room floor.

"We call this the Ozu shot," says Jarmusch of his little homage to the director of the 1953 classic *Tokyo Story*. Ozu, he explains, used a tripod for his camera with only two height settings—one near the floor, where his characters sat, and one few feet higher. "He almost never, ever moved his camera, and he always used only one lens," says Jarmusch. In this scene, the camera is static: Mitzuko, now barefoot, is working on her Elvis scrapbook while Jun takes pictures of her and things in the room. "He leaves the frame, and she's still working there, but we follow his activity by seeing his camera's flash go off to one side," explains Jarmusch. Though the camera cuts briefly away—to Jun photographing the aqua plastic radio that's chained to the bedside radio—and shots of Mitzuko's scrapbook are inserted, the basic setup shot doesn't change.

Mystery Train then cuts to a funny little scene down at the hotel desk, as the night clerk and bellhop puzzle over the Japanese plum. When the film cuts back to the couple upstairs, Jun is sitting on the floor, his back against the bed, another low "Ozu shot." The camera shows Mitzuko standing in the bathroom doorway, then cuts back to the first shot of Jun. Mitzuko comes into the frame and sits next to him, and a charming scene is played out, again in one long take, one of the longest in the film.

Mitzuko is trying to make the deadpan Jun smile. "Jun," she asks in Japanese, "why do you always have such a sad face? Are you unhappy?" "I'm very happy," he replies. "That's just the way my face is." She puts on a thick layer of red lipstick and plants a huge kiss on his mouth, leaving them both as smeary as children who have been eating red licorice. Then she slides onto the bed behind her—the only camera movement is to follow her feet up—and performs an amazing trick, using her toes to light his cigarette with a lighter. Jun remains impassive, but when Mitzuko finally leaves his side, we see the trace of a smirk on his ruby red lips.

Jarmusch contrives his comic cast of lowlifes and innocents, and he dreams up strange and slightly creepy subcultures for them to move in. But there aren't any fancy tricks when it comes to shooting. "I don't like to emphasize what is supposed to be dramatic," he says. "If a character is static and the camera tracks in on him and the music swells, the camera becomes a character. I like the camera to be invisible."

Home and Away

PETER KEOGH/1992

PETER KEOGH: *Is this your neighbourhood?*
JIM JARMUSCH: I live a little east of here. I've lived here for fifteen years.

PK: *It seems that each of your films moves further out of town. First to more distant American cities, and now this one* [Night on Earth] *is international. Is this a conscious trend?*
JJ: Not really. Though perhaps it has something to do with the fact that making my first film, *Permanent Vacation,* enabled me to travel. I got invited to different film festivals and travelled to promote my films and as a result I met a lot of people outside New York. And I tend to write things for specific people. This film is a good example of that.

PK: *Your films are inspired by the characters?*
JJ: Usually I write for specific actors and have an idea of a character I want to collaborate with them on. The story is suggested by those characters.

PK: *Does the gestation process take a long time?*
JJ: It differs. I carry them around for a long time, thinking about the actors and the characters to make for them. But then I usually write them pretty fast—for example, I wrote this one in eight or ten days.

Published in *Sight and Sound*, Vol. 2, No. 4, August 1992, pp. 8–9. Reprinted by permission.

P K : *I'm sure the production was more complicated than usual.*

J J : Just shooting in cars was complicated. Also shooting episodes in this way. Usually when you make a film it takes the first two weeks or so to understand how to work with your crew, but in this case, we prepared each story for about a week and shot for ten days and were out of there and on to the next place. And shooting at night outdoors in the winter and shooting with crews that didn't always speak English were complicated. But we had very good crews because we hired people in different cities based on their enthusiasm rather than on their experience. So we had enthusiastic people—they had to be to stand outside at night, all night.

P K : *This could be described as a low-rent version of Wenders's.* Until the End of the World. *Did you know he was making his film at the same time?*

J J : I knew he was making a project that was taking him to cities around the world. But the films are very different in that his plot criss-crosses through all the locations, whereas ours is simultaneous stories that take place solely in each place rather than intercutting.

P K : *Blindness seems to be a motif in each episode.*

J J : On a lot of different levels. Although I'm perhaps not the best person to be analytical about that, it's in there. I was more aware of it while editing the film than while writing or directing it.

P K : *Could you analyse it a bit?*

J J : Well, a lot of people have talked to me about the idea that people don't see what's right in front of them. In the Paris story, the girl is actually blind, but in a way it's the driver who's blind because he thinks her blindness must be a weakness, a flaw she has to deal with, a handicap. So he spends most of the conversation trying to find that weakness to support his preconception of her. And really she doesn't have a weakness. She's blind. That's it. It's who she is. In other stories people are also blind to each other and to their own situations.

P K : *Is any allusion to Béatrice Dalle's poking her eye out in* Betty Blue *intended?*

J J : No. I had forgotten that she had done that in *Betty Blue* until after making the film, when I saw *Betty Blue* again.

PK: *Another motif in your films, beginning with* Permanent Vacation, *in which the character leaves and an emigré from France replaces him, is that of immigrants and rootlessness. Why is this an obsession?*

JJ: People ask me about that a lot. I don't know. When I was a student I lived in Paris for a year. It was the first time I'd been outside the United States and it really changed the way I thought about the world. It also inspired me to make films because I saw a lot of movies I hadn't seen in New York and I became fascinated by the form of cinema.

PK: *Do you see your own style growing more complicated since* Stranger Than Paradise, *which consists of several long takes barely disrupted by a camera movement?*

JJ: It changes depending on what the story needs. This film is much more dialogue-oriented. Because we're in an enclosed space, I didn't have room for characters to express themselves physically or in moments when there is no dialogue as I could in *Stranger Than Paradise*. That's what I like most about that film: the moments between dialogue when you understand what's happening between people without them saying anything. If you think about taking a taxi, it's something insignificant in your daily life: in a film when someone takes a taxi, you see them get in, then there's a cut, then you see them get out. So in a way the content of this film is made up of things that would usually be taken out. It's similar to what I like about *Stranger Than Paradise* or *Down by Law:* the moments between what we think of as significant.

PK: *Your first film was very solipsistic and was focused on one character. This one deals with several characters and many points of view. It seems that each film has more characters, their stories are more episodic, people bounce off each other. Do you feel your scope is expanding in this way?*

JJ: No. In fact, it's accidental. After *Mystery Train* I never intended to make another film that was episodic, or whatever you want to call this form: I had another script I had written which was about a single character. But for reasons too complicated to go into, that film was postponed and so I wrote this one very fast, out of frustration.

PK: *It probably has the most impressive cast of any of your films, with Gena Rowlands, Armin Mueller-Stahl, Winona Ryder . . .*

JJ: Gena and Winona arrived through a very strange set of circumstances.
I had just finished the first draft of the script and had written the LA story
for two male characters. But I wasn't satisfied with it. I had written it for a
specific actor who found just as I finished the script that he would not be
available. And then in a two-day period I met Winona and Gena separately—
completely by accident. Gena is one of my favourite young, American, fe-
male actors. In the course of my conversation with each I described the
project and they both seemed interested. And then I rewrote the story for
them and gave them scripts and they both said yes. I wrote specifically for
other actors too: Rosie Perez, Isaach de Bankolé, Béatrice Dalle, Roberto Benigni and three of the four actors in Finland. So I already had about 70 per
cent of the actors in my head while writing and 30 per cent were due to
circumstances.

PK: *Do you improvise once you start shooting?*
JJ: We do a lot of improvisation in the rehearsal process: in fact, we rehearse a lot of scenes that are not in the film but are the characters in character. They are scenes I play around with, and out of that I get a lot of new
ideas. Then while we're shooting, how much improvising we do depends on
the actors. Obviously I prefer to improvise in rehearsals because you're not
burning money. But some actors need a longer leash. Roberto Benigni—he
has to improvise. That's the strength of his acting. Giancarlo Esposito impro-
vises a lot, too. The guys in Finland stayed much closer to the script once
we'd rehearsed it. To me, the essence of each scene is what is important, not
the exact dialogue. I like to find dialogue that I like and that the actors like,
but there is an infinite number of ways of expressing something, so as long
as the idea remains the same, the language can change. What's most important is that it seems natural and in character.

PK: *Has this always been your procedure or has it developed over time?*
JJ: It's always been my procedure, though I've become better at playing in
the rehearsals and gradually focusing towards the script. In a way, I do everything backwards. Most directors get a script that they didn't write and then
someone casts that. I start with the characters, the actors themselves. I'm
much more a filmmaker than a film director, in the sense that a director can
go in and take over a project, get it going, whereas for me it starts from a

basic perception, sometimes not even accurate, of a person, an actor, a quality of that personality, and I want to grow a character on it. It's more organic.

PK: *Do you feel a kinship to Cassavetes, Scorsese and other directors who proceed in this organic fashion?*

JJ: I admire that way of working. Scorsese is from this neighbourhood. The way people talk in his films is so realistic and strong, you never doubt that they are those characters. Language is very important to me. I love the way language takes on slang, gets mixed up by different influences, different cultures. And I like working in other languages. In *Mystery Train* I got the chance to direct actors in Japanese, which I don't speak. And I don't speak Finnish and I don't really speak Italian, though I understand it somewhat.

PK: *How do you write the dialogue in other languages—do you give the actors the idea and then let them work it out?*

JJ: I write the script in English and then I work with translators, or friends, or the actors themselves to find the right way to translate it. Language is just a kind of code we use, so as long as I know that the actors and I translate the script together and are very attentive to what kind of people these are, for example working-class Finnish guys and how they would talk, it's OK. In the Paris episode of *Night on Earth,* for example, the African driver speaks in a very different way from the girl, who speaks a kind of street French, slang, tough, rough French. His French is more like that of an immigrant. These things are important so that it feels real.

PK: *You're often referred to as a minimalist. Do you agree with that label?*

JJ: I think of minimalist as a label stuck on certain visual artists. But I don't really feel associated with them.

PK: *There are also literary minimalists—Raymond Carver, Anne Beatty.*

JJ: I think maybe what they're saying is that the films are very light on plot and therefore minimal stylistically as well. My style is certainly not Byzantine or florid or elaborate. It's pretty simple. Reduced.

PK: *Would you say that your use of film language is very minimal, but is growing in vocabulary?*

JJ: There are more cuts in it, but we're still limited as to what camera positions we can have. We also don't see nearly as much of the city from the point of view of the cab as I shot because when I was editing I couldn't find places to stick it in—it seemed superficial to go away from moments with the characters, which is what the film is about, just for the sake of other visual input.

PK: *Since* Stranger than Paradise *your sensibility and style seem to have been dominant in American independent filmmaking, and also in filmmaking around the world, such as the Kaurismäki brothers. How do you account for it?*
JJ: It's hard to respond to that. I don't know if my early films have influenced those people or whether it's a simultaneous reaction to things being glossy and quick cut—you know, using montage sequences *à la Miami Vice,* slap a music cue over a sequence in which the characters don't hear the music, the whole MTV aesthetic. Aki Kaurismäki is one of my favourite directors; I'm excited to see his new film, *La Vie de bohème.*

PK: *Do you see your films and those like yours as an alternative to a Hollywood that's encroaching on all independent cinema?*
JJ: I'm interested in types of film. In films there's such a wide scope—from porno films to Kung Fu to Michael Snow to Stan Brakhage and Scorsese. Yet at the moment it seems that in Hollywood the idea is to saturate markets and release films wider and wider, so the margins get smaller.

PK: *Do you read reviews?*
JJ: With my last film, *Mystery Train,* I reached a point where I was hardly reading anything, except when people told me about negative reviews, which I found more interesting. I respect other people's opinions of my films more than my own because I'm so inside—I don't even know if I like my own films, sometimes. I certainly never look at them again after I'm done with them. I'm at a point with this film where I don't need to see it again. I've been watching it for video transfers—the quality of prints and so on—so I'm only seeing the surface now; I've reached that point where I'm not seeing the film.

PK: *You like making the films, I imagine.*
JJ: My favourite part is shooting: collaborating with all those different people and everybody working together towards one thing.

P K :   *What are you working on now?*

J J :   I have two scripts in the works which are very different from each other. I've never written two things at once before, but I've been making notes back and forth and carrying them around for a while. I haven't had time to start writing them because I've been travelling and promoting this film, getting prints ready and so on.

P K :   *Which is your favourite of your movies?*

J J :   *Down by Law,* I think, because shooting it was so much fun. Being in New Orleans was great and we had a really wild time. In retrospect I don't know how we got through it—it seemed as if we had a celebration after each night of shooting and I don't know physically how we got the film made. I tend to see my films in retrospect like home movies—I don't see the film any more, but I remember the experience of making it.

P K :   *You have a mythic structure to that film: I remember the scene where they come to the crossroads. And with this film the basic structure is the rotation of the earth.*

J J :   I have a very classical way of thinking about telling stories; I still cling to that need to order things in a classical way. Like *Stranger Than Paradise* is three acts with a coda, as is *Down by Law:* before prison, in prison and their escape from prison, with a coda at the end. So formally, I use that even though the acts don't necessarily follow the classical form where there is a conflict presented and resolved. In *Night on Earth* the crossing time zones, being on the planet at the same time and the sun going down at the beginning and coming up at the end helped me give an overall form.

P K :   *Bentley College invited me to be in a panel to discuss one of your films: I was wondering if they asked you too?*

J J :   Yes, they did . . . when is that?

P K :   *It's tonight.*

Regis Filmmaker's Dialogue: Jim Jarmusch

JONATHAN ROSENBAUM/1994

JONATHAN ROSENBAUM: *How did you first get interested in movies?*
When did it start?

JIM JARMUSCH: The first movie that I remember really having an impact
on me was the Robert Mitchum film *Thunder Road* that I saw on a vacation
at a drive-in theater with my mom and my sister in Florida, when I was about
six years old, I think. Previous to that I'd only seen Walt Disney movies, like
Son of Flubber and those kinds of things. And to see a movie with all that
violence and action, that's when I really started being interested in the screen
. . . being alive like that.

JR: *After that, did you see lots of movies?*
JJ: I grew up in Akron, Ohio, and there wasn't a big selection. Well, there
was a theater called the State Theater that had Saturday matinees that would
show like *The Fly* or *Attack of the Giant Crab Monsters.* They would show a
double bill every Saturday and my mother used to drop me off there so that
she could, I guess, get rid of me for the afternoon. So I used to go there a lot.
I loved going to see those films. Other than that, in Akron, there really wasn't
much until I was a teenager and there was what back then they called an art
house, which meant they showed like European sex films on the weekdays,
and on Friday nights they had a program called Underground Cinema. We

This interview was conducted in conjunction with a Jarmusch retrospective at the Walker
Art Center in Minneapolis, 4 February 1994. Courtesy Walker Art Center. © Walker Art
Center 2000.

used to go there all the time. We had fake ID cards saying that we were old enough, and there we saw like a lot of different things, including *Chelsea Girls* by Andy Warhol and some Stan Brakhage films, mixed in with *Reefer Madness*, you know.

JR: *This was in the sixties?*
JJ: This was in the late sixties.

JR: *At what point in all of this did you decide you wanted to make films?*
JJ: I went to college to study literature, I really wanted to be a writer. My last year at Columbia I studied in Paris and it was there that, rather than attending classes I was supposed to be attending, I ended up spending most of my time at the Cinémathèque, or in movie theaters. When I returned to New York I had no clue what to do with myself. I was really interested in movies by that point, and my writing was starting to take on elements of screenplays. I don't know if you know the Burroughs book *The Last Words of Dutch Schultz?* That's written in a way like a faked screenplay. Some elements like that were entering into my own writing. And then I applied to go to NYU graduate film school, but I don't know why I even tried because I had no money and I'd never made a film. And for some reason they accepted me. I guess that's why. I got financial assistance and went and started studying film there.

JR: *That's interesting. Was the trip abroad with Columbia your first trip out of America?*
JJ: Yes. I don't even think I'd been in Canada, which was *way* out of America—if you're from Akron, you know.

JR: *I mention it because it seems to me one thing that's almost unique for your films is that they're the films of an American who actually seems to feel at home outside of America, in some ways, which is very unusual.*
JJ: I think I feel not at home in America, but not necessarily at home outside of America.

JR: *Well, that seems a better distinction actually. I take it that it was while you were at NYU that you made* Permanent Vacation?

J J : Yeah. I began making *Permanent Vacation* as my thesis film at NYU Graduate Film School. I had been given a fellowship called the Louis B. Mayer Foundation Fellowship. They mistakenly sent the money to me rather than directly to the school to pay my tuition. I used that money to make the film rather than pay tuition, so I did make the film, although it didn't, at that time, get a degree from the school. They weren't pleased with the fact that I didn't pay tuition. They also weren't pleased with the film I made.

J R : *Was that the very first film you made, or had you made any shorts?*
J J : I had made two or three short films before that, as a student, which I think are lost, hopefully, forever.

J R : *So it was basically the Mayer grant that paid for the film altogether, or did you have to go to other sources too?*
J J : I got some phony car loan too, from a bank, so I was able to make the film. The budget was about $12,000.

J R : *I have the impression that you actually do casting before you write your scripts, that when you write your scripts, it's with very particular actors in mind. And I'm wondering if that was true at all of* Permanent Vacation *also?*
J J : Yeah, it was. I still consider myself, and I don't consider this to be derogatory, as kind of a fake film director. Because I started making films with my friends, basically, and writing things with them in mind. And I have kind of continued that procedure although my availability to actors, or to people with more experience, has widened. That's changed, because I've made films and traveled, and because of the fact that I've made films I've met actors and people who also work in films. So now that scope is widened, but it's still pretty much the same premise. I write with an actor in my head for a particular character, and if I'm not able to hoodwink that person into being in a film, then I rewrite it thinking of someone else. But I still work that way.

J R : *Were many of the other actors also at NYU?*
J J : No, none of them. In fact, none of the people in *Stranger Than Paradise,* except for Eszter Balint, were actors at the time. John Lurie and Richie Edson were musicians and had not acted—although John had made several Super 8 films of his own, in a kind of Jack Smith style.

JR: *What about Chris Parker?*

JJ: Chris Parker was a kid that I met on the street, a friend of mine. He was fourteen when I met him, and we used to go to CBGB's almost every night back then. This is late seventies. Chris Parker was a real kind of fast talking con man, and he knew Hilly Chrystal who owns CBGB's still. Somehow he'd get in, and then he'd go to the back door where they load equipment in and open it for me to get in. Because we didn't have any money to pay to go in. Not every night. He was very interested in all kinds of music, particularly bebop and punk rock. Which seems like a kind of odd combination. Somehow makes more sense now, I guess.

JR: *That sounds like a pretty good lead into the first clip we're going to be looking at, which is from* Permanent Vacation *and features Chris Parker along with an actor named Frankie Faison.*

JJ: This is like the Jay Leno show. [*laughter*]

[1st clip–*Permanent Vacation*]

JR: *I would be very curious to know where exactly that story* [about the jazz player not remembering how to play "Over the Rainbow"] *came from?*

JJ: Well, I forget the comedian who originated it. I heard it on the radio, late at night once, and just lifted it, you know. I don't remember whose joke it is. But I think you can see why they didn't want to give me a degree. [*laughter*]

JR: *At the same time, though, the poster that you see behind them is for* The Savage Innocents *which is a film of Nicholas Ray, and Nicholas Ray was one of your teachers at NYU.*

JJ: Yes.

JR: *Did he play any role at all in advising you about this film?*

JJ: He was the main reason I went back to NYU. It's a three year program, and when I had ran out of money, on my third year, I went to the director of the school, László Benedek—who directed *The Wild One*. And he said, "Listen, Nick Ray is going to teach here this year and he needs an assistant and I think you'd be good." And I said "Yeah, but I came in here to tell you I'm not coming back here to school. I don't have any money." So he said, "Listen, come tomorrow and meet Nick, and I'll see if I can help you get this fellowship to come back to school"—this was the Louis B. Mayer fellowship. So I came and I met Nick Ray who was like a big hero to me at that point before I ever met him. He asked me that day if I would be his assistant in his school year. So that's why I returned to school, basically.

JR: *Did he advise you on* Permanent Vacation, *to some extent?*
JJ: He kept giving me advice about the script saying that the script is too slow, there is not enough action, this kid should kill his girlfriend, she should have a gun in her purse, etc. My script had much more action at that time than it eventually did. Because whatever he would tell me, I would go do the opposite, and so I kept taking the things out that he liked, somehow. At the time I didn't really know why I was doing that. Now I realize why, because I didn't want him to think that I was just a puppet and would do just whatever he said. I kept bringing him back the script with more of the action taken out, and I would watch his reaction. Usually he was, you know, dumb-founded, and would say, "It's getting further in the other direction." And finally when I gave him the completed script, he said that he was very proud that I didn't take his advice, that I had founded my own style. But I really wasn't conscious of why I was doing that at the time.

JR: *One thing that's interesting in this, it's sort of like a hallmark of your style, is that this sequence is mainly a very long take. There are two cutaways, I guess, to Chris Parker, but otherwise it's just kind of giving the screen to an actor and sort of letting them go. Was this something that you arrived at through a conscious decision of wanting to do that? Did economics play any role in it?*
JJ: Certainly. I only did one take, I remember, of the long joke, I didn't even have a second take to select from. Primarily that style came just purely from economics. And I made this film, too, partly inspired by a film by Amos Poe, called *The Foreigner*, that he shot for like $5,000 or something in '77/'78, which was kind of a punk spirited film. He and his friend Eric Mitchell, who became my friends, were saying, "Come on Jim, you can make a film too," you know. So I was inspired by them and they used that basically similar style because of financial reasons. But one thing I wanted to say; this scene's shot in the lobby of the St. Marks Cinema—that doesn't exist anymore—where at the time I was working as an usher. It was like a two dollar theater, or something, and I was the new usher so they used to make me do things

like, you know, "Jim, get your flashlight, go down there and tell those Hell's Angels there's no reefer smoking." [*laughter*] Stuff like that.

JR: *Actually I didn't recognize it was the St. Marks but it seems very appropriate because that was a Lower East Side movie theater. I remember seeing things like Howard Hawks's* Red Line 7000 *there. One thing that's curious, though, is that on the soundtrack, if I'm not mistaken, what one hears during the scene is not the* Savage Innocents, *but is it a Sergio Leone?*

JJ: Yeah. It was a double bill, but you couldn't see the other poster. It's from *The Good, the Bad and the Ugly.*

JR: *What happened when the film was finished? Did you find a way to show it or did it take a while?*

JJ: NYU was having a film festival of its films by its students, and I gave it to them. Not only did they reject the film and send it back to me but they sent a really nasty letter saying, basically "What is this shit?" So then I was lost. I was playing in a rock band at the time and I thought, "OK, I've made a film, I'm not gonna make any more because no one's gonna let me, but at least I made one film." And then this guy Mark Wise, in New York, somehow saw the film and said that he would like to select the film for a film festival in Mannheim in Germany. I didn't even know any film festivals *existed*— except, I'd heard of the Cannes Film Festival. So I said "Wow, great," and the film was shown in Mannheim. And not only that. He said, "Well, you know, they'll fly you there and you can go to the festival." I was amazed by that. I had no idea that, you know, I could get a free trip to Germany out of this film. I went there and the film won a prize that was about $2,000—I had no money, I was behind on my rent and I had these kind of Mafia landlords and stuff. So I came back not only with the $2,000 but then WDR bought the film for German TV which paid back the cost of the film. The film was then asked to be in the Berlin festival, and then the Rotterdam festival. Then it sort of started for me.

JR: *I remember that an issue of the German film magazine* Filmkritik *was devoted to your film.*

JJ: All which was a huge shock to me.

JR: *And at this point it hadn't shown in the United States apart from at NYU.*

JJ: *To this point* I don't think it's shown in the United States. [*laughter*]

J R : *That's interesting in itself, in the sense that you were discovered in Europe certainly well before* Stranger Than Paradise. *I know that started out as a short, with the intention of making it a feature, is that right?*

J J : Yeah.

J R : *And I know that there were ways in which you were helped at different times by things like getting footage, or maybe raw stock, by both Wim Wenders and Jean-Marie Straub and Danièle Huillet. At what point did that happen? How did you initially get it set up?*

J J : Nick Ray had asked me to be his kind of gopher during the making of Wim Wender's film *Lightning Over Water.* I'd of course *met* Wim, but I was the only person on the crew that was asked by Nick to be part of the production, so I was pretty much treated as an outsider. I started shooting *Permanent Vacation* the day after Nick died, actually. It was shot in ten days. Wim saw the film, and then a year and a half later Wim and his partner at that time, Chris Sievernich, said that they had some unexposed film material left over from the film, *The State of Things,* and said, "Look, you can have it, that's a lot of the cost right there. There's enough to make a thirty, forty minute film." So I wrote the first part of *Stranger Than Paradise because* I had that film material available to me. And then Jean-Marie and Daniell gave me other film material, to be exposed for the black sections, as leader. So they both helped me. While I was editing the first half hour version I wrote a script for the longer version, and when the short version was done I also had a script to try to continue it. I was then further helped by Paul Bartel, who loaned me some money to buy the rights of the first part back from Chris Sievernich, who did some kind of fishy things—legally—to me. He had the negative under his name in the lab, and things like that. He kind of held it up for ransom. Paul Bartel, who I'd met by chance also I think at a film festival, had just had some success with his film *Eating Raoul,* at that time. And he said, "What's the problem?", you know, and I explained to him and he said, "Oh, well, you know, I'd like to help somebody starting out because I'm in the position to. I have a little money. You can pay me back in a year." He was really kind of an angel, in that way, to help the film. Before that I couldn't get financing because I didn't own the film. Then I got German TV money and a German producer named Otto Grokenberger to help finance the remaining part of the film. So I had really amazing people helping me out. I don't know why, but they did.

JR: *One thing I've always been curious about is the Hungarian aspect of the film. Does that relate to anything like in your family background or in terms of people you knew?*

JJ: Well, it's two things. My family on my father's side was Czech, and my grandmother, who was a lot like the Aunt Lottie character, was Czech. And Eszter Balint was a member of the Squat Theater Group in New York, an experimental theater company from Budapest that were friends of mine. A lot of our friends used to hang out with them. Because they lived communally on 23rd Street in one big building which was also their theater. So it was a combination of those things, I guess.

JR: *Well, it sounds like we're probably at a good point where we can look at another clip. The clip that we're going to be looking at, from* Stranger Than Paradise, *is in the first section of the film. It's shortly after Eszter Balint turns up in New York and arrives at the apartment of her cousin Willie. Her name is Eva. This is actually the first scene when she gets to meet Willie's friend Eddie, played by Richard Edson.*

    [2nd clip–*Stranger Than Paradise*]

JR: *I noticed in this scene there's another sort of little film reference, when Eddie's reading from the paper. The one title of a film which is real, I think, is* Tokyo Story.

JJ: Well, they're the names of race horses. There's a few Ozu in there, *Late Spring* . . .

JR: *Oh, and* Passing Fancy.

JJ: I stuck a few in there.

JR: *Do you feel there was an affinity with the, let's say, simplicity of Ozu's style, the idea of just putting a camera in front of characters and . . . ?*

JJ: Very much. I mean, I have kind of contradictory tastes. I like things that are very pure. Ozu's films or the films of Carl Dreyer or things by Joseph Cornell or Cy Twombly or music by Anton Webern. Or The Ramones, for that matter. Things that are very pure appeal to me strongly. I also like very messy things, though. Like Blue Cheer or paintings by Jackson Pollock or de Kooning. I like *King of New York, Detour,* films like that. Things that are messy appeal to me as well, but my own aesthetics tends to go toward a more kind of pure form of things.

JR: *One thing I've liked about the sketches of black leader in* Stranger Than Paradise *is that they are a little bit like blues choruses. It's a way of bracketing scenes, in a way. You think of them as units. Did you spend a lot of time editing them, I mean in terms of timing and so on?*

JJ: I spent a lot of time trying to figure out how long they should be, and they do vary somewhat. They were originally in my script, because I didn't want to hard-cut form one place to another. Like a blues chorus, or almost like respiration, a way of letting the image sink in before another one hits you. So they were intended from the start but we did play around with exactly how long they should be, I remember.

JR: *The fact of having those kinds of long takes, would you say it made the shooting of this film harder to do or easier?*

JJ: It works both ways. I think it's better for the actors because it's more like theater where they maintain their character longer. Working with actors not really experienced with film acting, and myself not experienced as a director, that was helpful. It also makes it more difficult because we had very little film material, and if any one of us would make a mistake, then the take would be ruined. So it kind of worked both ways.

JR: *Both before and after you made this film, how easy or difficult was it that the film was in black-and-white? Did you encounter any resistance from distributors or people putting money into it?*

JJ: Definitely. They would always say "We can't get a good price for video" or "We can't sell it to television so we can't pay you much for it." Before making the film it was not a problem because the film material offered to me was black-and-white and when I wrote the story I knew that it would be black-and-white. But after the fact it was kind of problematic. At that point, in 1982 and 1984, black-and-white was not even fashionable on MTV, or whatever. So it was kind of problematic selling the film, although more so in the States than in Europe, for some reason.

JR: *I guess black-and-white hung on much longer there. It seems that even now it's still easier to make a black-and-white film, there are still labs for it, in Europe.*

JJ: It's getting difficult everywhere because the really great black-and-white technicians are old guys that have retired. They haven't passed that expertise along, really. And it's a very different thing to light black-and-white, also, than color. Now black-and-white's more expensive to shoot than color. The processing is more expensive.

J R : *Now it's the luxury, in a sense.*
J J : There's still a lot of resistance to it. I know that Tim Burton had a lot of trouble making *Ed Wood* in black-and-white. He had to leave one studio to make it.

J R : *Have you had some of the same problems when you use subtitles? Has there been a comparable resistance from anyone?*
J J : I've had trouble in Europe because I have refused, with few exceptions, to allow my films to be dubbed. In Italy it was very unusual to release *Down by Law* with subtitles, because the Italians dub their own films, even. Even the ones in Italian. So that's been a problem. I've not been able to make TV sales to larger TV stations or prime time viewing in Europe with subtitles.

J R : *It has always seemed to me that there's something contradictory about it. I mean, although a film with subtitles is considered box office poison in the U.S., people tend to forget that* Dances with Wolves *has lots of subtitles. More recently* Schindler's List. *There seem to be lots of films that have subtitles that don't bother people.*
J J : If you have an interesting actor their voice is fifty percent of their performance. So you're taking that away as well. It's kind of like getting ripped off when you dub an interesting actor. Sometimes dubbing is funny, though. I like the Kung-Fu style dubbing.

J R : *I've heard that in Italy one reason why it's so important to dub so much there is because accents are very important, that for different parts of Italy there have to be different kinds of regional accents, and if they do it wrong people laugh in the wrong places and so on.*
J J : But Fellini—the first time I met him was when *Down by Law* was being released in Italy—said to me, "But Jim, why you don't dub the film?" Fellini will shoot a film and have the actors just say numbers. Just count. And he'll write the dialogue later and put it in, "I like the face but not the voice, so I choose one for voice and one for face." So he was very confused why I was adamant about it. I like that in some of those Italian movies they have the same guys dubbing each film, you start to recognize those voices.

JR: *Speaking of Italians, how did you encounter Roberto Benigni?*

JJ: I met him in Salso Maggiore in Italy, in a small film festival where I was on the jury with him.

JR: *It seems like some of the strange English expressions he comes up with in* Down by Law *are things that he came up with.*

JJ: A lot of things, yes. His favorite English joke, he was so proud of it when I first met him, was: "When is a door not a door? When a door is a-jar." He loved that joke so much. He now speaks English fairly well, but I love just his way of constructing a sentence. If he wasn't sure he would throw everything in, like "Yes, this thing we should must for to do." Because he didn't know which to select.

JR: *Another thing that happened with your next film,* Down by Law, *apart from introducing us all in America to Benigni, was that you had a change of cinematographers. This was your first film with Robby Müller.*

JJ: Tom DiCillo, who shot *Permanent Vacation* and *Stranger Than Paradise*, I knew from film school. He never wanted to be director of photography. His films in film school were, visually, the most beautiful that I saw, just very lyrical int he way they were filmed. Now he's a director and has made the film *Johnny Suede* and is preparing a new one. I would have continued to work with him but he didn't want to continue working as a cinematographer. And I had the amazing chance to have met Robby Müller, whose work I really loved, especially since Wim Wenders's films *Kings of the Road* and *The American Friend*. In fact, when Robby saw *Permanent Vacation* he said to me, "You know, if you ever wanna work with me I'd like to." He really loved that film. Then after *Stranger*, when Tom didn't want to shoot anymore, I immediately called Robby.

JR: *I remember you once telling me something about the way you shot* Down by Law. *You said that at least part of the conceptual idea of the shooting was, if I remember correctly, to always have at least two actors in the frame. Am I remembering you correctly? It was a particular visual idea that you based part of it on.*

JJ: Boy, I don't remember. And I never look back at my films, so it's kind of weird even for me to see these clips.

JR: *In most of this clip that we're about to see all three of the actors are in the frame at the same time, which is quite interesting. It becomes even more compressed than in the last sequence where we had that one camera movement. Anyway, why don't we look at the sequence. I think it's pretty self-explanatory, it has the three leading characters in it. It occurs a little over halfway through the film,* Down by Law.

[3rd Clip—*Down by Law*]

JR: *"Not enough room to swing a car" something that Roberto would come up with?*

JJ: Well, we collected so many things I don't remember what came from where anymore, but possibly. When I first met Roberto he had subscribed to a magazine in Italy that was to teach you English and had a lot of ridiculous expressions. A lot of those we pulled together from there and they ended up in the film.

JR: *How did you hit on the idea of doing this in Louisiana?*

JJ: Mostly through music from New Orleans. I'm a big blues and R&B fan. I had never been to New Orleans when I wrote the script, but I had a lot of images in my head mostly just from the music of New Orleans. That just kind of drew me there.

JR: *Were you thinking of prison films that you'd seen?*

JJ: No, actually I wasn't really. I was trying to figure out how to get characters that don't like each other stuck together. Prison was one quick way of doing that.

JR: *One of the themes of* Stranger Than Paradise *is the characters saying that no matter how much you keep moving around, things stay the same. And there's a way in this film that certain things repeat themselves. After they break out of prison, they find themselves in a shack where even the bunks where they're staying at are similar to those of the prison. It's like a duplication of where they were before.*

JJ: Yes.

JR: *Was this a much harder film to shoot than* Stranger, *or was it easier?*

JJ: This film was a lot more fun to make. *Stranger* was harder. We had less time, less money. In *Stranger Than Paradise,* there's a sequence where they're in a motel in Florida, which had three rooms in it. The whole crew and cast stayed in those rooms taking turns who would sleep on the floor. So it was not that much fun, making *Stranger Than Paradise*. This was more fun, we had a real motel, we each had our own room, even. A run-down motel, but it was fun there.

J R : *Did you have lots of time to scout locations, and so on?*
J J : Yeah, I did for *Stranger* too, though. But I love New Orleans, I still love it. I just went back there a few months ago. I just really love that town.

J R : *Did you do much to change or redress the locations that you used, or were they pretty much as you found them?*
J J : Almost always the way we found them. We only changed them by the way we lit them, or moved some furniture around. There's a scene early in the film where Tom Waits's character and his girlfriend Ellen Barkin live in a house that has graffiti and things on the walls. It was a girl that we met there who lived there. Her former boyfriend had been a disc jockey, or something. There were records everywhere and we just used her house exactly as it was.

J R : *Was it an actual prison?*
J J : Yes. The central lockup, or the Orleans Parish Prison, in New Orleans proper.

J R : *So there were real prisoners there at the time that you were shooting?*
J J : Yes, there were. I don't know what was in my head, but I decided it would be a brilliant idea for Tom Waits and John Lurie and Roberto, and myself—since I was making them do it—to be locked up in the prison for a day, without the guards in that cell block or the prisoners knowing that we weren't real new prisoners. I was put in a cell with Roberto, and Tom and John were put in another. It was pretty scary, we had to do everything you do, and we were treated pretty roughly by the guards and the other inmates. It was good for Tom and John, not that Tom doesn't have experience in jail cells. They were actually kind of frightened by the experience. I was also, but I was in the cell with Roberto who thought the whole idea was useless and was only talking to me about "Yes, Jim, this is interesting but . . . tonight, which restaurant should we go? I would like Linguini al dente," you know. It had no effect on Roberto at all.

J R : *Through the experience of making this film, he must have learned English a lot better.*

JJ: Quite a bit, yes. He's very quick, obviously a very intelligent man. He learned really fast. But we played a lot of tricks on him, teaching him the wrong things. For instance, we taught that to piss, or to pee, was "to flame." He now knows it's not correct, but he didn't know for years. When he finally found out, he played the trick back on John Lurie in Cannes at the film festival where an Italian TV crew was interviewing John. They did not speak English, so Roberto said, "No problem, I translate for you." They would ask things like "How do you come upon your craft as an actor, Stanislavsky, or method acting, or is it intuitive, or what?" in Italian, and Roberto would say to John "I don't know why, but they want to know what did you have for breakfast?" And so, John's response would be "Bacon, eggs . . ." He looked like a real idiot. So he did get back at us.

JR: *It's interesting that there's almost a curve, that from* Stranger Than Paradise *to* Down by Law *to* Mystery Train, *your films become more and more bilingual, in some way. Or even trilingual. Foreign language is used more and more and becomes more central to what's going on. Do you think this is partly a consequence of the amount of traveling around yo did with your own films and being in other countries, and so on?*

JJ: It comes from two things, I think. From the fact that I traveled and met a lot of people who don't have English as their first language, and also because I've lived in New York for so long. I live on the Bowery downtown, and in my neighborhood there are Dominicans and Puerto Ricans whose accents are slightly different, there are Hasidic Jews and Sicilians and Chinese. You know, there's a lot of people mixed in there. So it's that, too, somehow. I hear different languages swirling around me every day. That's what America is, a lot of immigrants who committed genocide on the indigenous people here so they could take it over.

JR: *It seems like it's happening more and more that people are making films sometimes in languages they don't know. For example, I just discovered that Kieslowski hardly knows French at all, yet* Blue, *obviously, is in French. He had to speak to Juliette Binoche, the lead actress, in English, when he was making that. The independent filmmaker Jon Jost just made a film in Italy, in Italian, and he knows very little Italian.*

JJ: Max Ophüls always impressed me by making films in English, French, Italian, and in German. He probably spoke all those languages, though. But you know what, since I've been to Japan a number of times I bought a lot of videotapes there that were not subtitled. Films by Ozu and Mizoguchi and Suzuki and a lot of other people. I like to watch them without knowing what they're saying, I've sort of got into that. Language is a code that we communicate through, but even within that code you can tell through someone's inflection what their emotional state is. The language of acting is not primarily a spoken language. You can read how people feel or where they're at emotionally, without knowing what language they speak. My first experience was directing *Mystery Train,* directing the Japanese actors. French I understand, Italian I understand a little, I'm learning more and more. Finnish I don't understand, but Finnish people are very open, you can always read their emotions. I think language is secondary.

J R :   *It also occurs to me that it might have been part of your background that might have led to this. The year that you spent in Paris, going to films at the Cinémathèque. Because when I used to go to the Cinémathèque, Henri Langlois used to have this philosophy that he even preferred to show you a film without subtitles. Or if they did have subtitles, they wouldn't be the ones that would help you. I once saw a Mexican Buñuel film that was dubbed into German and subtitled in Portuguese, for example. He liked to do things like that. Most of the movies I used to see at the Cinémathèque were in languages that I couldn't follow.*
J J :   I saw Central European films at the Cinémathèque and other films I had no clue what they were saying. The heart of the story's still there, though. Unless it's a totally dialogue oriented film.

J R :   *It's a pity that there's so many films in the world that are automatically considered non-commercial, just because it's assumed that people won't be able to see something if it's in a language they don't understand. It seems like an awful lot of commercial decisions get made on that basis. In the case, though, of for example working out the dialogue for* Mystery Train, did you, in order to get the right kind of Japanese idioms, basically work with translators? Was it always a question of trying to translate English ideas into Japanese, or learning certain phrases and then trying to work with those?
J J :   No. I do a lot of rehearsing and improvs with the characters. The actors are in character but the scene we're doing I write on the spot and it is not in the film. It's maybe before the story begins. With the Japanese kids I would stick in, like, "OK, they're gonna go to the movies, and he wants to see a

movie with Steve McQueen, but she wants to see a movie with Elizabeth Taylor." Well, I have those two words I know. I know when he says Steve McQueen, so I have some little guide in there. I give them the dialogue and a translator tells them the idea of the scene, and then I watch their interactions with each other. Once my script was written we rehearsed it and discussed a lot of nuances of how to express things with the translator and the actors. We made joint decisions and eliminated phrases or replaced them. Even though I didn't know myself, the difference of the nuance was explained to me, and then we would discuss which one was appropriate. So it was not really a problem.

J R :   *Did you ever get to see* Mystery Train *with a Japanese audience?*
J J :   I don't think so, no.

J R :   *I'm just wondering if you found out if there were in any way different responses to the Japanese segment in Japan?*
J J :   I don't know. My films are very popular in Japan. I don't know why. All my films have been very successful in Japan. Probably due to the distributors that I have, which are really excellent.

J R :   *Where did you find the two Japanese actors?*
J J :   The first time I ever saw Youki Kudoh, the girl, was in a film in the film festival in Italy where I was on the jury with Roberto, in a film called *Crazy Family.* She was twelve years old at the time when she acted in that, and she was hilarious. I was really drawn to her face and her kind of expressiveness and wackiness, you know? Bernardo Bertolucci told me to see a film called *The Typhoon Club* that was not released here—I saw it in Japan—and she was also in that. I then wrote the part for her, and cast for the guy that I was lucky to find, Masatoshi Nagase, in Tokyo. I saw about fifty young actors before I found him.

J R :   *Did they speak English very much?*
J J :   Youki spoke a little. Masatoshi none. Except, you know, "rawk 'n' roll."

J R :   *So you were having to direct through interpreters to some extent?*
J J :   Yeah, completely. I mean I had an interpreter. It's funny, because even my language to them as a director was not hampered by my lack of understanding the words. We were still able to communicate somehow.

John Lurie and Eszter Balint, *Stranger Than Paradise*, 1984

Eszter Balint, *Stranger Than Paradise*, 1984

John Lurie, Tom Waits, and Roberto Benigni, *Down by Law*, 1986

Roberto Benigni, *Down by Law*, 1986

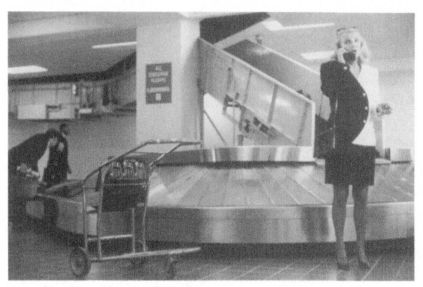

Gena Rowlands, *Night on Earth*, 1991

Paolo Bonacelli and Roberto Benigni, *Night on Earth*, 1991

Kari Väänänen, Sakari Kuosmanen, and Matti Pellonpää, *Night on Earth*, 1991

Johnny Depp, *Dead Man*, 1995

Johnny Depp, *Dead Man*, 1995

J R : *As with the experience you had with Benigni.*

J J : Yes. And I taught them to say some real foul things in English which they were very proud of.

J R : *Maybe we're ready to look at the fourth clip. It happens right near the beginning of* Mystery Train.

[Clip 4–*Mystery Train*]

J R : *The spiel that they get about Sun Records, is that a real spiel? Is that a real tourist guide?*

J J : Yeah. We got the tour guide text from Sun Studio, and just had it delivered in rapid fire.

J R : *Was it similar to* Down by Law, *in terms of getting to know Memphis and so on? It's again a case, I guess of being interested in a place because of the music.*

J J : Yes.

J R : *Did you spend much time there before?*

J J : Well, again I hadn't been to Memphis when I wrote the script. But as soon as I was done I went to Memphis to look for locations. So it was again music that kind of drew me to write something so that I could go there.

J R : *Is Chaucer Street something that you actually found there?*

J J : No. We had that sign made.

J R : *I see it as a maybe a remnant of your English major background. I know you had the idea of it being kind of like* Canterbury Tales *in some ways.*

J J : Yes, the form of the film is a little bit from *Canterbury Tales,* in a way. But there are a lot of streets in Memphis named after poets. Quite a few. Chaucer wasn't one of them, though.

J R : *You use a very small part of Memphis in this. Did Memphis wind up surprising you or being very different from what you imagined?*

J J : Yeah, it did, because the main center of Memphis, around Beale Street, was completely torn down in 1968/'69 after King was assassinated, to prevent, you know, disturbances. They just kind of razed the whole center of Memphis, which had been the largest inner-city black neighborhood in the South for years. So it was a really vibrant, amazing place prior to that, and they just kind of tore it down. The kind of empty lots and holes in places in the center of the city was very odd and kind of haunting and sad. But Memphis, anyway, consists of a lot of closed down gas stations and empty parking lots. And it still has a lot of ghosts around there. You feel a lot of weird stuff in Memphis. Also, a lot of this film takes place in a hotel. The building that we shot the interiors in, the back of it is right across from the Lorraine Hotel where Martin Luther King was assassinated. Supposedly, James Earl Ray assassinated King from that building. Which was weird. We really weren't aware of that when we selected it as a location.

JR: *Did you find it was harder to shoot in the city than out in the country? Does it make much difference?*
JJ: You know, you run into different problems depending on where you are. It's just different. I don't think you can say one is easier than the other.

JR: *There's an idea that you hit on in* Mystery Train *that sort of carries over to your next film,* Night on Earth, *which is the idea of all the different parts happening at the same time. Was there anything in particular that inspired you to start exploring that idea?*
JJ: Well, there was one thing that I can recall which was a book by William Faulkner called *The Wild Palms*. It's a book of two separate novellas that he wrote, about which the publishers at the time said, "Yeah, but Bill, we need a novel here. This is two short novels, that doesn't sell." I don't know whether they suggested it, or whether he thought of it, but he alternated chapters of two different stories that he wrote separately. And the kind of nuances and repercussions of doing that, the certain themes that exist in both stories and the way they work on each other is really, really beautiful and strong.

JR: *I agree, although I think I always heard it a little differently, the way he wrote it. That he started writing one of the stories, I think it was the love story, and then he felt it was missing something. So as a kind of counterpoint he started the other story and he actually wrote them in terms of alternating between one chapter and another. And then it was published. What happened, though, was that at one point they got printed separately. What's interesting is that when you read them separately as individual stories they don't have anything like the same impact.*

J J :   Yeah, I can't imagine reading separately, really.

J R :   *In that case, though, there's a simultaneity in the prose, but they're not necessarily taking place at the same time.*

J J :   Oh yeah, I didn't try to *imitate* that structure. I just found it really inspiring. Somehow inspiration came from that. Certainly *The Canterbury Tales* as well, because it's a beautiful structure, of people traveling and telling stories as they travel.

J R :   *There's even a parallel with the religious idea, because it's a kind of a religious pilgrimage that's being made, at least by the Japanese couple. You could say it's like going to shrines, actually.*

J J :   And there's also Boccaccio's *Decameron*, where they're waiting out the plague, sitting around telling stories, which contains some of the same stories as *The Canterbury Tales*.

J R :   *When you were writing* Mystery Train, *were you working on the three stories at once, or just writing them quite separately? There's a way in which, in the third at least, our memory of the first two become very important.*

J J :   As I always write, I make a whole lot of notes and collect them and then sit down and write them into the script. That simultaneity, that structure, was in my head before I started writing.

J R :   *It's interesting, in a sense what you've done, in a quite different way from other filmmakers, is returned to the possibility of making shorts. Even though they're interconnected shorts. Of course there was* New York Stories *a few years ago, but that was by three different directors. There are very few cases where you have one filmmaker making short stories that are put together.*

J J :   Well, there's a Japanese tradition, like Kobayashi's *Ghost Stories,* and a few other directors, I think, that have made episodic films like that. And it's a kind of Italian light comedy tradition. But like you said, it's usually different directors doing each section. After making *Mystery Train,* I never intended to make an episodic film like that. With the exception of this thing I'm working on over a period of time, a collection of short films called *Coffee and Cigarettes.* But those I write as I go along, you know. I'm sort of collecting them here and there. But I never intended to make another film like that. *Night on Earth* was just kind of an accident, because another script I'd written, for reasons I won't go into, I was not able to make and was frustrated, and I wrote *Night on Earth* extremely fast. In about eight days. Initially just to shoot outside of America and work with some friends of mine in Europe and stuff.

JR: *Was it hard to set up?*
JJ: It was complicated.

JR: *I bet. Actually, why don't we look at it. What I selected for a clip in this case is from the New York episode, which is the second episode in the film. This occurs about halfway through that episode.*
JJ: Is everyone still awake here? [*laughter*] *Some* people are awake . . .
   [Clip–*Night on Earth*]

JR: *I should have explained, maybe, for those of you who haven't seen the film, that Helmut Grokenberger, who's last name incidentally is, I guess, an homage to your producer?*
JJ: Yes.

JR: *He is in fact the one who's the cab driver. But because he can't drive, it's Giancarlo Esposito who takes over the driving, which is why he's at the wheel. One thing I really like about this sequence is how the foreigner/outsider really sort of humanizes the other two, or at least makes a real change in the emotional tempera-ture. Well, I've been monopolizing Jim up to now. Maybe some of you have some questions of your own.*

Q: *You and so many other great artists are from Akron. What is it about Akron?*
JJ: Well, I think the key is to come to Akron. I don't know, Akron is a pretty dismal place. When I grew up there everyone's father worked for the rubber companies, including my own and my uncle. It was just a place my friends and I knew we wanted to get out of. There was nothing to do there.

Q: *A lot of the settings that you choose are the kinds of settings where there's nothing to do. How carefully do you choose those sets?*
JJ: Well, I think the locations are as important, or almost as important, as the characters in the film. So, I choose them very carefully. I guess because I'm from Akron, I have a kind of weird, or perverse, nostalgia for kind of post-industrial places. You know, I find them beautiful somehow.

J R : *I've just found out that there's still time to look at one of the* Coffee and Cigarettes *shorts. I've heard that you're going to wait until you've made enough of those in that series and possibly release them all as a feature?*

J J : Yeah, I think I will. My intention is for them to work on their own, but at the same time there are little things that reappear. I've shot five of them now and eventually, when I have about twelve or however many makes up eighty minutes or something, I'll at least release them on video together. I don't know if anybody would release them theatrically.

[clip–*Coffee and Cigarettes—Somewhere in California*]

J R : *I gather this was a series that actually started with* Saturday Night Live, *is that right?*

J J : Yeah, they asked me to make a short film for them, and they gave me the money, so I made the first one. This is the third, and then I have two more that are shot but not edited.

J R : *Are they all in different cities?*

J J : No. I shot three of them in New York, and one in Memphis and one in California.

J R : *Well, I believe this is the most recent of Jim's works. Perhaps we've got time for just a couple of more questions before we call it a night . . .*

Q : *You talked earlier about your early cinematographers. How did you come to work with Frederick Elmes?*

J J : I had seen his work, the films he shot for David Lynch, and particularly also a film called *River's Edge,* in which I really loved the way the photography fit the story. It didn't seem slapped on, it seemed to grow out of the nature of the film, the subject and the feeling of the film. I was very impressed by his work and had met him briefly, and also, I'd read an interview with him where what he said was very strong. It was a lot like what I felt about cinematography, the way that it should grow from the essence of the film, and not be a signature put over the film. So I called him up and talked with him and then went to LA to meet with him, and he agreed to do the film, *Night on Earth.*

Q :   *How heavily do you tie your actors to the dialogue in the script?*

J J :   We change the dialogue a lot in rehearsals. Very much. I'm not interested in tying the actors to the script at all. Except to the ideas of an exchange of dialogue, but not exactly how they phrase it. So, I like to keep them within the way the script works, how things go back and forth, but *how* they say things I am rarely adamant about. Sometimes I am, if it's a very particular joke that I want them to retain. But I'm interested in them being the character, and believable as the character. We change things quite a lot, and a lot of the best things in my films have been things actors came up with during rehearsal periods and improvs that I'd then note down and put into the script. Really, a lot of it comes from them.

J R :   *Well, I think we're out of time. Thank you very much, Jim, and thank you all for coming.*

J J :   Thanks a lot.

Jim Jarmusch

DANNY PLOTNICK/1994

IN THE WORLD OF FILM—particularly American film—
one is either cranking out studio fodder or wallowing in independent obscurity. Jim Jarmusch is one of only a handful of American
filmmakers who has managed to bridge the gap, making intensely
inspired personal works while keeping complete creative control,
and getting enough distribution to make his name known, if not
to all of America, certainly to a tasteful cross-section. Though he's
kept a low-profile as of late—it's been more than a year since his
last feature, *Night on Earth,* and his next feature isn't scheduled to
shoot until this coming fall—he has been working on his ever-
expanding collection of short works, *Coffee and Cigarettes.* Now was
as good a time as any to chat.

DANNY PLOTNICK: *Is* Coffee and Cigarettes *a short or long film?*
JIM JARMUSCH: It's a series of short films that are also designed to eventually be put together. I started them in 1987. The first one was for
Saturday Night Live. That one was with Roberto Benigni and Steven
Wright. I've made four more since then. A couple of them are not
edited yet. They are intended to work as short films independent
of each other. They're all called *Coffee and Cigarettes,* but they do
have running jokes in them, that when you eventually see them all

A shorter version of this interview was published in *The Village Noize,* Vol. 6, No. 16, pp.
18–21, 48. Reprinted by permission.

together, when I get enough of them, they will also work as a
group—as a sequence of shorts. I try to make them so they're suffi-
cient in and of themselves, but I also, in the back of my head, stick
little things in that will recur when I put them all together. I don't
know when that will be. I don't even know if I'd be able to release
them all together theatrically, but certainly eventually on video.
But I'll need about twelve of them or so.

D P :   *Why don't you think you'd be able to release them theatrically as a collected*
        piece?
J J :   I don't know. Maybe I would. I'm not sure how interested people would
        be to distribute that theatrically. I would like it if they did.

D P :   *Have you been able to show the shorter works in places beyond festivals, or*
        even festivals at this point?
J J :   I have on European television and even theatrically they have licensed
        them to show before features. But in the States I can't really find an
        outlet for short films. It's frustrating because it's such a beautiful
        form and it's a great way for younger or new directors that don't
        have much experience to work out. . . . It's a great way to learn and
        to make interesting things. But there's no real place to show them.
        Why don't they have short films in the theatres before films, espe-
        cially in whatever remaining so-called art houses there are? In Eu-
        rope they do that sometimes and it's great. But they just don't do
        that here. You'd think they'd at least try that. And with cable televi-
        sion, why isn't there . . .

D P :   *. . . An independent short film channel?*
J J :   Why not? Or even on Comedy Central or something. Why don't they
        have a program of one hour a week that was just short films? But
        maybe that will change. Cable could be so great if you could have
        more. . . . Instead television is like a big river that everyone goes
        down and throws their garbage in. It could be so great, but it's so
        weak.

D P :   *These kind of interdependent short pieces tie in with your recent films,*
        wherein things hold together thematically in a segmented way, rather

than being held together by some constant narrative strain. I think that's a great device, but unfortunately, that's not how most people are accustomed to looking at films.

JJ: Frankly, I didn't intend to do that—to repeat it. I designed *Mystery Train* to be episodic but simultaneous. While writing, I was interested in playing around with time and things happening simultaneously and in the same place, but without intercutting them. So the pieces within the film remained sequences or episodes in a way. I had no intention of doing that again. I had already started these *Coffee and Cigarettes* films as a separate project, but as a long term project between longer films. I then wrote a script, which for a lot of complicated reasons I wasn't able to do after *Mystery Train*. I got very frustrated and ended up writing *Night on Earth* very fast—in about eight days. It came out accidentally as a film that consisted of short stories or episodes within a longer thing. It wasn't any kind of master plan. It was really an accident. I don't really intend to do that again, except with *Coffee and Cigarettes*. I do have a couple other projects that are a series of short films that could be shown independently as shorts, but I haven't started on those yet.

DP: *What kind of connection do you have to short independent filmmaking? Your work seems to tie into a more independent or experimental framework, yet you get distributed on a wide theatrical scale compared to some. How do you see yourself fitting into those two camps?*

JJ: I'm not really sure. It's kind of complicated to answer because I don't really analyze it. You can see some people who obviously start out independent for financial reasons and then they cross that line into commercial filmmaking by making films with or for the studios. I certainly don't look down on that. And I think there's room in the world for all different kinds of films and hopefully there will continue to be all different kinds of films. It's really the nature of what you want to say in a film that determines what you need in order to make the film. For example, a film like *Lawrence of Arabia* is a huge film that needed that kind of structure, that kind of financing to tell that story, whereas a film like *Slacker* doesn't need that. But the categories kind of bother me. I know they exist because they're enforced by the commercial world, but in my head, I see myself

somewhere in between without paying a whole lot of attention to
those categories. I feel very lucky that my films get distributed.

D P :   *You seem to bridge both those worlds.*

J J :   Somehow I did. Often, especially in Europe, they put me in a difficult-
to-describe category of being half-American and half-European in
terms of the style of my films. I think that just comes from what
has moved me cinematically or things that have inspired me, and
they're not purely American films.

D P :   *What kind of things do you consider very influential on your work?*

J J :   I'd rather say inspirational rather than influential. But all kinds of
things from Hollywood films, especially in the past, especially the
more outsider directors like Nick Ray, Sam Fuller, Douglas Sirk,
Edgar G. Ulmer, and Henry Hathaway. A lot of Hollywood stuff I
really love.

D P :   *Have you seen the recently released Fuller film* Street of No Return?

J J :   I didn't get a chance to see it, but I love Sam Fuller. I just went to the
Amazon this summer with Sam and Mika Kaurismäki, a young
Finnish director. In 1954, Sam was sent to the Amazon by Darryl F.
Zanuck to prepare a story based on a book that Zanuck had bought.
And he sent Sam down there and Sam went with a 16mm camera
and made a lot of footage, particularly of an Indian tribe called the
Karaji in the Amazon basin. He came back and wrote the story. The
film was cast with John Wayne, Ava Gardner, and Tyrone Power,
which was going to be a big thing for Sam. And then the insurance
company would not insure those stars in the Amazon. Zanuck tried
to get another insurance carrier and they kind of banded together
and refused to insure the film and so the film was never made. Sam
was cleaning out his closets and house in Los Angeles four or five
years ago, and he found all the footage that he had shot, so he sent
it to Kaurismäki, and said, "Here, you can have it, maybe you can
think of something to do with it." Mika decided to go back down
to the Amazon with Sam forty years later and go to the same places
he filmed, film him there, show the footage to the indigenous people that he stayed with and see if they recognized themselves or

relatives. I somehow got pulled into this project. In the film, I'm
just traveling with Sam. So that was a fascinating experience. I
haven't seen the finished film, but I know it showed in the Berlin
Film Festival this year and had a good response.

D P :   *It sounds a bit similar to the Falkenau film where a French director documents Sam's reactions to the footage he shot during WWII of the libera-
tion of a concentration camp.*
J J :   I've never seen that. I'd love to see that. It was great being down there.
I've known Sam for quite a few years, but I've never spent three
solid weeks with him.

D P :   *He seems pretty crazy . . . in a good way.*
J J :   He is so energized. The man is like eighty-six and you can't stop that
guy. You can't shut him up. He never stops talking. He has so many
amazing stories. He's like some kind of historical artifact. I love that
guy. He used some footage of this tribe in *Shock Corridor.*

D P :   *The hallucination scenes?*
J J :   Yeah.

D P :   *What's this Finnish director's deal?*
J J :   You probably know his brother's films more than his—Aki Kaurismäki.
He made *The Match Factory Girl, Shadows in Paradise, I Hired a Con-
tract Killer, Leningrad Cowboys Go America,* etc. . . .

D P :   *Are these people you made connections with making* Night on Earth?
J J :   No. I've known these guys a lot longer than that. I've known Mika and
Aki since 1986. We're been friends for a long time. I appeared briefly
in *Leningrad Cowboys* and in a film Mika made in 1987 called *Helsinki
Napoli All Night Long.* Sam was also in the film, and Eddie Constan-
tine and Wim Wenders had cameos, too.

D P :   *How do you like doing cameos?*
J J :   It varies. Sometimes I've liked them a lot and other times I just hated it.
I think it depends how comfortable I feel with the director and the
material. Sometimes when I've just been left alone, I've learned

from that how terrifying it is. When I feel comfortable I feel like
I've done a good job.

D P :   *Which ones do you think you haven't done a good job in?*

J J :   I don't know if I should say. It's kind of negative. *Helsinki Napoli* was
not good on my part, nor was Alex Cox's film *Straight to Hell*. But
these were my fault, not the directors'. I had fun in *In the Soup*
though with Carol Kane. I got to be Carol Kane's husband and we
were two sleazy promoters that had a television show called *The
Naked Truth* on which our guests appear nude. We had fun doing
that.

D P :   *You work with people who aren't "actors" like Screamin' Jay Hawkins and
Iggy. What's your experience with working with someone like that as
opposed to people who are "actors"?*

J J :   I think certain people are capable of being good actors or being relaxed
and becoming real in front of the camera. They could be someone
who studied acting academically for years, or they could be your
plumber. It really depends on the person and the character and
how you work. There's no one way to direct all actors. There's only
one way for a single director and single actor to collaborate. When
you find that, you can collaborate and get a great performance. But
in the case of people like Iggy or Screamin' Jay, they're already . . .

D P :   *. . . personas . . .*

J J :   . . . and they're performers too. Although it's very different. I would say
performing rock'n'roll live is closer to acting on the stage in a theatre, whereas filmmaking is maybe a little closer to making a record
in a studio because you can overdub or do other takes. It's not live.
I have to qualify that because I'm sure there are a lot of musicians
that are terrible actors. It really depends on the person. But those
guys are performers and they're also, as individuals—although very
different personality-wise—very observant and intelligent, so
they're pretty good as actors.

D P :   *Do you also find that you gear your writing of their parts to what you perceive
them to be as performers?*

JJ: I do that even with "actors." I try to write with specific people in mind
     for a character. It's often someone I already know, so even if I'm
     not conscious of it, my impressions of them, whether accurate or
     not, filter into the character I write for them. And that's not to say
     I'm writing for them to be themselves. But I use certain aspects of
     their personality to develop the character from. And I'm not always
     accurate. Sometimes I misread people, but so far I've been pretty
     happy with the results of that.

DP: *How did you hook up with Roberto Benigni?*
JJ: I first met Roberto in a small film festival in Salso Maggiore in Italy. We
     were both on the jury of this festival. It's the first and last time I
     would ever be on a jury because Roberto and I caused a scandal, by
     not voting for the film we were being pressured to vote for. Even
     the head of the festival yelled at us.

DP: *Was it a more theatrical or independent festival?*
JJ: It was a more independent festival. In fact, I met Jean-Luc Godard there.
     It's the only time I've ever met him. But Roberto and I met there
     and he didn't speak English and I didn't speak any Italian and
     somehow we became really good friends during that two week pe-
     riod babbling on endlessly in very bad French. We kept saying that
     if some French person had a hidden microphone and heard what
     we were saying, they would be horrified by the way we were butch-
     ering the language, but we still could understand each other com-
     pletely. We really had fun. I had started sketching out a story for
     Down by Law, but was kind of lost. Then I met him there and from
     there I went to Rome and wrote the rest of the script in about a
     week or two. I gave it to him and he said, "Yes, I will do this."

DP: *He's incredible in both* Down by Law *and* Night on Earth.
JJ: He's amazing in general. He's more of a wild man in real life, in fact. A
     lot of the things we did in *Night on Earth* came from things we had
     talked about or done together. Once I stayed with Roberto for a
     couple of months in Rome. We would go out at night and on the
     way home, he would try to drive all the way back to his house
     going only the wrong way on one way streets as a kind of game.

He'd flash the lights and honk the horn at every intersection. We almost got killed several times. He loved that game. One way is "senso unico" in Italian so he would say, "Now Jim, do you want to play senso unico?" I would be terrified and we'd drive home and almost get t-boned at every intersection.

DP: *How much of his bit in* Night on Earth *was scripted beforehand and how much did he improvise?*

JJ: All of his dialogue was initially scripted, but he had a very long leash. Of all the actors in that film, he improved the most, but always around what was scripted. I remember while shooting we did a take that was really great, but it was five minutes long. After that take I said, "Roberto, that was hilarious, but it should be more like two and a half minutes." And he said, "No problem, I do it again," and the next take was about eight minutes. He was really going crazy improvising. A lot of the most hilarious stuff was just stuff he was coming up with as we shot. He stayed to the text, but his interpretations of it and way of delivering it was really wild.

DP: *When you do these segmented films, my guess is, in your head, you have a sense of how they'll all hang together. But, when you get the film back from the lab and begin to piece it together, do things start changing? Do sections maybe not flow as smoothly as you expected and you then have to rethink how you're going to edit?*

JJ: Not so much actually. In *Night on Earth,* that didn't happen very much. It happens more in my little short films. The *Coffee and Cigarettes* films are also scripted, but they are more cartoon-like in our approach to them. So I encourage them to improvise or go off on tangents if they want to. But then I have to really piece the thing together in the editing and a lot of the shots don't match. There are jumps of continuity in the finished films that I don't really care about. Those ones are more of a surprise in terms of how do I fit the pieces together. In the long films, it's been less that way mostly, because I encourage improvisation in the rehearsals more than in front of the camera, and that's due only to financial restrictions. I wish I had more time or could shoot in a different way. Did you see *Naked?* I was so envious of Mike Leigh's way of working. I guess he rehearsed for months beforehand as well. I would love to have the chance to work that way, but my budgets have been pretty restricting. I would rather be able to work the way Leigh or John Cassavetes worked and have more play while rolling. But I haven't had that luxury.

D P : *Have you seen much of Mike Leigh's work?*

J J : Only a few. My favorites are *Naked* and *Abigail's Party*. Some of his other stuff I've seen and don't really remember because it was too sweet and didn't really hit me the way *Naked* did. I really liked *Naked* 'cause it was so funny and so brutal.

D P : *It's impressive how he can infuse humor into grim situations. People's reactions to that kind of stuff is interesting—that "it made me uncomfortable so I didn't like it" approach that some people have to a certain style of film like* Naked.

J J : Some girl that I didn't know accosted me in a bar asking me if I liked *Naked*. I said, "Yes, a lot," and she started railing against me for saying I liked the film because she thought it was misogynistic, and I said, "It's really more misanthropic," but it was more just the cynicism or nihilism of the character. But it's such a ridiculous argument. I said to her, "Well, I guess you should really see films and read books about people you know you would like." It's so ridiculous. There's a great book by Honoré de Balzac called *The Wild Ass's Skin* that I like a lot and the character in it is a total fuck-up. It's a great book, but do you have to like the guy and want to have dinner with him in order to read it. It's just so ridiculous to me.

D P : *So* Coffee and Cigarettes *is scripted?*

J J : Yeah, but we play around with them. We rehearse them too, but we only have a little time, like a day, to rehearse them. The one with Tom Waits and Iggy Pop, we didn't have much time to rehearse. Tom was exhausted and we had just shot a video the day before for "I Don't Want To Grow Up" [from *Bone Machine*] and he had been doing a lot of press and was really exhausted and he's very surly in the film. He was kind of in a surly mood as he is sometimes, but he's also very warm. But he came in that morning—I had given

him the script the night before—and I was there with Iggy and Tom
came a little late and threw the script down on the table and said,
"Well, you know, you said this was going to be funny Jim. Maybe
you better just circle the jokes 'cause I don't see them." And then
he looked at poor Iggy and said, "What do you think Iggy?" And
Iggy said, "I think I'm gonna go get some coffee and let you guys
talk." So I calmed him down and I knew it was just early in the
morning and Tom was in a bad mood. Then his attitude changed
completely and he was really great the whole day and worked really
hard. But I wanted him to keep some of that paranoid surliness in
the script. We worked with that and kept that in his character. So
it turned out a good thing. If he had been in a really good mood, I
don't think the film would have been as funny.

DP: *That's the version which showed in Cannes last year and won big prizes?*
JJ: It won the short film award, whatever that is. I don't really know. Those
kind of award things I think are kind of ridiculous. When Sam Fuller's *Shock Corridor* came out he was given a humanitarian award in
San Sebastian, Spain. He went up and said, "I don't want your god-
damned award. This isn't a god-damned humanitarian film. This is
a hard hitting action packed melodrama. Give your award to Ing-
mar Bergman." And he walked off without accepting it. And the
next year, they gave the humanitarian award to Bergman. I've had
films in competition, so this is somewhat duplicitous on my part,
but I've really done that for reasons of selling my films to distributors. But I think it's kind of funny and it's why I also would never
be on a jury again. It's like sending eight people into the Louvre
and having them decide collectively what's the best painting in the
museum and then what's the best painter and then which painting
is the most artistic. It's kind of ridiculous to me. But it's all political.
It's for money. It's just to get publicity for those films and the companies behind them. It's like the Academy Awards, which someday
maybe will change with new blood, but it's like a big company
picnic with people slapping each other on the back. And that's ok,
but you've got to know how ridiculous and absurd it is from the
start.

D P :   *So now you're working on another film?*

J J :   Yeah. I'm preparing a film that I will shoot in August, September, October—somewhere in there. I'm also laying the groundwork for another film that I would like to make in the fall of 1995. So I'm
getting ready for a long stint of work, because for the last year and
a half I really didn't do anything at all. I didn't feel like doing anything. I hit a funny period and I felt like I had absolutely nothing
to say. I did make three short films and a video with Tom, and I
acted in a biker film in Finland that was directed by a young French
guy called *Iron Horsemen* and then I went to the Amazon with Sam
and Mika. So I did some things that were fun, but I just didn't want
to make another film. And then I kind of burst through that and I
spent three months this winter alone up in the country and wrote
this script and sketched out the other film I want to make next
year. So now I'm ready to work again. I don't want to talk about
them yet because I'm sort of superstitious about it. It's not to be
secretive. It's more just 'cause I feel like I'll jinx myself.

D P :   *You'll still be shooting* Coffee and Cigarettes *shorts periodically?*

J J :   Yeah. I have two in the can that aren't edited yet, and then I have two
more that are loosely scripted. So, I'll certainly do one or two or
three in between these next two films and edit the two that I
haven't cut yet.

D P :   *Do you ever do the lecture circuit?*

J J :   No, I never have, although I just got a bunch of requests to lecture and
I was thinking of actually doing it because it sounded like it would
be fun. I would like to do a lecture. It would certainly be meander-
ing. I don't know how interesting I would be, but I would like to
try it and see if people thought it was fun or not and if they don't,
I'll never do it again, I promise. Have you ever heard John Cage
lecture?

D P :   *No.*

J J :   When he died they started playing them on college radio stations and
stuff. One lecture is about "nothing." It's about an hour long lecture about "nothing." It's really great. He's like saying, "I'm speak-

ing about nothing and the subject of my lecture is nothing, so as I talk, we are going nowhere and I'm speaking about nothing, and if you wish to go to sleep, feel free, because I will still be talking about nothing. And if you want to leave, go ahead, we will still be going nowhere and talking about nothing." It's very lulling and hypnotic and it's very beautiful. So if he could give a lecture about nothing that was interesting, then I figure I should be able to come up with something.

DP: *What kind of things do you think you might talk about? Would it be film related or maybe more philosophical stuff tied into film?*

JJ: I think I would throw together a bunch of disconnected things. Talk a little bit about films I liked or experiences I've had or anecdotes that aren't related to film at all or maybe read a couple poems that I like. Or maybe stop and play a piece of music for no reason at all except as a musical break. Maybe even play a little excerpt of that particular John Cage lecture. I don't really know. I think it would be kind of a collage thing. I have been writing a little book. Do you know this little publisher—Hanuman Press—that does those little tiny books? There is a Burroughs one about painting and guns, there's a Patti Smith one. They asked me to do a book. I haven't finished it yet, but I've been writing just little anecdotes of things that have happened in my life, not related to films at all, but just stupid little things that have happened that I think are maybe funny. As a kind of like memoirs, but in a random order. Maybe I could stick a few of those in and pad the lecture.

DP: *In* Night on Earth, *did you have any language problems communicating and directing with the Finns or the French?*

JJ: Strangely, I didn't. It's interesting—you find out how much language is just a code that we use. People express their emotions in a lot of ways other than just by language. It was interesting. I like Japanese cinema, I've been to Japan a number of times and I've brought back a lot of video tapes by directors like Suzuki, Ozu, Oshima, and Kurosawa and other less known directors, and I spent time watching them. They're not subtitled, so I don't know what the fuck they're saying, but it's amazing how much you can follow. Of course you miss certain plot points that are intimated only in the language, but you still know how people are feeling and what they're expressing without knowing what they're saying. That helped me on working in languages I didn't speak. Of course, I had translators all the time and I speak French and I understand maybe sixty percent of what Roberto says in Italian, so those were less difficult. It really wasn't a problem at all and I had had some experience working with the two Japanese kids in *Mystery Train*. The Finns were following a script that I had written, so as long as I knew where they were in the dialogue, I could assess what I felt about their performances.

D P : *So you would write it and someone would then translate it into Finnish?*

J J : Yeah. I worked with the actors while it was being translated. We all sat around together for a whole day and discussed the nuances of the translation to make sure, for example, that the way they talked was working class. We collectively made some changes in their Finnish by discussing it with them. They would explain nuances and together we would make decisions. So we worked a lot on the way the Finnish was spoke, even though I couldn't judge it without working with them on it.

D P : *What kind of reactions did you get from Finnish or French audiences? Did that give you a sense of whether your translations or methods of working succeeded?*

J J : Everyone said it was really strong, that it was very realistic. Both in the French, Finnish, and Italian sections of that film. So I was very happy about that.

D P : *From a technical standpoint, was it difficult to coordinate crews for each country?*

J J : It was. It was also complicated because in each section of *Night on Earth* we had to have two identical cars. We'd pull the engine out of one and build a little rigging area that we could place our camera in. We'd use one car for the exterior shots and then one for the interior and that was really complicated. It was also complicated having new people each time. We had the same basic crew—the same soundman, director of photography, gaffer, grip, myself, and the line producer. But everyone else was a new crew in each place. But we were pretty lucky because we tended to hire people on the basis of their enthusiasm rather than their experience. That worked out well, because we had dedicated younger crews that were really great. We had a few problems in Italy where they didn't want to shoot after certain hours or they wanted an hour and a half for lunch and they wanted to drink wine. But that was just cultural. Once we got over that, everything worked out pretty well.

D P :   *How long did it take to shoot?*

J J :   It took about three months but we were only able to shoot for about seven or eight shooting days for each section. We would have a week to prepare and rehearse and get our vehicles and locations ready. I had gone there beforehand and rehearsed and set up and got the actors together and locations. But once we were in production we would arrive a week before and then shoot for a week. It was pretty hectic, but it was fun. I liked doing that. I devised the film to see a lot of my friends or work with them.

D P :   *Good reason to go to Finland.*

J J :   One of the few good reasons, yeah. I actually like Finland because I have good friends there. I met some crazy people there. This motorcycle gang called Overkill M.C. invited me out to this party in their headquarters. We drove about forty minutes outside of Helsinki to this Quonset hut in the middle of the night where they were having this wild Finnish biker party. Two huge leaders of the gang came up to me—I'm 6'2" and they were much bigger than me—and they pushed me in a corner and said [in menacing Finnish biker-tone] "You—You are Jim Jarmusch, no? I want to tell you something. We are liking so much your films. Come and have beer with us now." I thought it was trouble. They're spitting it out and spitting on me, and I'm looking at the scorpion tattoos on their necks and stuff. But they were good guys.

D P :   *In* Mystery Train, *were the Japanese kids actors or people you knew?*

J J :   They're actors. The girl Youki Kudoh was an actress who, ironically, I first saw when I was on that jury in Salso Maggiore where I met

Roberto. We saw her in a film called *Crazy Family* which was a very funny Japanese comedy—really wacky. She was fourteen at the time and she was really funny. She made a big impression on me, so when I wrote that part of *Mystery Train,* I wrote it thinking of her as the actress. Then I went to Tokyo and cast the guy. I saw like thirty or forty young Japanese actors and then found Masatoshi Nagase through casting sessions.

DP: *So you went to Japan just to cast?*

JJ: Yeah, and also since the film was being financed mostly by Japanese money, I had to conclude some business deals, as well. But mostly I was there for casting.

DP: *Do you have a regular film company or do you shop your films around?*

JJ: Well, all of my films thus far have been produced through my own company or companies. They change just for insurance reasons, but it's the same company. I own all the negatives, but I finance them with different people and that changes each time. On the last two films, JVC from Japan has been a large part of the financing and the remainder has come from France and Germany. I try to work with the same people, but it doesn't always work out that way.

DP: *Does that put a lot of added pressure on you or are you always confident you can find someone else to back you?*

JJ: So far I've been very lucky—knock on wood. Now I'm trying to finance my new project, which is bigger, budget-wise, than anything I've done so far. So this one's a little trickier and I'm seeing if I can still piece together financing, or if I have to try to go to one place that will then try to put restrictions on me creatively, which I'm desperately trying to avoid. At the moment we're scrambling around trying to finance it by split rights. It's looking good, but it's not completely in place yet. We have other people in American that have offered to fully finance my next project, but they want to have script conferences or they want to discuss certain creative things. So far I'm just keeping them on a back burner. I'd certainly rather not have to do that and I'll avoid it at all costs. We'll see what happens.

End of the Road

SCOTT MACAULAY/1996

IN JIM JARMUSCH'S NEW *Dead Man,* Johnny Depp plays William Blake, a mild-mannered accountant who travels by train across the frontier West to work in a bookkeeping firm run by a crazed, gun-toting Robert Mitchum. When, as in a Kafka novel, the job vanishes before it's even begun, Blake finds himself a hunted man, pursued for a murder he didn't commit while his life force ebbs away through a bullet wound in his chest.

With its fixation on mortality and transcendence, *Dead Man* stands alongside a number of death-obsessed contemporary works—the revisionist Yakuza dramas of Takeshi Kitano, Nick Cave's new *Murder Ballads* and, of course, Mike Figgis's *Leaving Las Vegas.* But where Figgis's film cannily turns its protagonist's death trip into a Romantic quest successfully completed by film's end, Jarmusch remains more open-ended in his storytelling. He freely mixes dollops of existential absurdism with English poet William Blake's mystical poetry—an aesthetic fusion echoed by the film's poetry-reading Native American character, Nobody.

But while Depp's character may carry the poet's moniker, it is Jarmusch himself—with his dedication to a personal sense of film rhythm and pace, his use here of poetic, unexplained symbols, and, finally, his ability to finance his films in ways that ensure his ultimate creative control—who most strongly echoes Blake. An engraver and printer by trade, Blake controlled the means of production, ensuring that his unique and eccentric work would always find a way out into the world. And with this sixth feature, a "mini-

Published in *Filmmaker,* Vol. 4, No. 3, Spring 1996, pp. 46–47, 70. Reprinted by permission.

malist epic," Jarmusch, who has inspired a generation of filmmakers after him (look up "independent film" in Microsoft's *Cinemania '96* and you get a still of *Stranger Than Paradise*) continues to make unpredictable and highly personal cinema in a climate that prioritizes neither.

FILMMAKER: *I thought a lot about Neil Young and Crazy Horse while watching the movie. It wasn't just because his guitar sound is all over the soundtrack. A lot of the movie reminded me of* Sleep with Angels—*a couple of albums ago. That record had the low-end, distorted guitar played somewhat softly and the honky-tonk piano but also similar themes—death, the corrupted American myth, Native Americans, industrialization as destroyer . . .*
JARMUSCH: That's in a lot of Neil's songs. "Cortez the Killer," "Pocahontas"—

FILMMAKER: *"Powderfinger."*
JARMUSCH: Well, we're interested in a lot of the same things. *Dead Man* is a very simple story on the surface but there are so many things the film is about—history, language, America, indigenous culture, violence, industrialization. I wanted these things to be important but in a peripheral way. The film has a lot more levels than any of my other films but I wanted to stay focused on the simplicity of the story and let those other levels coexist without one taking precedent.

FILMMAKER: *Was it a concern of yours that your William Blake, played by Johnny Depp, is such a passive character?*
JARMUSCH: It's hard to be a passive character, a vessel that carries us through the story. I wanted to work with Johnny in advance but he only arrived a day before shooting. But I was really amazed by how precisely he had mapped out his character's emotional flow throughout the piece on his own.

FILMMAKER: *Well, he does ultimately step into his role as an outlaw. In the trading post scene, it seems as if he's even enjoying it.*
JARMUSCH: By that point, he's given up any thoughts of going back to the person he once was. And I think [the change] happens too because when Nobody leaves him alone, something happens to him that is not told to you by the film. We don't say, "A vision quest has changed his character." But

something happens. When he comes out of the tunnel and he and Nobody ride through that cathedral-like redwood forest, the next scene is the trading post.

FILMMAKER: *And that's the scene where you most explicitly deal with this idea of the corrupted American myth. The traders are selling the Indians' blankets contaminated by smallpox, tuberculosis . . .*
JARMUSCH: It's funny, whenever Neil sees that scene with Alfred Molina, he says, "Oh man, there's that South African guy." He's an English actor and I was wondering why was he obsessed with him being South African. Then I realized—biological warfare, not serving the heathen aboriginal—it's the same thing.

FILMMAKER: *Are you the kind of director who finds the film in the cutting room or do you do the montage in your head as you shoot?*
JARMUSCH: I'm in-between. When I go in the cutting room, I have a pretty good idea of how a scene was intended to be cut together. The editing is very important because you get to a Zen-like place where the film starts telling you how to cut it. A lot of scenes were shot for *Dead Man* that are not in the film. Shooting is like cutting up big pieces of granite that are sort of in the right shape of the thing you want to sculpt out of them. And then you go back, and the shape is not exactly what you had in mind so you sculpt them some more. I like the process. That's why I never use a storyboard and on *Dead Man* I didn't even have shot lists in advance. I don't want to know in advance what we're going to do because then we are not thinking on our feet.

FILMMAKER: *How did you work out the conception of the film's look with d.p. Robby Müller? It's a black-and-white film with lots of shades of gray. And the landscapes were quite ugly but beautifully so.*
JARMUSCH: We worked hard to use black and white like it was used in the '30s and '40s when the gray scale was the color palette. We wanted to avoid the recent "hard" black-and-white look, although the blacks are very black and the whites are very white. We wanted a feeling like a film by Mizoguchi. And when we were scouting for locations, whenever we saw any magnificent view, like a postcard type, we would appreciate it, Robby and I, and then turn out backs and look for our location with that out of view.

FILMMAKER: *A lot of recent movies about death have adhered to that Elizabeth Kubler-Ross model—the five stages. I think* Fearless *even used it as a structuring device. Anyway, one level is acceptance. Does Johnny Depp ever reach that state?*

JARMUSCH: Not an obvious one, but certainly he does in that he accepts that his physical life is limited in time and he has to go on a journey. Does he make a realization that he's going to die? I didn't want to make that obvious. In fact I tried to throw it away at the end. The last piece of dialogue before he's shoved out into the ocean—there are jokes in there. "Now you have to go back to the place you came from." "You mean Cleveland?" I didn't want a heavy handed scene.

FILMMAKER: *You are someone who is making films not only outside of the Hollywood system but also outside of this new mini-major system—Miramax, Fox Searchlight, Fine Line, the Polygram companies—*

JARMUSCH: —I'm still broke and a lowlife, I tell you.

FILMMAKER: *But* Dead Man, *you sold it blind to Miramax—meaning they couldn't see it even though you had a print—for a good amount of money just before Cannes. That testifies to a strong interest American distributors have in your work. Yet, look at the credits of the movie and it's all European financing.*

JARMUSCH: Mostly European, there's some Japanese money in there and some bankers finished it but I don't want to go into that.

FILMMAKER: *My point is, if you wanted to make a movie with one of those American companies, you could have. You wouldn't have to mess with stitching the financing together from all over. Yours is a more complicated method of financing but I suspect it offers you more freedom and autonomy.*

JARMUSCH: Exactly. The only thing that matters to me is to protect my ability to be the navigator of the ship. I decide how the film is cut, how long it is, what music is used, who the cast is. I make films by hand. I'm there every day in the editing room. I'm there in the financing. I write the script. I collaborate with a lot of great people. I don't believe in the auteur thing but somebody has to say, look, a filmmaker should make the film, not businessmen. My films are ghettoized by being called art movies. When people describe a rock-and-roll group as art rock, I want to put on Motorhead. And then I wonder, why is that? What's wrong with art? But they will make anything a dirty word to make commerce and corporate control the priority.

That's Hollywood. Who has the most powerful agent and how much money can the lawyers suck out of the above-the-line? It's one of the most overpaid of any field in America, entertainment. The Academy Awards—why don't we have awards for short order cooks or bus drivers?

FILMMAKER: *Have you explored these new, "filmmaker-friendly" companies?*
JARMUSCH: Yes, there were two of those companies that wanted to be involved with *Dead Man* but they wanted script approval, editing approval. They wanted to be on my set. Hey, man—I don't work that way. I do it my way or I don't do it. It helps me in negotiating to know that I will walk away if I don't have control.

FILMMAKER: *As you get older, are you still finding films that turn you on as much as stuff did that you encountered in your twenties?*
JARMUSCH: It continues to happen. I didn't discover Ophuls until eight years ago and I had to see every one of his films. But I go through periods, like I had to see every film Steve McQueen was in. I don't know why, but it had to be Steve McQueen. I go off on binges. Could be Brigitte Bardot, could be Dolph Lundgren. But I don't think I've seen every film Dolph has been in.

FILMMAKER: *Have you seen many of them?*
JARMUSCH: Yeah, of those guys—Jean-Claude Van Damme, Steven Seagal and Dolph Lundgren—I prefer Dolph.

FILMMAKER: *Why?*
JARMUSCH: Van Damme I find annoying. There's something smug about his face. I like how Dolph Lundgren is so robotic. He doesn't pretend to have to play a character that has some emotional dilemma.

FILMMAKER: *What about directors?*
JARMUSCH: I liked *Slacker* a lot. I like Gus Van Sant. I liked Leos Carax's early film, *Mauvais Sang*. I like Tarantino's sense of how he structures stories. I hate what he's done for soundtracks, though. It's not all his fault. It started before him. "Let's buy pop songs by the yard and put them over the film."

FILMMAKER: *Well, Scorsese does that too.*

JARMUSCH: He does it in a very different way. I don't think he does it to have a marketing tool, a record. And Scorsese didn't even start doing it until *GoodFellas.* And it's used very precisely to cue your emotions, your memory, to specific periods by the year. That's different from collecting a bunch of shit and slapping it on and having a good ancillary marketing device.

A Gun Up Your Ass

JONATHAN ROSENBAUM/1996

A DOZEN YEARS AGO, when his second feature, *Stranger Than Paradise*, catapulted him to worldwide fame, Jim Jarmusch seemed at the height of arthouse fashion. Having already known him a little before then, I could tell that the extent to which he suddenly became a figurehead for the American independent cinema bemused him in certain ways. Given the aura of hip, glamorous downtown Manhattan culture that seemed to follow him everywhere, how could it not? I can still recall a *New York Times* profile a few years back that was so entranced by his image that it suggested that, simply because Jarmusch chose to live in the Bowery, that neighborhood automatically took on magical, transcendent properties.

When *Dead Man*, his sixth feature, premiered at Cannes last year, it suddenly became apparent that Jarmusch's honeymoon with the American press was over—although is international reputation to all appearances survives intact. There are multiple reasons for this, including *Dead Man* itself, and before getting around to this visionary, disturbing black-and-white Western—which I regard as his most impressive achievement to date—it's worth considering what's happened to the American independent cinema over the past decade, which has a lot to do with Jarmusch's changed position in the media.

When thinking about today's ambitious American filmmakers, one of the easiest ways to distinguish between Hollywood employees (current or prospective) and those with more creative freedom is to look for logical and

---

Published in *Cineaste*, Vol. 22, No. 2, June 1996, 20–23. Reprinted by permission.

consistent developments from one film to the next—a clear line of concerns that runs beyond fads and market developments. Though it's possible to see a director such as Alfred Hitchcock developing certain formal and thematic ideas in his fifties movies, there's little likelihood of such an evolution being possible in a studio director today, what with agent packages, script bids, multiple rewrites, stars who get script approval and/or say over the final cut, test marketing, and so on. Within such a context, it's significant that Jarmusch as a writer-director, virtually alone among American independents who make narrative features, owns the negatives of all his films. This means that, for better and for worse, all the developments—and nondevelopments—that have taken place in his work between *Permanent Vacation* (1980) and *Dead Man* are of his own making.

This provides one model of American independent filmmaking, but not the one that most of the media are currently preoccupied with. Their model tends to gravitate around the Sundance Film Festival, where success in the independent sector is typically defined as landing a big-time distributor and/ or a studio contract—the exposure, in short, that goes hand in glove with dependence on large institutional backing. And though it would be wrong to assume that Jarmusch isn't himself dependent on such forces to get his films into theaters (Miramax is distributing *Dead Man*), the salient difference between him and most other independents is that he's strong enough to afford the luxury of brooking no creative interference when it comes to making production and postproduction decisions. (*Dead Man* has been trimmed since its Cannes premiere—without apparent injury, in my opinion—but all of the recutting was done without Miramax's input.)

So where does Jarmusch belong in the present, reconfigured independent scene constructed around the Sundance myth? One disheartening clue is offered by Sundance star Kevin Smith, the director of *Clerks* and *Mall Rats*, who was recently quoted as saying, "I don't feel that I have to go back and view European or other foreign films because I feel like these guys [i.e., Jarmusch and others] have already done it for me, and I'm getting filtered through them. That ethic works for me." Another clue is provided by the mixed response of the American press to *Dead Man* at Cannes.

Prior to *Dead Man*, when Jarmusch's three features since *Stranger Than Paradise*—*Down by Law* (1986), *Mystery Train* (1989), and *Night on Earth* (1992)— could be partially taken as light, comic entertainments with serious undertones, it was possible to assume that Jarmusch might have continued in such a vein. But *Dead Man*—which might be described as a serious art film with colic elements—flings down the gauntlet of proposing a much more ambitious direction for Jarmusch's work, daring an audience to follow it. The plot hinges on a recently orphaned accountant named William Blake (Johnny Depp)—though, characteristic of Jarmusch's white heroes, he's never even heard of the poet of that name—traveling out West with the promise of a job at a steelworks run by someone named Dickinson (Robert Mitchum in a cameo), only to discover that the position has already been taken. Soon afterwards, in bed with a woman named Thel Russell (Mili Avital), he suddenly finds himself killing her former lover (Gabriel Byrne), who happens to be Dickinson's son, in self-defense just after he has shot her. Seriously wounded by a bullet in the same skirmish, Blake spends the remainder of the movie dying—mainly in the wilderness, and chiefly in the company of a renegade Native American named Nobody (Gary Farmer) as they proceed through various encounters with strangers, many of them bounty hunters dispatched by Dickinson and seeking a reward.

Even though *Dead Man* contains many familiar Jarmuschian elements—a "foreigner" (Nobody) who offers a poetic, comic critique on the viewpoint of the other characters (such as the fact that he knows the poetry of William Blake and Blake himself doesn't); an episodic structure; a starting-and-stopping rhythm punctuated by fadeouts (hypnotic and haunting in this case, if one feels sympathetic to what the film is doing, and accompanied by a powerful and minimalist improvised Neil Young score); and a preoccupation with death (a constant in Jarmusch's work since *Down by Law)*—this is the first substantial alteration of the Jarmusch formula since the one that took place between *Permanent Vacation* and *Stranger Than Paradise,* in large part because of the changes brought about by a period setting and a Hollywood genre (the Western). And the film's carefully researched, multifaceted approach to various Native American cultures makes for a sobering contrast to the scary portrait of white America as a primitive, anarchic world of spiteful bounty hunters and bloody grudge matches—a portrait that can be read without much difficulty as contemporary.

Perhaps the film's most courageous defiance of commercial conventions is a response to the current cinema of violence that is so unsettling that audiences generally can't decide whether to wince or laugh. Every time someone fires a gun at someone else in this film, the gesture is awkward, unheroic, pathetic; it's an act that leaves a mess and is deprived of any pretense at existential purity, creating a sense of embarrassment and overall discomfort in the viewer that is the reverse of what ensues from the highly estheticized forms of violence that have become de riguer in commercial Hollywood ever since the heyday of Arthur Penn and Sam Peckinpah, and which have recently been revitalized by Tarantino, among others.

My phone interview with Jarmusch took place in April, eleven months after the Cannes premiere of *Dead Man,* and two months after I saw the film a few more times in its final form at the Rotterdam Film Festival. In part because we'd already discussed the film more casually the previous August, the interview often took the form of a conversation, with me offering some of my reactions to the film and then getting his responses to them.

C I N E A S T E : *I know that the main passage from William Blake that Nobody quotes—"Every Night & every Morn /Some to Misery are Born . . ./Some are Born to sweet delight/Some are Born to Endless Night"—is from* Auguries of Innocence. *But I've heard you say that some lines are quoted from* Proverbs of Hell, *and I don't recall any.*
J I M   J A R M U S C H : Nobody says, "The eagle never lost so much time as when he submitted to learn of the crow." And when he and William Blake meet again toward the end of the film, he says, "Drive your cart and your plow over the bones of the dead."

C I N E A S T E : *The funny thing is, they sounded like Indian sayings in the film.*
J A R M U S C H : Yeah, that was the intention. Blake just walked into the script right before I was starting to write it. There were a bunch of other quotes that didn't get into the film that seemed very Native American: "Expect poison from the standing water." "What is now proved was once only imagin'd." "The crow wish'd every thing was black, the owl that every thing was white." And Nobody quotes from "The Everlasting Gospel" when they're at the trading post: "The vision of Christ that thou dost see/Is my Vision's Greatest Enemy."

C I N E A S T E : *How long was the rough cut that Neil Young improvised his score to?*
J A R M U S C H : Two and a half hours. He refused to have the film stop at any moment. He did that three times over a two-day period. Neil asked me to give him a list of places where I wanted music, and he used that as a kind of

map, but he was really focused on the film, so the score kind of became his emotional reaction to the movie.

Then Neil came to New York to premix the stuff and we thought in a few places we'd slide it around a little, but it almost never worked—in general it was married to where he played it.

CINEASTE: *Was your final editing influenced by what he did?*
JARMUSCH: No, oddly enough. Or maybe it was, subconsciously. The final movie is two hours long and very little of Neil's music is missing, so we didn't cut much where there was music. But it wasn't a conscious decision.

CINEASTE: *One thing I really like about* Dead Man *is that it's the only film of yours, apart from* Stranger Than Paradise, *that really establishes a rhythm all its own, one that's not the rhythm of any other film. It seems that part of this has to do with the fadeouts.*
JARMUSCH: Yeah, I think you're right. But I'm the worst person to analyze the stuff and I hate looking back at it. I unfortunately had to look at *Stranger* again recently to prepare the laserdisc release in the U.S., which was really painful; I hadn't seen it since 1984. But I think there is something similar to them in that they do have very particular rhythms that seem to grow out of the stories themselves. It doesn't seem imposed in the same way that it might in *Down by Law* or the more formally episodic ones. It does have a very odd rhythm. I think of it—and I don't know if this is accurate at all, it's just in my mind—as being closer to classical Japanese films rhythmically. We had that in the back of our minds while shooting, that scenes would resolve in and of themselves without being determined by the next incoming image.

CINEASTE: *When Blake is travelling west on the train and sees other passengers firing at buffalo, there's a line that says "A million were killed last year." Was there a year in which that many were actually shot?*
JARMUSCH: I think in 1875 well over a million were shot and the government was very supportive of this being done, because, "No buffalo, no Indians." They were trying to get the railroad through and were having a lot of problems with the Lakota and different tribes. So that's factual. I even have in a book somewhere an etching or engraving of a train passing through the Great Plains with a lot of guys standing upright on the top of cars firing at these herds of buffalo, slaughtering them mindlessly.

CINEASTE: *I've heard that Nobody speaks four languages in the film— Blackfoot, Cree, Makah, and English. How did you write the Indian dialog?*
JARMUSCH: Well, Michelle Thrush, who's in the film, spoke Cree and is Cree. We wrote some dialog together and then she translated it with someone else who was even more fluent.

CINEASTE: *As I recall, one of the native American dialog is subtitled.*
JARMUSCH: No, I didn't want it subtitled. I wanted it to be a little gift for those people who understand the language. Also, the joke about tobacco is for indigenous American people. I hope the last line of the film, "But Nobody, I don't smoke," will be like a hilarious joke to them: "Oh man, this white man still doesn't get it." Makah was incredibly difficult; Gary [Farmer] had to learn it phonetically and read it off big cards. Even the Makah people had trouble, because it's a really complicated language.

CINEASTE: *Why did you make Nobody half Blood as well as half Blackfoot?*
JARMUSCH: Well, I wanted to situate him as a Plains Indian, so I chose those two tribes that did intermix at certain points historically but also were at war with each other. So his parents in my mind were like Romeo and Juliet; there was even a reference to that in the original script.

CINEASTE: *The funny thing about the tobacco joke is that, like so much in the movie, I took it as a commentary on America right now. Like the fact that Dickinson hires three bounty hunters to go after Blake and then sends other people out, too. Kent Jones said to me that was like the way Hollywood studios hire screenwriters.*
JARMUSCH: [*Laughing*] Good point—that's true. But to talk about tobacco, there were indigenous to North America some forty strains of tobacco that are far more powerful than anything we have now. I have a real respect for tobacco as a substance, and it just seems very funny how the Western attitude is, "Wow, people are addicted to this, think of all the money you can make off it." For indigenous people here, it's still a sacrament, it's what you bring to someone's house, it's what you smoke when you pray. Our cultural advisor, Cathy, is a member of the Native American Church and even uses peyote ceremonially.

We used to go up on these hillsides sometimes early in the morning before shooting, usually with just the native people in the cast and crew, and pray and smoke. She'd put tobacco in a ceremonial pipe and pass it around, and you'd wash yourself with the smoke. She prays to each direction, to the sky, to the earth, to the plants and all the animals and animal spirits. And what cracked me up is, as soon as the ceremony was over, we'd be walking back down the hill and she'd be lighting up a Marlboro. She was very aware of the contradiction herself because I used to tease her about it.

CINEASTE: *It seems like a key exchange when Blake asks Thel why she has a loaded pistol and she says, "Cause this is America." I believe you had a gun as a kid, didn't you?*

JARMUSCH: I still have guns. And I'm not into killing living things, you know, but I'll always have guns. It seems so ingrained in America, but—well, the country was built on an attempted genocide, anyway. Guns were completely necessary. I find it very odd that the amendment about the right to bear arms, laws that were written so long ago, still pertain and don't get adjusted properly. Because the right to bear arms doesn't mean automatic weaponry designed specifically for human combat. I think people should have the right to bear arms, but they should be limited as to what kinds of guns they can have.

CINEASTE: *In a recent essay about the dumbing down of American movies, Phillip Lopate writes, "Take Jim Jarmusch: a very gifted, intelligent filmmaker, who studied poetry at Columbia, yet he makes movie after movie about low-lifes who get smashed every night, make pilgrimages to Memphis where they are visited by Elvis's ghost, shoot off guns and in general comport themselves in a somnambulistic, manner."*

JARMUSCH: I don't know, man. Once I was in a working-class restaurant in Rome with Roberto [Benigni] at lunchtime. They had long tables where you sit with other people. We sat down with these people in their blue work overalls, they were working in the street outside, and Roberto's talking to them, and they started talking about Dante and Ariosto and twentieth-century Italian poets. Now, you go out to fucking Wyoming and go in a bar and mention the word poetry, and you'll get a gun stuck up your ass. That's the way America is. Whereas even guys who work in the street collecting garbage in Paris love nineteenth-century painting.

I don't know, am I supposed to put on a false voice and say, "Here are the rare exceptions, and we should be like them?"

CINEASTE: *A subjective impression I had when I first saw* Dead Man *at Cannes is that it's your first political film. The view of America is a lot darker than in your previous films.*

JARMUSCH: I think it is a lot darker. You know, you can define everything as being political and analyze it politically. So I don't really know how to respond to that because it wasn't a conscious kind of proselytizing. But I'm proud of the film because of the fact that on the surface it's a very simple story and a simple metaphor that the physical life is this journey that we take. And I wanted that simple story, and that relationship between these two guys from different cultures who are both loners and lost and for whatever reasons are completely disoriented from their cultures. That's the story for me, that's what it's about.

But at the same time, unlike my other films; the story invited me to have a lot of other themes that exist peripherally: violence, guns, American history, a sense of place, spirituality, William Blake and poetry, fame, outlaw status—all these things that are certainly part of the fabric of the film, that maybe unfortunately, at least for the distributors, work better when you've seen the film more than once. Because they're subtle and they're not intended to hit you over the head with a sledgehammer.

CINEASTE: *Incidentally, why is the smoke that you see coming from the Dickinson Steelworks animated?*

JARMUSCH: I wanted it to look more realistic, and I didn't have enough budget to do that matte shot to my satisfaction, so the smoke looked kind of cartoonlike. But I couldn't redo it and I didn't want to not have the smoke.

CINEASTE: *In the sixties and seventies, there was an attempt at a sort of make-shift genre that might be called the Acid Western, associated with people like Monte Hellman, Dennis Hopper, Jim McBride, and Rudy Wurlitzer, as well as movies like* Greaser's Palace; *Alex Cox tapped into something similar in the eighties with* Walker.

JARMUSCH: Yeah, I think of them as peripheral Westerns.

CINEASTE: Dead Man *struck me as being a much-delayed fulfillment of that dream. Part of it has to do with certain literary ideas about the wilderness and*

travelling from the East to the West. And if you think of all the white people that
Blake and Nobody run into, they all seen to fit into two categories—some version
of capitalism or some version of the counterculture, sometimes the two mixed to-
gether.
JARMUSCH: Yeah, they coexist somehow. And the counterculture is always
repackaged and made into a product. It's part of America. If you have a
counterculture band, you put a name on it, you call them beatniks, and you
can sell something—books or bebop. Or you label them as hippies and you
can sell tie-dyed T-shirts.

CINEASTE: *But then there's also Iggy Pop in a dress. What's disturbing about*
Dead Man *is that the whole sense of society—which is always pretty attenuated in*
your films to begin with—is pretty nightmarish whenever it turns up. And some of
the film's stylistic ruptures evoke Acid Westerns as well, like that creepy yet
strangely beautiful moment when the bounty hunter, Cole Wilson (Lance Henrik-
sen), crushes the head of a dead marshal under his heel, as if it were a rotten
watermelon. Was that a homage to Sam Raimi?
JARMUSCH: Not specifically Sam Raimi, but I was aware of that genre of
films, whether it be something from *The Evil Dead* or even Raúl Ruiz. I was
definitely conscious that it was somewhat out of style in relation to my previous films, and maybe this film, too, but I left it in. It's stylistically over the
top, but it seems to fit with that guy's character. The cannibalism, too, is
over the top.

CINEASTE: *You get the feeling that between these isolated outposts of civiliza-*
tion, anything can happen. You can't always distinguish between what's interior
and what's exterior, what's real and what's inside your head.
JARMUSCH: Yeah. And I think when Blake encounters the trappers [Iggy
Pop, Jared Harris, and Billy Bob Thornton], it's the same thing. It's like here
is a trace element of the family unit that has gotten so perverted out here,
because these guys live out in the fuckin' nowhere. Yet there's some slight
thread of a family unit that they've adapted between themselves—which is
absurd on one level, but on another level it's exactly what you're saying.
They're way out there.
   I don't know if you can hear it, but when Iggy's trying to load his shotgun,
he's complaining, "I cooked, I cleaned . . ." Incidentally, I recently came
across this interesting Sam Peckinpah quote: "The Western is a universal

frame within which it's possible to comment on today." Of course, I only saw this quote after I made the film.

CINEASTE: *I'm reminded of that 1972 Robert Aldrich Western,* Ulzana's Raid, *which a lot of people said at the time was really about the war in Vietnam.*
JARMUSCH: In Hollywood Westerns even in the thirties and forties, history was mythologized to accommodate some kind of moral code. And what really affects me deeply is when you see it taken to the extent where Native Americans become mythical people. I think it's in *The Searchers* where John Ford had some Indians who were supposedly Commanche, but he cast Navajos who spoke Navajo. It's kind of like saying, "Yes, I know they are supposed to be French people, but I could only get Germans, and no one will know the difference."

It's really close to apartheid in America. The people in power will do whatever they can to maintain that, and TV and movies are perfect ways to keep people stupid and brainwashed. In regards to *Dead Man,* I just wanted to make an Indian character who wasn't either A) the savage that must be eliminated, the force of nature that's blocking the way for industrial progress, or B) the noble innocent that knows all is another cliché. I wanted him to be a complicated human being.

CINEASTE: *Right, but he's an outsider too, even to his own tribe. And given where we're at in terms of Native American consciousness, it somehow seems significant that in order to give him coherence, you have to route him through Europe.*
JARMUSCH: I don't know. Like the slaughtering of buffalo, that was based on real accounts that I read. I read accounts of natives that were taken all the way to Europe and put on display in London and Paris, and paraded like animals. I also read accounts of chiefs that were taken east and then murdered by their own tribes when they got back because of the stories they told about the white man—which becomes part of Nobody's story.

CINEASTE: *The notion of what Nobody calls "passing through the mirror" seems to have a lot to do with the way the movie is structured: there's the industrial town at the beginning and the Native American settlement at the end, the train ride and the boat ride . . .*
JARMUSCH: Yeah, and they do somehow connect with that abstract idea that Nobody has to pass Blake through this mirror of water and send him

back to the spirit level of the world. But what was more fascinating to me is that these cultures coexisted only so briefly, and then the industrialized one eliminated the aboriginal culture. Those specific Northwest tribes existed for thousands of years and then they were wiped out in much less than a hundred years. They even used biological warfare, giving them infected blankets and all kinds of stuff—any way to get rid of them. And then they were gone. And it was such an incredibly rich culture.

I don't really know of any fiction film where you see a Pacific Northwest culture. I know there's the film *The Land of the War Canoes* made by Edward Curtis, the early twentieth-century photographer—he shot some Kwakiutl people, but it's sort of a *Nanook of the North* deal where he used them pretty much as actors. But their culture was so rich because where they lived provided them with salmon, and they could smoke that and exist all winter long without having to hunt very much. Therefore they spent a lot of time developing their architecture, their carving, their mythology, and their incredibly elaborate ceremonies with these gigantic figures that would transform from one thing into another, with all kinds of optical illusions and tricks. That's why the long house opens that way in *Dead Man*, when Nobody goes inside to talk to the elders of the tribe and eventually gets a sea canoe from them. It seems to open magically, but it's based on a real system of pulleys that these tribes used.

CINEASTE: *It's interesting how Blake picks up bits and pieces of his identity from other people in the film, including Nobody.*
JARMUSCH: Yeah. He's also like a blank piece of paper that everyone wants to write all over, which is why I like Johnny [Depp] so much as the actor for that character, because he has that quality. He's branded an outlaw totally against his character, and he's told he's this great poet and he doesn't know what the hell this crazy Indian guy is even talking about. Even the scene in the trading post where the missionary [Alfred Molina] says, "Can I have your autograph?" and then pulls a gun on him, and Blake stabs him in the hand and says, "There, that's my autograph." It's like all these things are projected onto him.

When Nobody leaves him alone after taking peyote, Blake is left to go on his own vision quest briefly, whether he knows it or not, because he's fasting—not because he wants to but because he doesn't know how to eat out there. That's a really important ceremony of most North American tribes—a vision quest where you're left alone to fast, usually for a three-day period.

CINEASTE: *How many Native Americans have seen* Dead Man *so far?*
JARMUSCH: At this point very few. But it's going to show in Taos, and I know there's a big Native American contingency that goes there. Gary Farmer's having a benefit in Canada, and I'm going to take the film eventually to the Makah reservation to show them. And then Gary and I are going to make sure that videos are distributed to every reservation video store we can get them in. That's really important to us.

Like a Hurricane

MARJORIE BAUMGARTEN/1997

TWO MONTHS HAVE PASSED since this interview with Jim Jarmusch took place in Toronto. *Year of the Horse* was the first film I saw after arriving in Canada for the film festival in September and Jarmusch's movie about the music of Neil Young & Crazy Horse set the perfect mood. This movie rocks. It consists mostly of uninterrupted concert footage, although it's interspersed with snatches of interviews with individual members of the band, some backstage and on-the-road flavoring, and fragments of Crazy Horse clips shot by others in 1976 and 1986.

Year of the Horse was filmed in 1996, following Young's contribution of the score for Jarmusch's ethereal Western, *Dead Man,* in 1995. The match-up of the Jarmusch and Young sensibilities has turned out to be an inspired fit. Just as Young's music provided the perfect jangly dreamscape for *Dead Man*'s trippy American journey, Jarmusch's choice to shoot *Year of the Horse* in a low-tech combo of Super 8, 16mm, and Hi-8 video formats creates an ideal visual equivalent of the ragged passion that characterizes the Crazy Horse sound. Music has always been a major factor in Jarmusch's films: Musicians such as John Lurie, Tom Waits, Screamin' Jay Hawkins, and Iggy Pop have been regularly cast as fictional characters in his movies *(Permanent Vacation, Stranger Than Paradise, Down by Law, Mystery Train,* and *Night on Earth)* and have also contributed to his soundtracks. And Young's history of making and releasing film documents of his musical efforts is extensive. The originality

Published in *The Austin Chronicle*, Vol. 17, No. 10, 10 November 1997. Reprinted by permission.

of *Year of the Horse* has little to do with any new or radical techniques of making rock & roll concert documentaries. The movie stands out because it gets the music right: The complement of music and movie here is total. *Year of the Horse* is a rock & roll movie through and through.

Using material from three different decades also emphasizes the movie's sensitivity to the passage of time—echoing one of the band's constant if un-acknowledged preoccupations. It's a theme with universal resonance, this idea of improving with age, moving constantly closer to the source, and dis-covering the preciousness of things only as a result of time's passage. The differences between working solo and working in concert with others is an-other recurrent theme acknowledged by the band members, all of whom recognize that there is a greatness to their sound that can only be achieved in unison.

Jarmusch's primary collaborator on this project, Larry A. Johnson, also participated in this interview. Johnson, an associate of Neil Young's since producing his 1972 feature *Journey Through the Past,* also produced *Year of the Horse* and shot all the footage along with Jarmusch. His sound work on *Woodstock* received an Academy Award nomination and in addition to his nearly three decades of work with Young, Johnson has also worked on such films as *Marjoe,* Bob Dylan's *Renaldo and Clara,* Martin Scorsese and the Band's *The Last Waltz,* and directed the award-winning CD-ROM title *Forrest Gump: Music, Artist & Times.*

The interview ranges from topics directly related to the movie and the music to the meaning (or meaninglessness) of so-called independent film-making and Jarmusch's experience of acting in other people's films, espe-cially the adventure of making *Tigrero: A Film That Was Never Made,* which Jarmusch made with his beloved Sam Fuller, the legendary film director who died just last week at the age of eighty-six.

AUSTIN CHRONICLE: *How did this movie come about?*
JIM JARMUSCH: Larry [Johnson] produced and we made a video for Crazy Horse on their last record, *Broken Arrow,* for a song called "Big Time." That was all shot on Super 8 and Neil really liked the way that looked. Then he called me a month or two after that saying, "Let's shoot some more stuff that looks like that video." And so I just went out on the road, Larry orga-nized it all, we went on the road and just started shooting. We had no road map, no plan, we didn't know if it would end up being a video for another

song, or a half-hour film they might give away with their record, or a feature
film . . . we didn't know. So it wasn't really a decision, it's just kind of like
it's the Neil Young way: Just start in and see what happens.

A C : *How long were you out there with the band?*
J J : Not very long. We were with them in Europe for a week or two and then
we went and filmed them outside of Seattle at the Gorge.

A C : *What about the three performances that are intercut for "Like a Hurricane"?*
J J : That's a collage of France in 1986, outside of Seattle, and this 1976 footage
from the Odeon Hammersmith.
L A R R Y   J O H N S O N : The Odeon Hammersmith in London. That's from the
archive collection.
J J : That's the only song that has sections from different places.

A C : *That song as captured here effectively raises the dead.*
J J : But still, man, I think live it was much more hallucinatory. We tried to
re-create that feeling but, man, live it was extraordinary.

A C : *How far back does your relationship go with Neil Young?*
J J : Larry, from years and years. For me, only since he did the [*Dead Man*]
score. I met him while I was shooting *Dead Man* and then he did the score.
It only goes back a couple of years.

A C : *Who shot the 1976 footage?*
J J : In 1976, I was in New York, at CBGB's probably.
L A J : The band was on tour and hired local cameramen. Throughout the
years, different times, we decided to document different episodes for the ar-
chives. We dug in there and told Jim about some of the footage and he
wanted to look at it and thought it would be appropriate to use our '76 tapes
in '96, as a journey.
J J : Larry now has the formidable task of organizing a lot of Neil's archives.
L A J : It's another one of Neil's ongoing projects.
J J : Never-ending.
L A J : Never-ending, ongoing. Neil has a motto: Anything worth doing once
is worth doing over and over again. So that's what we do.

J J : They called me on the HORDE Tour. They said, "Come and film this." I was like, "Oh man, I'm writing a script. Please, leave me alone."

A C : *Looking back on it, there really does seem to be a Neil Young master plan to get all that stuff on film.*

L A J : Yeah, we have a lot in the archives, a lot of stuff, going back to Buffalo Springfield days and then all through when he first . . . there's a little bit of a gap we discovered in the Danny Whitten slot in terms of real footage and still photographs, there's not very much documentation, that's the only period . . . a little bit of material on *Tonight's the Night,* and a whole bunch on the rest of it. *Harvest* and all that is well-documented.

J J : I keep trying to convince Neil to make a film out of that '76 stuff. There's a great film in that.

L A J : But it's very hard to live near it. It's like Neil, living today, it's hard to look back into the past. He's afraid his past will catch up with him.

A C : *To me, the most effective thing about the film is not that it dwells on the past but rather that there's just this palpable sense of time that permeates the film and the band's reflection on it. They talk about not realizing how precious something is until you've been doing it for this length of time. It had a lot of resonance for me.*

J J : Yeah.

L A J : I think Jim was the one who really appreciates that and brought that to the Horse and got them in the interview to talk about it, to look back on it. Jim really brought that out in them. I don't think anyone has ever successfully gotten them to sit down and reflect on that.

J J : But still, the film is a celebration of their longevity and where they are now. It's not intended to analyze their past in any kind of a deep way.

A C : *No, it's more in the sense that the past helps the present make sense, and you keep getting closer to the source. There are all sorts of phrases like that.*

J J : Yeah.

L A J : Yeah, in the movie, you're right.

A C : *And I keep thinking about all these songs, so many of the song titles or album titles have time references:* Journey Through the Past *and* Tonight's the Night *to concepts like* Harvest *and* Rust Never Sleeps.

L A J : They say that rock & roll will never die but how long can rockers go?

J J : Well, Link Wray's on tour. He's seventy-eight. He fell off the stage and hurt his leg but he's rockin' away. He's killer. He kicks ass.

A C : *How many songs did you record altogether for the film? Was it tough to whittle it down to nine?*

J J : Yeah, it was actually. We had a few more in an earlier cut of the film but it was like three hours long, so. And Neil was totally cool. He let me pick what songs. I would call him up and run by lists and he would say, "That's cool. Whatever you think." We took out "Danger Bird," we took out "Pocahontas," we took out some other stuff too. But it was kind of hard. I got two in there from Zuma . . . dammit.

A C : *[whiningly] But there's no "Cinnamon Girl."*

J J : There's no "Cinnamon Girl"; there's no "Cortez." You've heard those enough.

A C : *Oh, okay.*

J J : You've heard those enough [repeated schoolmarmishly]. I know, I love "Cinnamon Girl" too. And "Down by the River" too, man. They played that live on this HORDE tour. It was amazing. It was great.

A C : *What did you see as your greatest challenge in making this movie?*

J J : Oh, waking up and having to look at Larry every day.

L A J : Pretty much the same.

J J : No, ah, there wasn't a challenge. You know it was really fun and Larry was so amazingly organized. I wish my feature films could have the same kind of organization because Neil's people, his road people, man we should make a movie just about them. Cause his road crew are like pirates, or a biker gang, or something. Very organized. And they were great. And then Larry, whatever we needed was suddenly there. Like Neil asked us to go on the road and in three days—I was in New York, Larry lives in L.A.—he had all the equipment together, all the film material, everything was on the way. It was amazing. I guess the challenge to it came after collecting the material and sitting down and being open enough so that the material told us—me and Jay Rabinowitz, the editor—what the film wanted to be. You know, to just not try to bludgeon it into any form at all, just sort of in a Zen-like way say, "Okay, what do you want us to do with you now?" That was like the most challenging thing. It was a fun film to make.

A C : *How did you decide which segments would be filmed in each different format? Did that just depend on what you had available at the time you were doing the segment?*

J J : Yeah. We started shooting interviews at one point in Super 8 and quickly realized that we had two and a half minutes to a load. That's pretty hard to get someone to really talk, you know. So we just switched to video, which we had available.

A C : *Where was that space where the interviews were shot?*

L A J : That was one of the hardest things, you talk about grace and finding things out. That was a location in Dublin . . .

J J : backstage . . .

L A J : . . . backstage, and it was the last day of the tour and Jim said, "We need a place to interrogate these guys."

J J : An interrogation room.

L A J : And when we found that room we went, "This is perfect." We got exactly what you wanted. You were really pleased with that.

J J : Yeah, we even had German accents for interrogating. "Vy did you steal zees guys from another bahnd, Neil. Confess," you know.

A C : *How much of the footage did you shoot?*

J J : Well, Larry and I shot all the Super 8 stuff and most of the good Super 8 onstage stuff Larry shot because my camera malfunctioned through a lot of it. But most of the stuff shooting out of car windows and stuff like that, I shot.

L A J : All the dreamy stuff. Obviously, the stuff that Jim's in, I shot.

J J : All the stuff that looks really sloppy and amateurish, we shot.

L A J : Yeah, exactly.

J J : And we're proud of it.

L A J : Very proud of it.

J J : We don't distinguish between whose is whose.

A C : *"Proudly shot in Super 8" [as it says in the film's opening credits].*

J J : We were proud of our Super 8 photography. Dammit.

A C : *So this shouldn't have been a very expensive film.*

J J : It's a lot of expenses. It's a 40-track mix, the recording. Dolby Digital. And it was expensive because we shot Super 8, 16, and Hi-8 video. Then we made a digital video of that and from that they make three 16mm strands, like the old three-color process, and from that they make a color 35mm negative. So, technically, it was a little trickier than it seems.

L A J : If we had a plan—which we didn't, never did, not even a desire—I don't know if we would have done anything different. But actually, it's at the end when we tried to get it on 35mm and mix the audio, that was the most expensive part. The actual going out and shooting on Super 8 and getting the film and the transfer was pretty humble. Which is how we wanted it to be.

A C : *Have a lot of the roadies been with Young a long time?*

L A J : Yes, there's a core group of people. I've been with Neil twenty-seven years. And Jim, as we say in the film, is the new guy. Which is why he gets all the abuse from the band members.

J J : Especially from Poncho, who's been known as the new guy for twenty-five years.

A C : *What convinced you that your ideal for* Dead Man *would be Neil Young to do the music?*

J J : Oh man, that was my dream even while I was writing it. I just never thought it would really happen. But I was lucky, very lucky. Then *Sleeps with Angels* came out while we were filming, and I'd go to the set in the mornings and hear Neil Young & Crazy Horse coming from different trucks. Different people listening independently. It was kind of a magical thing. It just was right for the film, so it's just how it happened.

A C : *But he came into it after it was shot and assembled?*

J J : Yeah, I met him while we were shooting. We all went to see him play, our whole crew, in Sedona, Arizona. That's the first time I met him. I got to go backstage. I had been corresponding, trying to get through to him and finally did, and got to talk to him there. It wasn't until I sent him a rough cut of the film, he responded saying he loved it and wanted to do the music.

A C : *Did you ever consider not shooting* Dead Man *in black-and-white?*

J J : No, never. I thought of it while writing as black-and-white. And I'm pretty stubborn. I've done three films in black-and-white.

A C : *Do you think you'll start any trends with Super 8?*
J J : Hey, it's a trend that already exists. It's beautiful material. You know they said that when photography was invented that was the death of painting. But painting just got more interesting in a lot of ways. Sometimes you need a hammer and a chisel instead of a chainsaw. Just because there are computers doesn't mean you can't write with a pen anymore. It depends on what material suits what you need. I like technology. I use Avids and stuff to edit, you know. I love all that stuff but that doesn't mean that anything predating that is dead. It depends on what you need to use. I'm not a Luddite. I find a lot of uses of technology highly suspicious, but it's not involved with the technology itself.

A C : *The film is a perfect merger of the music with technology, that rawness of both of them.*
J J : I think it fits and I think the Super 8 stuff is beautiful. Some people won't, but people have different tastes.

A C : *Did you play around with different titles?*
J J : Well, our working title was *Horseshit*. And one of the band's slogans always is: "Smell the Horse," a *Spinal Tap* take-off. I liked *Horseshit* but I decided *Year of the Horse* would be better.

A C : *What determines which cameo roles you take in other people's films?*
J J : I do it if they're friends of mine and think it might be fun, basically. Because I'm not an actor. It's good for me to do it because it helps me as a director to know what it's like on the other side. But mostly I do it because it's like people I know, Billy Bob Thornton [*Sling Blade*], the Kaurismäki brothers [*Leningrad Cowboys Go America, Tigrero*]. I knew Paul Auster who was writing the Wayne Wang film [*Blue in the Face*]. I knew Wayne too.

A C : *What about Tigrero?*
J J : I was with Sam [Fuller] who I love. And Mika [Kaurismäki] is a good friend of mine. But I'd do anything for Sam. He's the man. It was just a pleasure to be there. It was also really interesting to be with the Karajá people, and the Amazon, and I like Mika Kaurismäki [*Tigrero*'s director] a lot. And I love Sam Fuller. So that was just selfishly having a great experience with those people. And Sam. I'd like to be with Sam anywhere in the world,

you know. He's such a character. He's the only guy that didn't get sick. Every-one on the crew, everyone got sick. Sam didn't get sick. [Switching to Fuller's craggy, rapid-fire voice] "What is the matter with you? You're all falling apart here." He was like eighty-four years old. What a guy. I remember one scene—I don't know if it's in the movie—where he's telling me how to kill a jaguar and I'm saying, "Why don't you just shoot it?" [In Fuller's voice again] "Ah, you just can't shoot it. You've got to use a spear. Don't you un-derstand the whole concept of the thing? We're in the Amazon. They don't have guns here right now." He just explodes on me. He was great.

A C : *Do you go back and look at your previous films?*
J J : Never. I don't like to look back. It's very uncomfortable. Don't look back.

A C : *Except that it's ever-present in* Year of the Horse, *that inescapable sense of time that's an undercurrent. And the differences between the things you do solo or do in concert with others. Do you find any resonances in that as a filmmaker?*
J J : Yeah, time goes by too fast. I like getting older. I'm not afraid of age. In our culture people are supposed to think about being young and it's bad to be older, whereas in a lot of cultures being older is really a cool thing. It's like with Native Americans if you're old, if you get to the top of the moun-tain, you get the cool view. It's just kind of strange. Time goes so damn fast but I just try not to look back. I still try to keep my films out there if I can, I just don't want to look at them myself.

A C : *Is it as good a time to be a so-called independent filmmaker as the media would like us to believe?*
J J : It's just a load of shit. It's just another brand slapped on something to market it. I don't know what it means anymore. It's like "alternative" music. It means nothing now. It's used to make alternative music commercial, you know, mainstream. I've never liked titles slapped on things anyway. So I don't know what it means. I'm getting really annoyed at even hearing the word. When I hear the word independent I reach for my revolver. At this point, what the hell does that mean? *The English Patient* is an independent film. I don't know. I'm getting annoyed though. Hootie and the Blowfish are alternative music. I'm the Queen of Denmark. I don't know what it means anymore.

A C : *It's like when I asked if you expected to see any trends with Super 8 . . . I would expect more people to say, "Oh look this is independent filmmaking. You can do it on the cheap, and just go out with Dad's Super 8 camera." Which is great if it makes sense, if it's right for the material. And it's a great way to learn. I just see it mushrooming into something that doesn't make sense.*

J J : Yeah.

L A J : It's just a matter of using the tools. It's always been there. The unfortunate part is that Kodak stopped making the stock, and it's hard to get the cameras. But you can do a movie and it could be great. If you can afford to do the blowup. The problem is you can spend the money cheap but then you're going to spend extra money doing a 35mm blowup—spend $50–60,000—which is probably twice what you spent on making the movie—just to get it into a theatrical venue.

J J : But there's a real problem, it's all screwed up because people go to Sundance and they want to get a studio deal or something. I know of a few films where distributors overpaid for the films for more than they were worth and then they couldn't get their money back out of them, and then it was the filmmaker's fault if it was a failure. And the failure was that too much money was put on the film. So maybe it was a really great film but now the filmmaker is struggling to get another one because of being labeled a failure. But the failure was because of some system that wanted to keep them alive and make them a product without being sensitive to what was the thing they did, you know. So the problems run pretty deep and it sort of started with Ronald Reagan when he allowed studios to own theatre chains again, which is a big disaster. It's changed a lot since I started out. But I always have hope for people who love movies because of what they can do with it.

Jim Jarmusch Interview

GEOFF ANDREW/1999

GEOFF ANDREW: *How did you get into movies as a spectator and when did you decide to become a filmmaker?*

JIM JARMUSCH: Before she married my father, my mother was a film reviewer for the Akron *Beacon Journal*—a small newspaper—but in Akron, Ohio, there wasn't a real variety of films. When I was a kid, in order to get rid of me on Saturday afternoons, my mother would drop me off at a theatre called the State Road Theatre that had double and triple features—usually *The Blob, Attack of the Giant Crab Monsters, Creature from the Black Lagoon*. I used to go there a lot and I saw all of those films as a kid, and I really loved it.

When I left Ohio when I was seventeen and ended up in New York and realised that not all films had the giant crab monsters in them, it really opened up a lot of things for me. I've always loved films, always. I studied literature at Columbia in New York and I went to Paris for part of one year and ended up staying there. I didn't go to classes, but ended up at the Cinémathèque, and there it opened up even wider because there I saw a variety of films from all over the world.

I'd wanted to be a writer and when I came back to New York worked as a musician too. But I found my writing starting to get more and more referential to cinema. I was writing prose poems, but they were starting to echo not

This interview was held at the 43rd London Film Festival, 15 November 1999, in collaboration with the National Film Theatre and *The Guardian*, and was published on the London Film Festival website. Copyright © Geoff Andrew. Reprinted by permission.

film scripts, but descriptions of scenes in a cinematic way. Then I didn't have any money and I didn't know what to do with myself. I applied to graduate film school at NYU. I'd never made a film, but submitted some writing and I guess to fill in their group of students with some potential writers, I got "financial assistance" and I was accepted there. Really it was just a whim that I applied and then studied there for two years. I didn't get my degree there; I got it later, they gave me an honourary one.

I didn't get the degree because in my last year, for my thesis film I made a feature called *Permanent Vacation* and they'd given me a scholarship, the Louis B. Mayer fellowship and they made a mistake. Instead of sending it to the school for tuition, they sent it directly to me, so I spent it on the budget of the film. The film school did not like the film, nor did they like the fact that I hadn't paid tuition and used the money for the film and I didn't get a degree. Later they started using my name in ads for the school and I said in an interview, "That's odd, cause they didn't like my film and they didn't give me a degree." And then they sent me a degree. [Laughter] And with that degree and a $1.50, you can buy a coffee in New York.

G A : Permanent Vacation *was made for $12,000 and then you made* Stranger Than Paradise, *which originally was a half-hour short. How much did that cost?*
J J : About $7,000, something like that.

G A : *And it got a very enthusiastic reception.*
J J : What I did was I completed the half-hour film, but before really showing it, I wrote two more sections for a potential feature film. I didn't think would really happen, but at least I had it in case. I was very lucky and eventually showed the film, got some good responses, and some people helped to make the longer version of the film.

Wim Wenders gave me some unexposed film material that was left over from—that was actually for the half-hour version—*The State of Things*. In the longer version the black sections in-between had to be a certain type of exposed negative to get a true black, and I got a roll of black negative film from Jean-Marie Straub. So I had some help from some pretty amazing people. I don't know why they helped me but . . . [Laughter]

G A : *It is entirely made up of discreet shots—every scene consists of one shot interrupted by black film—which is quite a formal or experimental way of telling the story. Why did you decide to do it and what is your interest in those formal things?*

JJ: I think it comes from really liking literary forms. Poetry is very beautiful, but the space on the page can be as affecting as where the text is. Like when Miles Davis doesn't play, it has a poignancy to it. I was interested formally from literature and musical structures. I don't remember exactly where it came from. At that time, I was also inspired by very formally pure films, films by Carl Dreyer or Bresson.

Those things were very moving to me, especially at a time when MTV was just starting, and there was this barrage of images that was not so interesting to me at the time. It seemed like filmmaking was starting to imitate advertising. It was something that wasn't my aesthetic at the time. It came from those things.

GA: *The film has certainly got a serious side to it, but it is also very full of humour and that's something that's coursed through all of your work. Why is an element of comedy so important to you in your movies?*
JJ: Laughter is good for your spirit and Oscar Wilde said: "Life is far too important to be taken seriously," which is a quote I really love and I feel that way about the work as well. In *Ghost Dog: The Way of the Samurai*, there's a quote from *The Hagakure*, a Japanese text, written by an old samurai, that has to do with how things of great concern should be treated lightly, and things of small concern should be [treated] seriously. That kind of contradiction was something I really like when it is embraced in that kind of philosophy.

GA: *With* Stranger Than Paradise *and* Down by Law, *you cast John Lurie and you were quite involved in the music scene before you started making films?*
JJ: It was a really interesting time in New York in the late '70s and early '80s. The music scene was interesting because you didn't have to be a virtuoso to make music. It was more about your desire to express things. That period was important, because there were a lot of different artists— musicians, filmmakers—that had this "make-it-in-the-garage" aesthetic that was really inspiring and really good. It was not about trying to be famous or have a career, or be a virtuoso, or be flashy. It was more like having real emotional feelings that you expressed through whatever form, mostly by picking up guitars you didn't really know how to play and bashing away on them.

That gave way to a lot of interesting things. I always think of the Sex Pistols and the Ramones as very important because they stripped things down. Dogme 95 owes some debt to the purity of so-called punk rock. But I also love The Clash because they were the opposite. They were into synthesis in that they said: "Bring us reggae, rockabilly, R&B, we'll take all that and charge it up with our feelings." Two opposite aesthetics which appealed to me and inspired me. Still do.

G A : *You talk about these musicians making music in an emotionally expressive way, but when* Stranger Than Paradise *came out some people didn't quite understand your attitude towards the John Lurie character, who is anything but emotionally expressive; he's very concerned about his own self-image. And also in* Down by Law *so is Tom Waits. You do seem to have this interest in puncturing their self-image and pretensions to coolness and showing that much more innocent, straightforward people can transform those people. Would you say that's a valid interpretation of those films, and if so what is your interest in that?*

J J : In what? Sorry, I drifted off. [Laughter] To me, John Lurie's character is not non-emotional. He tries to be not emotional, he tries to be cool, but it's transparent. I have to tell everyone that when I finish a film and it goes out and is released, I never look at my films again. I don't like looking back. I don't even like talking about 'em! [Laughter] So I'm really digging back in my memory because I don't like to sit and look at my films again.

But my recollection is that the character of John Lurie is made very human by the fact that he cannot disguise his emotions, and when Eva leaves, he's upset even though he treated her badly. But he didn't want her to leave and that's a contradiction that's very human and flawed, but transparent. I don't think he's able to hide his emotions. Does that have anything to do with the question? [Laughter]

G A : *Absolutely. I think it confirms what I said.*

J J : Let's talk about baseball.

G A : *I don't know anything about baseball.*

J J : Baseball is one of the most beautiful games. [Laughter] It is. It is a very Zen-like game. I don't like American football. I think it's boring and ridiculous and predictable. But baseball is very beautiful. It's played on a diamond. [Laughter]

GA: *I've seen a few movies about it.*

JJ: Cricket makes no sense to me. [Laughter] I find it beautiful to watch and I like that they break for tea. [Laughter] That is very cool, but I don't understand. My friends from The Clash tried to explain it years and years ago, but I didn't understand what they were talking about.

GA: *From sports to William Blake and Robert Frost, because in* Down by Law, *you have the Roberto Benigni character frequently quoting from Frost, and in* Dead Man, *you have references to William Blake. What is your interest in poetry, because it's not very often that we see characters in movies quoting and referring to poetry?*

JJ: Yeah, if you go into a bar in most places in America and even say the word poetry, you'll probably get beaten up. [Laughter] But poetry is a really strong, beautiful form to me, and a lot of innovation in language comes from poetry. I think that Dante was hip-hop culture because he wrote in vernacular Italian, and at the time that was unheard of; people wrote in Latin or Petrarch wrote in high Italian, and so Dante was talking street stuff. Poets are always ahead of things in a certain way, their sense of language and their vision.

Language can be abstracted; language can be used as a very beautiful code in poetry, the nuances and the multiple meanings of things. It has a music to it. It has so many things in it. It is also reduced from prose and therefore can be both mathematical, or very abstract. A lot of poets too live on the margins of social acceptance; they certainly aren't in it for the money. William Blake—only his first book was legitimately published. For the rest of his life, he published everything himself and no one had any real interest in it during his lifetime, which is true of many, many poets. I think of poets as outlaw visionaries in a way. I don't know. I like poetry. Dammit, I like poetry; anyone got a problem with that?! [Laughter]

GA: *Going on to* Coffee and Cigarettes. *You've made five little shorts revolving around this theme of people meeting up in cafes and sharing coffee and experiences.*

JJ: Don't talk about my shorts! [Laughter]

GA: *You were talking about doing enough so you could eventually put them together to make a feature. Do you still have plans to do that?*

J J : Yeah, I do. In fact, I have plans to shoot some more this coming year. But it's a project that I'm not in any rush to complete. I'm behind my schedule because I wanted to shoot one or two each year, but I haven't shot any for four years now. The intention was to shoot short films that can exist as shorts independently, but when I put them all together, there are things that echo through them like the dialogue repeats, the situation is always the same, the way they're shot is very simple and the same. I have a master shot, if there's two characters, a two shot, singles on each, and an over-the-table overhead shot which I can use to edit their dialogue.

So they're very simple and because the design of how they're shot is worked out already, it gives complete freedom to play. They're like cartoons almost to me. It's a relief from making a feature film where everything has to be more carefully mapped out. I like doing them. They're ridiculous and the actors can improvise a lot. They don't have to be really realistic characters that hit a very specific tone as in a feature film. They're really fun. I want to make more of them definitely. Sometime I will release them all together, but I don't know when.

G A : *You do seem to have written roles with specific actors in mind and you trade off their personalities a little bit in the film. How do you decide to work with a certain person and do you consult with them about their dialogue?*
J J : I started working with friends of mine and that, to some degree, continues. I always start with characters rather than with a plot, which many critics would say is very obvious from the lack of plot in my films—although I think they do have plots. But the plot is not of primary importance to me, the characters are. I start with actors that I know personally or I know their work, and there are things about their work or their presence or their own personality that make a character, that exaggerates some qualities and suppresses other qualities. It's always a real collaboration for me.

What I like to do also is to rehearse with the actors scenes that are not in the script and will not be in the film. What we're really doing is trying to establish their character, and good acting to me is about reacting. I'm not a big fan of the theatre because, often, I know what their intention is. They know what the intention of the scene is and they're following a line to achieve that intention. But that's acting, and in real life, if you're at a table with four people, you don't know which one is going to speak next. It's not scripted in that way. If you can work with the actor to get to a place where they are confident in their character, then you let their character react to the scene that you're filming.

All actors are different. Nicholas Ray said to me: "There is no one way to work with all actors and anyone who tells you that is full of shit"—in his words, 'cause I don't talk like that myself. [Laughter] So what you do is work with each actor individually to find out "How can I work with this person, how can the two of us collaborate?" and it's always that there's a different way. Different actors have different strengths. Some are really brilliant at improvising; others want the dialogue set for them, they want a map.

I love rehearsing because in rehearsals there are no mistakes, nothing is wrong. Some things apply or lead you to focus on the character and the things that don't apply are equally valuable because they lead you towards what does. I'm not a director who says, "Say your line, hit your mark." That's not my style. I want them to work with me and everyone I choose to collaborate with elevates our work above what I could imagine on my own. If not, it's not working right. I'm like a navigator and I try to encourage our collaboration and find the best way that will produce fruit. I like fruit. [Laughter] I like cherries, I like bananas. [Laughter] Poor Geoff Andrew didn't know what he was getting himself into. [Laughter]

GA: *I had some idea. [Laughter] Moving on to* Mystery Train. *It's another three-part feature. But in this one it seems like you've taken three different genres, a romance film, a supernatural, and a thriller, and yet your films don't fit easily into any one genre. What is your approach to genre?*

JJ: When I was writing *Mystery Train*, I was not thinking at all about cine-matic genres. I was thinking about literary forms and I was very interested in Chaucer, things that have smaller stories within that make up a larger work. I was playing with the idea of things happening simultaneously. It's hard for me to answer that because I really wasn't thinking about any of those genres, although I was aware of Italian episodic films that are like romantic come-dies. There is a tradition in Japanese cinema of ghost stories that have sepa-rate stories together, although I don't think I ever thought of that till just now, or actually he (points to Geoff Andrew and then adopts deep voice of seniority), "Yes, I was referring to the supernatural . . ." [Laughter]

But I like that form very much. I liked playing with things happening at the same time and characters being in the same place, but not interacting and yet being somehow connected by some little threads, like the bellboy and the night manager of the hotel, the gunshot, the fact that they're in the same hotel, the fact that you see them walking down the same streets. But it really was more from a literary form than from playing with cinematic genres.

G A : *It is an incredibly detailed film because we don't actually see Steve Buscemi until the last episode, but he's there in the first one because you see him as the Japanese couple walk past him; he's referred to in the second episode. It must have been a nightmare to put together, how did you do that?*

J J : It was fun. It was fun to write something where you could see a character that you don't know is going to appear later and be a main character. It was a little bit like a puzzle, not a real complicated one, but it was fun trying to make the pieces fit together while writing the thing down.

G A : *How did you decide on the cities to use in* Night on Earth?

J J : To be honest I had written a script for another film, but was not able to make it due to things that were very frustrating and I felt somewhat betrayed due to certain circumstances, so I thought to hell with that then, I'll just write something else real fast. I wrote *Night on Earth* in about eight days and what I was thinking was, "There's friends I'd like to work with and friends I'd like to see and I'm just going to write something that will get me to work with them and see them." They included Roberto Benigni, Isaach de Bankolé, all the actors in the Finnish section, and Gena Rowlands. The cities were really based on what actors I wanted to work with, or people I wanted to see. It wasn't very calculating; it was just, "I've got to do something" because I was very frustrated by this other project that didn't work out.

G A : *But each episode is coloured by the culture in which it is set. With the Finnish, you have the moroseness; with the Italian influence you not only have the influence of the Catholic church, but very broad Italian comedy; in New York you have the cultural mix and the aggression. Was that calculated or did that just come naturally?*

J J : That comes as soon as you decide, "I want to work with these actors in Finland." Then my impressions of Helsinki or Finland or their culture certainly filter in, and that is the atmosphere that I'm thinking of while writing. I love cities, they are almost like lovers. I'm attracted to many cities I've been in, often cities other people don't like at all. I like Detroit and Gary, Indiana, cities other people would avoid like the plague. The cities become characters even though they're enclosed in a cab; the atmosphere, the colour, the quality of light in each city is very different and has a different effect on the people who live there and on your emotions when you are there.

GA: *Those things do come over, but as you say, shooting virtually within a cab all the time—you get shots looking out of the cab and establishing shots of the cities—it must have been a very difficult film to make given all those constraints you set yourself.*

JJ: That was ridiculous. I wrote the film really fast and I was saying to myself, "This will be something real easy to do and I can do it fast." Then I stepped back in pre-production, realising, "Oh man, this is in four different countries in five different cities all inside of cars." Shooting in a car is really difficult and anyone who has made a film in a car interior will tell you, "Don't ever do that again."

I had people locked into the cars because there was a speed-rail built on the outside of the car to put the lighting rigs on. If they had to get out and use the bathroom, it was a big nightmare. We had to roll the windows down and put sandwiches in for them just to keep them alive at times. [Laughter] It's really not fun shooting in a car.

At one point in Helsinki, we were towing a car. A rig broke and the car with the actors in it was stopped on the line of the streetcar and a streetcar was coming. And my Finnish actors are, (puts on Finnish accent) "What the bloody hell, are we going to die here in a jam?" on the walkie-talkie. We had to run and get these guys to stop the train. But just physically shooting in a car is really hard.

Fred Elmes was the director of photography. In some of the shots when we were towing the car, we had taken away the engine out of the engine cavity and mounted the camera in there. He was riding on the car, operating, sometimes holding a diopter—which allows you to have two different focus areas in the frame—and it was 14 degrees below zero. It was really cold and we were out all night. It was really not an easy film to make. I was deluded when I said, "This'll be easy, little stories, a few characters." It was hell.

We were stopped in Italy because we drove by the American embassy in a car that looked like some sort of gun mount. We were held there by the police for a long time, asking for our passports. Of course, our passports were all in the hotel, so we each had to tell a young Italian person working on the film, "Okay, there's a shelf in the closet, it's got a green bag, it's not in the green bag, but underneath that is a red bag, if you open that . . ." Five hours later the guy comes back (puts on Italian accent), "I have ze passports!"

It was really insane. We were shooting over a holiday and we told this Italian guy, "Please make photocopies of this schedule." He came back about nine hours later and had copied them by hand. [Laughter] I said, "Why?" and he said, (puts on Italian accent) "Because there was no photocopy place to make. It's all closed, it's a holiday. Now I copy for you the schedule." [Laughter] Lots of absurd things like that going on. Fred Elmes is very interested in using silks over the lens for different light diffusion in each city, and he uses very expensive lingerie. In Paris, he'd see a lingerie shop and he'd rush in there and he'd be saying, "Could I see more of these stockings please?" which got a little bit embarrassing. "Jim, do you think that this is nice?" [Laughter] French girls waiting on us were looking around thinking, "Strange Americans . . ."

G A : *Was it difficult working in different languages?*
J J : It's not, surprisingly. I can understand Italian somewhat, French I can understand very well, and Finnish I don't understand at all, but I wrote the dialogue and I worked with the actors in advance and with a translator. The actors spoke English in Finland, and we were able to discuss the nuances of their translation to make sure it was the right way; for example, working-class guys would speak. I'd already worked with Japanese actors in *Mystery Train*. It sounds funny, but it is not difficult at all.

When I came back from Japan, I came back with a load of videotapes of Japanese films that I couldn't find in the States that, of course, had no subtitles. If you watch an Ozu film not subtitled, believe me you understand what the characters are feeling. Nick Ray also compared acting to piano playing and he said, "The dialogue is just the left hand, the melody is in the eyes." Language is very important, but it is not necessarily the primary way of knowing what someone is feeling. Actors are expressing a lot of things through many tiny things, not just the language, so that was not a problem at all for me.

G A : *Many people were surprised by* Dead Man: *it wasn't urban, it was set in an historical era, it had a much more linear structure. Did you feel you were breaking new ground and deliberately trying to do something different?*

JJ: I certainly was doing something I had never done before, which was to make a film in a period other than the present. I was also making a film in which natural landscapes were almost like characters in the film. It's very difficult to take trucks with horses and wardrobe and find places to shoot where you can't see a road or a telephone pole or anything. It was a very physically exhausting film to make.

It was very different, but at the same time everything I do is intuitive and it was still an extension of that. Each film I make I learn a lot from. Maybe, some day, I'll learn really how to make films, but probably not. Kurosawa said in his eighties, "I'm still making films because I'm still trying to figure out how to make them." If you ever think you know everything about it you should stop, and that's not why I will stop because I won't learn completely how to make a film.

Dead Man was also dealing with a subject like death and having violence in a film, those things I had not done before.

GA: *Which is something you've carried on with in* Ghost Dog: The Way of the Samurai, *in that you're looking at a different belief system and trying to juxtapose that with modern western ideas. What is your fascination with these belief systems?*

JJ: I don't subscribe to any organised religions because I think they are often used to control people and I find that very suspicious. At the same time I'm very interested in different religious philosophies and things that are spiritual, because I don't think we know a lot of things about life and there are so many things we just don't understand.

Just to change the subject a little bit, I think it's really funny that they're always trying to study the language of dolphins. You see some guy with all these millions of dollars of computer trying to decode what the dolphins are saying. Meanwhile, the dolphin swims up and says, "I want fish" in English. They can learn our language easily, so it just seems so odd to me. We don't look in the right places for the answers to things. Some insects can communicate over long distances. It doesn't seem people are interested in understanding those things. Anyway, I don't know what that has to do with the question. "I want fish." [Laughter] And dolphins don't have to pay rent, they don't have to pay insurance. They eat, they play, they have sex, they cruise around, they talk to each other. I think they're more highly evolved.

G A : *In* Dead Man, *the two marshals are called Lee and Marvin. Can you explain that?*

J J : And also two of the killers are called Wilson and Pickett. [Laughter] I'm a huge Lee Marvin fan, You see Lee and Marvin makes Lee Marvin, get it? It's a tribute to Lee.

G A : *Aren't you a member of some unofficial group?*

J J : Yes. It's not unofficial, it's a secret organisation. It's called The Sons of Lee Marvin and I'm a card-carrying member, although I don't think I have my card on me. There are a number of us who really admire Lee Marvin. He was a really great actor and he must have been a really amazing man, too. I never got to meet him, but I've talked to a lot of people that knew him. Sam Foley knew him well, John Boorman, of course.

G A : *After* Dead Man, *you made a concert documentary,* Year of the Horse, *with Neil Young. How did that happen?*

J J : Neil had done the music for *Dead Man* and then he asked me to make a video clip for a song called "Big Time." I shot that video on Super 8, and Neil loved the fact that it was just me and Larry Johnson shooting with these little cameras, and he liked the way it looked. While we were shooting he said, "Why don't people use these to make longer films?" And then he called me up a couple of months later and said, "Do you want to make a film that looks like the video we did?" I said, "How long a film are you talking about?" to which he said, "Hey man, when I start writing a song I don't think how long it's going to be!" [Laughter]

And then he said, "Look, I'll pay for it, just shoot some stuff and see if you like it. We'll continue if you do, and if you don't, I'll just put it on a shelf somewhere." How could I refuse that? And then I said, "When do you want to start?" and he said, "Well, we're on the road in a week and a half. Meet us in France." So in a week and half, we organised all the equipment, and we shot two or three weeks on the road. It was really a great experience because there was no road map at all. What could be better than Neil Young as the producer of the film who says, "Hey man, I don't know just shoot whatever you want. We'll figure it out later, maybe it'll look cool." [Laughter]

It was my dream. We just went off and shot whatever we wanted and hoped that it looked cool. We took the material back into the editing room, and Jay Rabinowitz, who I work with, played with the footage and allowed it to tell us what it wanted to be. We didn't have a plan or anything we were trying to bludgeon the footage into. We just listened to it and made a film which I don't think of as a documentary as much as a kind of a concert film really.

But it was really a lot of fun and I think that it is successful in capturing a viscerally raw visual style that is somehow closely associated with their style of music. Also, I was having some business problems with my own company at the time, which was sucking a lot of my energy out. I was getting very frustrated, and it was delaying me from making another film, or writing a new script so it saved my soul. It was a nice gift to make.

G A : *How did* Ghost Dog *come about?*

J J : It really came about from wanting to work with Forest Whitaker, who I met when I was going to the Super 8 lab when I was working on *Year of the Horse,* or maybe on the video. I ran into him a couple of times and we would just start talking. He said to me the first time, "Hey, if you ever think of anything for me, let me know. I'd love to work with you." I couldn't get him out of my head, certain qualities that he has, and it was more from talking to him as a person than his work.

I was moved by his portrayal of Charlie Parker in *Bird.* I thought it was a beautiful performance, although I'm a big be-bop fan and I did not like the movie in terms of its slant on depicting the life of Bird—how can you make a film about Bird in which Miles Davis is never even mentioned? There were a lot of things really odd to me about it. Miles' estate probably refused to let them use his name. With good reason.

They usually use this very soft, gentle, poignant side of Forest and he gets cast as the loveable soft guy. I'm really attracted to that quality, but there is a whole other side to him, just physically, his presence. There's more there than that and I wanted to get both of those things in a character. So I started thinking how can I do that? He should be a warrior and I thought he should be a hitman, that sort of cliché. Then the samurai thing came to me because in eastern-culture warriors, there is a whole spiritual side to their training. If you look at the Shaolin monks in China, they're martial arts experts, but they are priests. They are enlightened religious teachers, but the physical side is also completely intertwined. So that gave me the idea to give him some depth.

Then there's the book *Hagakure,* a text from the 1750s written by an old samurai as a guide to samurai life and philosophy. It contains so many things, from minor, mundane details about the food you eat, how your house is built, how often you clean your armour, to incredibly deep Zen philosophy. It's all in this book and it jumps from one to the next.

Then I just started collecting disparate ideas. I was interested in the decline of organised crime families in New York because I used to live right across from the Gambino family social club in Little Italy. In the late '70s and early '80s when they were unravelling, I would always see them on the street—John Gotti and Sammy "The Bull" Gravano and Neil Belacroche and all those wise guys.

So I collected some ideas about them. The idea of pigeons came from the fact that on the roof behind me, there was an old Italian guy who had a pigeon coop for years. He died just before we started filming actually, and his birds were moved away. I used to watch him fly his birds a lot and there was something very beautiful in that movement. Sometimes I'd just look out the window on a Saturday morning and see them moving, and the light would shift and they would go from black to white to black to white to black to white, and that was a detail. I would just collect and collect, and then I sat down and tried to weave all these disparate things into something.

G A : *Did the Melville film about the samurai have any shape on the movie?*
J J : Inspiration certainly. Not so much on the shape of the movie, but certain thematic things. Melville always has killers wear white editor's gloves, which is a private joke between him and his editors, I guess saying his editor kills his films. So Forest wears white editor's gloves in the film. But there are references to other films. My favourite hitman films of all time are *Le Samouraï*, and *Branded to Kill* by Suzuki. I made quotations from those films in ways.

But I was also inspired by Don Quixote, which is in some ways a similar situation—an oddball character following a code that the world doesn't really recognise or care about anymore. Also, the books from which *Point Blank* comes, by Richard Stark with the character of Parker, were favourites of mine when I discovered those books in my late teens.

Of course, *Rashomon* and Kurosawa's depiction of samurai culture in his films. Mary Shelley's *Frankenstein*. I think music was really an inspiration because in be-bop and in hip-hop Charlie Parker can play at what was at the time considered an incredibly outside solo, but he will quote a standard within that solo. He's not playing the standard, but he is referring to it and weaving it into something completely new and his own. And in hip-hop, the backing tracks are made from other things and put together to construct something new out of them. In the past, when I was writing and I thought of a reference to another film or another book, I always pushed it away because it was not original. But this time I just opened that door and I think music convinced me to do that.

GA: *Was that partly to do with working with RZA?*
JJ: Yes, because even before I started writing, I was just kicking around the disparate ideas that make up the film. RZA was my ideal composer and by luck I got him to do the music. And he got us to work in a hip-hop style with the music. The total opposite was Neil Young in *Dead Man*. He played the music directly to the film passing in front of him, and reacting to it emotionally himself at the moment. Even when Neil and I together tried moving some of the music and sliding, it lost its magic. Something just deflated so it stayed where Neil put it, where he reacted to it.

RZA, on the other hand, would go away for three weeks, having seen the film only in a rough cut on an Avid editing machine, and then would call me up and say, "Yo, I got some music, I got a tape. Meet me in a blacked-out van at 3 am on 38th Street and Broadway." So I go there, get in the van, RZA gives me a little DAT tape with nothing written on it and says, "Yo, check this shit out" and I'd say, "Does it go anywhere? Any ideas for a particular place in the film?" "Nah, nah you guys figure that shit out, you gotta use hip-hop style, you can edit it, you can change it, you can put two together, here's some stuff."

So I got three tapes from him over a two-and-a-half-month period and this guy is a genius; I got real respect for him. He gave me so much incredible music by the end that I couldn't use it all; it would have drenched the film in music. But he taught me to adapt to his style in the same way Neil did. Neil said, "I really want to play right to the picture," and RZA style was, "This is the way I work, hip-hop style, you gotta play with them, you gotta play with them how you wanna." So I learned a lot from both of them in different ways. And RZA made beautiful, beautiful music for the film.

QUESTION 1: *What was it like working with Robert Mitchum in* Dead Man?
JJ: Robert Mitchum is an actor who does not like to improvise, and liked to have all of his dialogue in his hands a few days at least before shooting. I was

a little bit intimidated by him because, hell, he's Robert Mitchum, one of my all-time favourite screen actors. But he's a very self-effacing, really funny, intelligent man, and it was a real honour to work with him. But it was also very funny. He has a shotgun which is a prop in the scene. I knew he had some guns and thought he was maybe interested in them. So I got several vintage shotguns from the period for him to choose, put them in my car, and drove from LA to Santa Barbara where he lived, and went to his house.

His wife let me in and I laid out the guns on a carpet in the living room to let him come and look at the shotguns. He came in and said, "What the hell's this?" I said, "Well, I wanted you to choose the gun that you use in the film," and he said, "Why the hell should I care which one it is? You're the damn director!" I had spent a day going to the place, picking the guns, researching everything, and I said, "You don't care which one it is?" He said, "I gotta hold the damn thing in several scenes, right?" and I said, "Yeah," and he said, "Well, which one's the lightest?" [Laughter]

Also, when we were shooting that scene when he was talking to the three killers, he was basically in two positions: one leaning over the desk and one standing up. I kept shooting it with different lenses and different sizes. He got confused where we were picking up a certain section from and he said, "Well dammit Jim, was I in the receiving position, or was I fully erect?" I said, "You were fully erect," and he said, "Goddamn right I was!" [Laughter] What an amazing man I tell you.

QUESTION 2: *How were you influenced by Wim Wenders?*
JJ: I would not cite Wim Wenders as a particular influence any more than any other filmmakers whose work I like. Wim works in a different way and often prefers, I think, not to have a script at all and just start filming and then finding the story that way. That's not the way I work. I like his visual sense and a lot of things about his films, but I would not cite him as a primary influence. But he has inspired me and also helped me personally by giving me film material in the very beginning and being supportive. I have a lot of respect for him.

QUESTION 3: *What do you feel about films, such as* Four Rooms, Go, *and* Pulp Fiction, *which use the same structure as* Mystery Train?
JJ: I've only seen *Pulp Fiction* out of those three films, but I know that *Four Rooms* is very similar and people have mentioned *Go* to me. I guess I'm flattered in some way. I liked *Pulp Fiction*.

QUESTION 4: *What was it like working with Robby Müller?*

JJ: I loved Robby Müller's work and I asked Wim Wenders in 1980 how I might meet him. I was going to the Rotterdam Film Festival to show my first film, *Permanent Vacation*. At that time in Rotterdam the people who visited the festival stayed on a boat that was harboured there. It had a bar in it, and Wim said, "Just go on the boat and in the bar next to the peanut machine, Robby Müller will be sitting there."

So I went to Rotterdam, I went on the boat, I went in the bar, and next to the peanut machine Robby Müller was sitting there. [Laughter] Seriously. So I sat down next to him and started talking to him. And we hung out quite a bit at the festival and he saw my first film. He said to me eventually, "If you ever want to work together man, let me know." That was a big thing for me. I made my next film *Stranger Than Paradise* with my friend Tom DiCillo, because Tom was working then as a director of photography. But he really wasn't interested in shooting films, so when I wrote *Down by Law*, I immediately called Robby Müller.

The beautiful thing about Robby is that he starts the process by talking to you about what the film means, what the story is about, what the characters are about. He starts from the inside out, which is really, really such a great way. I've learned that you find the look of the film later after you've found the essence of the film, what its atmosphere is, what it's about. Then you look at locations together. You start talking about light and colour, about what film material to use and the general look of the film. We've worked together a lot now, so we don't have to discuss as many things as other people might because we understand each other.

He considers himself to be an artisan in a way. I remember, especially in *Dead Man*, the crew and I were joking a lot by saying, "He's Robby Müller, but don't tell him that!" He considers he has a lens, he has film material and he has light. Sometimes crew members would mention some modern piece of equipment, "We could do that shot with a lumacrane," and Robbie would say, "What is a lumacrane?" I think he's like a Dutch interior painter, like Vermeer or de Hoeck, who was born in the wrong century.

QUESTION 5: *A lot of your characters seemed to be touched by loneliness and melancholy, what draws you to that?*

JJ: My own loneliness and melancholy. [Laughter] It's part of life and I've always felt like an outsider in a lot of ways—I'm sure you can't imagine why!

But in the same way that I'm drawn to humour, miscommunication, and things that arise out of misunderstanding. All those things coexist, so I try to have them coexist in a character or in a film.

QUESTION 6: *A lot of characters in your films are foreigners. Do you enjoy seeing films through the eyes of the foreigner?*

JJ: It's several things. One is that America is made up of foreigners. There are indigenous people that lived here for thousands of years, but then white Europeans tried to commit genocide against them all. I'm a mongrel, I have Irish blood, bohemian blood, some German blood. All of America is a cultural mixture, and although America is very much in denial of this, that's really what America is.

And the other thing that attracts me is that I love to travel and I love to be in places where I don't understand everything culturally, or even linguistically, because my imagination opens up. I try to imagine things or understand, but I'm sure that I misinterpret them and misunderstand them. For me, it's imagining things that's a kind of gift I enjoy. You know when dogs don't understand something and they go like that? (cocks head on one side and takes an asking look) I feel sort of like that sometimes.

QUESTION 7: *How do you get funding for your films while retaining creative control?*

JJ: I'm really stubborn and I started out with an attitude that I was going to make films the way I and those people I chose to collaborate with want to make them and I've just stuck to that. I'm not seduced by money or the things that Hollywood tries to offer you, and in exchange you have to make the film the way some businessmen tell you to. I just would not be good at that. So I have a system where I try to avoid having American money in my films, because with that comes a lot of strings attached and script meetings and casting consultations. I can't work that way. I don't tell the business people who finance the films how to run their business, so why should they tell me how to make a film? I've been very lucky to find people to collaborate with in that way.

Since *Mystery Train*, JVC in Japan has been very supportive and has invested money in all of my films. Pandora in Germany has done the same. For the last two films, I've worked with BAC films in Paris. All of them, in my contract, I'm not even required to show them a rough cut of the film. I could just deliver them the finished film. But I do show them a rough cut because they respect me, so I respect them. And if they give me comments, I listen to them and sometimes their comments are helpful. But if they're not, I can discard them. I'm not obligated in any way to do anything they suggest.

It comes from stubbornness. I've walked out of a lot of deals where people were offering to finance a film under certain conditions. The Hollywood people are really shocked when you say to them, "I don't do it that way, I'm going to go now." They think, "Who does he think he is anyway? He doesn't want our money to make a film. People are banging on our doors to get us to do this and he's just going to walk out?" And I do, because I can't do it that way. I would end up in jail for kneecapping some guy in a $4,000 suit. And I'd also make bad movies that way. I'm not saying I don't make bad movies, but I make 'em bad in my own way! And when I get depressed about business things, I get a copy of Sid Vicious's "My Way" and turn it up to 11. Really it does your soul good.

QUESTION 8: *Do you have any comedic influences?*
JJ: Certainly, many. My favourite director of all time is Buster Keaton, and it goes deeper than just being a comedian, because he is a great director and actor and funny in an extremely human way. I like Charlie Chaplin, but he's not on the same level as Buster Keaton, who is someone really I have a deep respect for.

I love the Marx Brothers very much, although some of their films have shockingly racist things in them and things which disturb me. I know it's a reflection of the period, but their sense of comedy is incredible to me. I read an article about a guy who had cancer, who they said could not be cured. He watched Marx Brothers movies over and over, and his cancer went into remission and the guy says he owes it to the Marx brothers.

Lennie Bruce is important to me. I like To-To, the Italian comedic actor. I like Chris Rock. Sometimes I like George Carlin, sometimes Eddie Murphy. Richard Pryor was one of the great comedians. There is a film by Steve Martin called *All of Me* which is very funny; he can be very funny. There's a lot of funny cats out there. In the days before he was ever in a film, Steve Buscemi and another actor, Mark Boone Jr., used to perform in little clubs in the lower east side of New York, doing little two-man half-theatre half-comedy sketches that were really, really hilarious.

QUESTION 9: *Are you trying to get away from "The Jim Jarmusch Film"?*
JJ: I'm not really very self-analytical. I don't want to know what a Jim Jarmusch film is. I'm just a guy from Akron trying to learn films and I just move on to the next thing. It's not superstition in that case. It's not feeling comfortable looking backwards and the same in my life as well. I know Robert Altman and I know he likes to watch his old films over and show them to people. I wish I could be like that because he really loves them, he's proud of them, they're like his children. And my films are like my children, but I send them off to military school. [Laughter]

QUESTION 10: *In* Blue in the Face, *you play a man who is having his last cigarette. Were you trying to quit smoking yourself?*
JJ: Well, I hope I'm not a notorious smoker. [Laughter] I'm insulted. They approached me. Paul Auster had an idea about someone quitting smoking, and he asked me. I wrote most of my dialogue, but it was based on a conversation I had with him. As far as giving up smoking, films aren't really real, it's all set up. [Laughter] There's a camera there, those people aren't really doing those things.

QUESTION 11: *What happened to the project which fell through because of* Dead Man?
JJ: Parts of it were rewoven into *Dead Man,* so it's not something that exists that I'm going to do ever.

QUESTION 12: *How do you feel about* Dead Man *being banned in Australia?*
JJ: I thought it was very strange because they banned it for the scene where one character is getting a blow job at gunpoint. I don't know what they thought that meant, because the guy is walking through a town with a lot of skeletons and images of death and very negative examples of this civilisation's effect on the land. The idea that they might think that the film is condoning that was really strange, strange to me. I never thought that *Dead Man* was promoting going out and getting blow jobs at gunpoint. [Laughter]

QUESTION 13: *Why do you like Aki Kaurismäki so much?*
JJ: He's one of my favourite filmmakers. I love his films. I love the simplicity of them. I love the dry sense of humour of them. I love the bleakness.

Here is a filmmaker who uses limitations as a strength, and that's something I've tried to learn to do myself. I get very moved by Kaurismäki's films.

There's a scene in one, *Ariel,* where the guy meets a girl and they're in bed together having a cigarette after making love and she says, "Does that mean you will love me forever and ever?" and he says, "Yes." [Laughter]

East Meets West

CHRIS CAMPION/2000

CHRIS CAMPION: *Can you tell me where the initial idea for* Ghost Dog *came from?*
JIM JARMUSCH: I can't really because I did everything backwards. I started with a really vague idea, but wanting to work with Forest Whitaker was really the beginning. So I was trying to think of what kind of character I could make for the qualities in him as an actor that I liked. That contradiction he has of being both gentle and imposing. So it really started from there. I thought of a warrior character, but with a spiritual side so that I could get both aspects of him as an actor. Then the samurai thing became interesting to me. Unlike Western warriors, who trained just as warriors, Eastern warriors like samurai—or more particularly, Shaolin monks in China—are also priests and teachers. Although samurai are not priests, there is a spiritual depth to their training. So it seemed like an interesting thing. Then to make a kind of Don Quixote character who follows an ancient code that is not part of the modern world seemed interesting to me. I started collecting ideas, as I always do, and eventually I sit down and weave them together and see what the hell I've come up with.

CC: *Did the connection with RZA come later on?*
JJ: Well, I had imagined The RZA doing music for the film before I had even started writing it. But I didn't know RZA. Not until the film was shot and I

A shorter version of this interview was published in *Dazed & Confused,* No. 64, April 2000. Reprinted by permission.

had a rough cut did I find RZA and show it to him, meet with him and hoodwink him into collaborating on this. But somehow it worked out.

CC: *The story could almost come from one of the little episodic scenarios you find within Wu Tang Clan lyrics.*

JJ: Yeah, well it's interesting. I've loved the Wu Tang since they started. I love that mixture of things, like their interest in martial arts films. And it goes deeper into Eastern philosophy for them, and for RZA. I was talking with him a while ago and he said, "Y'know, I make my songs like little movies and you make your films like songs." So we found working together worked out very well. Even though we come from very different places, we understood each other's processes and our own philosophies meet somewhere as well.

CC: *It seems as if his music matched the pace of the movie and became more languid.*

JJ: Yeah, but it's deceptive because if you listen to RZA's instrumentals without the lyrics, they are languid sometimes. They have an edge to them but they're also very visually inspiring. There's a dream-like rhythm thing to them that is very unusual. RZA is one of the first guys too to start sampling strings and violins. Now everyone imitates RZA, which is why he is also now Bobby Digital. There's something very poetic and cinematic to his music without the lyrics. If you listen to Raekwon's "Ice Cream," which is the only old thing we used in the film actually, it's incredibly languid.

CC: *All the travelling footage at the beginning leads you into the film very slowly. Was that meant to invoke that dream-like quality, as if you're entering Ghost Dog's world?*

JJ: Yeah, it's not something I can say was calculated or intended. Jay Rabinowitz, my editor, and I started editing the material. We always try to listen to the material and have it tell us what it wants. It sounds odd but . . . There's some way not to bludgeon the material into your expectations or pre-designed thinking, but let it sort of speak to you. We liked this opening where you're introduced to Ghost Dog. You literally drop in on him from the bird's point of view, then you follow him on foot, stealing a car and driving into the night. It's sort of the world that he travels through to establish the film. If it were a studio film, they would not allow such a languid opening, to use your word, but we really liked it atmospherically just to let him move. There's a track by Killah Priest that he listens to. The lyrics are very strong and reflect a lot of the themes in the film. So we just played with that and let it go.

CC: *There's almost a comic book element to the film. Just like Wu Tang Clan create these alter-egos and identities, Ghost Dog has his origin story that you flashback to, like a traumatic event that caused him to follow this path?*
JJ: Yes, almost like "why is Batman who he is?" That's true, there is that element to it. But I didn't want to give a whole back story. Forest and I have one, but it's not for the audience. For me, sometimes it's too condescending to have to explain why someone is the way they are. So there's only really that flashback. So it is like a comic book structure in a way. We're given a glimpse of it and this is all we know. But we don't really know why he became a samurai, why he's fixated on this book, what changed him. There are little clues. There's a picture of a girl in his house that's part of our back story, but I didn't want to explain that. I just wanted to drop in on him and enter his world. We only get that little flashback, which happens twice and the two are different. In Ghost Dog's memory, this kid aimed a gun at Ghost Dog and Louie shot this other kid. But in Louie's flashback, the kid aimed the gun at Louie and he shot the kid. That's the Rashomon part of the story.

CC: *How did you first stumble across the Hagakure? And how did that help with the formulation of what* Ghost Dog *came to be?*
JJ: I had read some books before, not concerned with researching the film, just out of interest. I had read a book called *Code of the Samurai,* which is a book written by a samurai. And I had read *The Book of the Five Rings* and stuff like that. When I actually started writing the script [for *Ghost Dog*] a friend gave me *The Hagakure,* which was formally the most beautiful of those books because it's written in little aphorisms with a little symbol between each piece of text. The translation we have in English is very small compared to the actual book, which is 600 or 800 pages long. It includes information for a samurai on all levels, from the philosophical to the mundane. Like how you cook your food to how you build your house, how often you clean your armour or your sword. The funny thing was that the way the text looked in the book influenced the form of the film. There are symbols that separate each text in the book. In a way, the film is like the inverse of that where I use

the quotes from *The Hagakure* almost like those little separations. So it even visually and formally influenced the writing or the structuring of the film somehow.

c c : *Did that symbol that's used in the film come out of the book?*
J J : No, it didn't. I was already looking for symbols. And the one that's used in the film is one that Forest chose from a number of symbols that I had found.

c c : *Does the symbol he chose have a particular meaning?*
J J : Well, it has birds in a circle so it has meaning in terms of a cyclical sense of nature. But I'm not sure exactly whether that was like a family crest or what. They call those symbols "monsho." Sometimes they are family crests in Japan or identify certain allegiances and things like that. Doing some research later, I found out that the monsho of the pigeon is a messenger of the Shinto god of war. But [laughs] I didn't find that out until after we made the film.

c c : *Are you very much concerned with the details in your movies?*
J J : Yeah, I'm somewhat obsessive about the details. Even the colour of an ashtray in a scene, as well as anything that resonates through the film even as a small detail. The monsho that Ghost Dog wears is very important in that it identifies him as someone who is seriously inspired by another culture. I picked a number of them—with birds—and really wanted Forest to choose the one that he wore.

c c : *So that it would have some meaning to him?*
J J : Yeah, and to collaborate with him. I collaborated with him on things that were in his shack, in Ghost Dog's house. I chose a lot of books and then asked Forest which of them he thought Ghost Dog would have. I wanted him to collaborate as much as possible on those things that directly affected or described his character.

c c : *Do you generally let people build their own environments?*
J J : Well, no, not on their own. We always work together. There's a beautiful essay by Carl Dreyer, I can't remember what it's called, on furniture in film. He said, and I'm paraphrasing, "The less furniture you have, the more the

design of each thing you see is related to the character in the viewer's mind."
So even the kind of chair, or whatever else you see on a very simple set, will
have some impact on your feeling about the character who inhabits that
room. So I try and work really carefully, especially in this case with Forest. I
don't always do that with all actors. I do try to collaborate in some way with
all of them. Some details are things that we work on together so that they
feel they are their own and help define aspects of the character, like wardrobe
or any objects that they use.

C C : *Which film school did you go to, and did anything you learnt there help train
your technique in this direction?*
J J : It was NYU Graduate Film School. I studied literature at undergraduate
school in Columbia. Film school was problematic because a lot of things I
learned there, or was supposed to learn there, I found out that you have to
later fight against and erase from your memory.

C C : *In what sense?*
J J : A specific example was that I took an acting class because I wanted to
prepare as a director, theoretically. And I wanted to learn about how actors
prepare. The acting class was taught by an idiot, a guy who broke people
down emotionally in front of each other to, I don't know, manipulate them.
It was more a class in manipulation. I was so furious with that that I stopped
going to the class and complained both to the professor and the school itself.
Although, you know, I was just some student and they didn't really listen to
me. But it was really horrendous.

   Then there were other really good people. I had great teacher named Elea-
nor Hamerow, who was an editor and taught us how to think about a scene
in terms of shots and cuts which was really invaluable. There were also people who taught there who treated the information they had as if it was secret.
And you had to prove to them that you were on the right wavelength in
order to receive it, which I thought was pretty disgusting, really. But then I
also got to work with Nick Ray by going to film school and became his gofer
and assistant. I learned so much from him. So film school was a mixture of a
lot of really great things and a lot of nonsense that you either had to forget
about at the time or unlearn later.

C C : *Working with Nicholas Ray must have been a schooling in itself?*
J J : Well, I've been very lucky to be able to hang around with some people
that I really respect and would have learned from even if I'd never met

them—particularly Nick Ray, Sam Fuller, and Robert Frank, the photographer, people like that. To know and get to talk to and learn from them and discuss all kinds of things, not just about movies. I got some real gifts just having the chance to be around those guys.

cc: *How did you become involved with Nick Ray?*
JJ: Well, the head of the school was László Benedek—he's gone now but he directed *The Wild One*—and he was really helpful to me. It was a three-year programme and I went back after two years to tell László Benedek that I wasn't going to come back to school because I didn't have any money. He said, that's really unfortunate because I want you to meet someone I brought here to teach who I think you'll really like. It was Nicholas Ray. So I went into the other room and talked to Nick Ray for like half an hour and then he said, "You're my assistant!" László Benedek subsequently helped me get a fellowship to be able to come back to school—a Louis B. Mayer fellowship [laughs], the guy who destroyed Erich Von Stroheim's film *Greed*. So I did get to come back to school and worked with Nick mostly that year.

cc: *Was he actually in production with anything?*
JJ: No, but eventually he made *Lightning Over Water* with Wim Wenders and I was on set, assisting on Nick's side. He worked on that film and then he died.

cc: *Was that your first experience on a set?*
JJ: No, I had done other films here and there. I had done sound on Eric Mitchell's film *Underground USA* and had worked on a few other Super 8 films being made on the Lower East Side.

cc: *What kind of Super 8 films?*
JJ: I worked on another film by Eric Mitchell. One called *Red Italy*. There was a group of people that were really inspiring at the time. They had a place called the "New Cinema" which was a storefront. James Nares, who's an English painter but lives here, made some films back then. Also Amos Poe, Charlie Ahearn, Betty Gordon, Tim Burns. There were a lot of people that were making Super 8 films and showing them at this storefront. Charlie Ahearn made *Wild Style*, the seminal hip hop film, a few years later. Those people were really interesting so I was always trying to work on films with them anytime I could. This was 1977 through '79.

c c : *How did you first meet Samuel Fuller?*

J J : I don't remember. I think he first came to film school while I was there and then I kept meeting him all over the place with Wim Wenders, with Mika and Aki Kaurismäki. Then I would visit him if he was in Paris or New York and got to spend a lot of time with Sam.

c c : *A classic example of a director who wasn't appreciated in his own country but recognised and reappraised abroad.*

J J : Yeah, it's sort of sad. But in a way you can't worry about those things. I know that hurt Sam Fuller at times, emotionally, but at the same time he did what he did and you can't take that away. I'm always drawn to things, in my personal tastes, that are in the margins, not in the mainstream. The mainstream doesn't attract me so much. If you think about someone like Béla Bartók, who died pretty much in misery in New York with his music not being respected. Someone like Franz Schubert died impoverished and nobody cared at all about his music. Or William Blake—only the first book of his poems was published legitimately in his lifetime, and everything else he published himself in little pamphlets. Thelonious Monk said, "If I'm fifteen years ahead of things, it's not my responsibility to worry about that. I've got to do what I do. They'll either catch up to me or will never get what I do. It's not under my control." So Sam Fuller is Sam Fuller, and he left us these incredible gifts. It's sort of sad when people aren't respected in their time, but things do catch up. I mean, look at Vincent Van Gogh. Nobody gave a shit about him and now his paintings sell for $15 million or whatever. You can't worry about how people value things. I'm not that interested in time periods anyway, or in the delineation of things by boundaries, borders, nationalities, time periods. I find it kind of odd the way they categorise periods. Like you have the "beatniks," then the "hippies," "punks" and so on. It's all just waves. If you look at the ocean from above, you can't number the waves. They're all part of the same ocean and keep coming in, as they overlap and affect each other.

c c : *But history by it's nature has to be concrete.*

J J : It's compartmentalised.

c c : *You once said that* Stranger Than Paradise, Down by Law *and* Mystery Train *formed a trilogy. There seems to be a similar connection between* Ghost Dog *and* Dead Man *in that they both play with classic American genres.*

JJ: Yeah, there's two connections and, again, they're not conscious. I'm not analytical about my work. The obvious one is that they're playing with genres and allowing them to be departure points for something that maybe subverts them or uses them in a way that's not necessarily formulaic. The other thing is the theme of death being part of life. It's the cyclical nature of life that comes from aboriginal or Eastern philosophy, much more so than the Western or Christian philosophy of "behave in this world and you'll get a reward later." It's the idea that life and death are part of the same thing. Those two things connect *Dead Man* and *Ghost Dog*. Beyond that I don't know, and I don't really want to analyse them. Better to leave that up to someone smarter than myself who can explain it to me sometime.

CC: *It's almost as if you're deconstructing genres and rebuilding them in your own way.*
JJ: Well, I'm attracted to things in those genres, so I just take the things I'm attracted to and weave them into something of my own.

CC: *You've said in the past that you have a very European sensibility.*
JJ: I've said that? People always say that about my films. See, I don't know because America to me is a place of great denial as a country. For thousands of years there was indigenous culture and then white European culture came and took it over, basically. I live in New York which in a way is not part of America. In fact, I saw some graffiti on the Lower East Side a few months ago which said, "US out of New York!" which I like a lot. New York is a mixture of all kinds of cultures. I'm mixed up. I'm Irish and Bohemian. There's also some German and other things in my blood. Everybody's mixed, even white people. There's Asians, Muslims, people from everywhere, and that's what America really is. But America doesn't want you to think that way because when you watch TV, it's all white people. Then there's one or two black shows, with just black people, who don't interact with anyone else. That's not the world that I live in, so it just seems very odd to me. Fifteen years ago people used to joke about New York being the cultural capital of Europe. So there's a lot of inspiration from Europe in New York, but also from Asia, Africa, and all kinds of places. The reality is that's true all over America. In New York, it's just more visibly obvious. I'm also interested in all kinds of different cultures within America—pop culture and especially music. Music coming from blues, jazz, R&B, rock 'n' roll, funk, and hip hop—that's the most beautiful gift, in a way, that America has given the world. But I also

love other cultures—Japanese culture, obviously European culture, India, China. I'm really interested in Aboriginal cultures and they're philosophies. I'm very drawn to those, which somehow seem very pure. They seem to understand things that we have either lost or ignore. So anything that you take from another culture that goes into your heart, or your soul, part of it becomes part of you. And I want those things to enter me, the things that move me. I want to learn from them and incorporate them somehow into my life. Consequently, they find their way into my work, somehow—again, I'm not analytical about how, where, or why, I'm just happy that they do. There's funny cycles too that I'm getting off them. For example, I was drawn to a lot of so-called Hollywood directors like Fritz Lang, Douglas Sirk, and Billy Wilder—they're from Europe, right? But when I read about the French New Wave directors who were writers like Rivette, Godard, and all those guys, they lead me to Nicholas Ray and Sam Fuller in a way. So it's a weird circular thing.

c c : *Was it an ambition of yours to become a filmmaker when you first went to New York?*
J J : No, I had no idea. I studied literature. I got to go to Paris for a semester from Columbia and ended up staying there for like ten months. I didn't go to school much there but ended up going to the Cinémathèque almost every day. I was so amazed at the variety of films in the world that even in New York I wasn't really aware of. I was aware of a lot of things in New York that I wasn't aware of in Akron, Ohio. But then the Cinémathèque was amazing to me. Then I worked as a musician in New York. I didn't really know what to do. I loved the form of film and the idea of making them but I had never done anything like that. I applied to graduate film school on a whim, because I had no money and hadn't made any films. I submitted a lot of writing that I had done. They accepted me into the school on financial aid because I guess they wanted to balance out the students with some potential writers. It was a big shock to be accepted on financial aid because, believe me, I didn't expect it would happen. I started attending and there were a lot of interesting people there like Spike Lee, Tom DiCillo, Sara Driver. Susan Seidelman had been there a year before.

c c : *What kind of films did you see at the Cinémathèque?*
J J : Oh, films from India, films from China, a lot of Hollywood films that I wasn't that familiar with—by people like Sam Fuller and Douglas Sirk—a lot of classic French and Japanese films.

c c : *So you spent all your time there?*

J J : Pretty much, then I came back and found I had a lot of incompletes in my classes because I hadn't really been attending them [laughs]. But it was OK because, man, I saw so many amazing movies. Henry Langlois, the guy who ran the Cinémathèque, was still alive back then.

c c : *Were you given a good grounding in being self-sufficient as a filmmaker?*

J J : In film school? No, you were pretty much guided towards one function. My thinking of it in a more open way came from music and the whole punk rock scene, because the whole idea was that you didn't have to be a virtuoso if you had something to express. You could express it in a crude or slightly-damaged sounding way, but it was what you wanted to say. Then there were people like the New Cinema people I mentioned, including Amos Poe, who had by then made *Unmade Beds* and *The Foreigner,* which were two really guerrilla/street/punk films. He and Eric Mitchell were very inspiring to me. They were always like, "Jim, when are you going to make your first feature film? C'mon!" So I made my first film in 1979, *Permanent Vacation,* which was inspired by those guys. That was more valuable in a way than film school.

c c : *What were you doing as a musician?*

J J : I was in a band that played a lot in New York clubs. [sheepishly] I'm not going to say the name. I played a primitive Moog synthesiser that I could patch other sounds through. This is pre-sampling. I played oddly-tuned guitars and shared vocals with the guitar player in our band. For some reason, we opened a lot for English bands like Echo & The Bunnymen and the Psychedelic Furs, and a band called Blurt—I don't know what happened to them [laughs]. We played a lot in New York. We weren't getting rich but we were playing pretty steadily.

c c : *Was this around the time of Television and Teenage Jesus & The Jerks?*

J J : It was a little bit after. It was more like 1979 through '82.

c c : *Did you know all those people?*

J J : Yeah, I did. I wasn't that close with Television, but I knew a lot of those people like the Ramones, the Voidoids. I knew Johnny Thunders, Debbie Harry. Everyone sort of hung out together at CBGB's and Max's Kansas City.

c c : *So you were leaning towards a career in music?*

J J : Well, music to me had been the most beautiful form of expression and still is. I still get the most inspiration from music. Music has always been, I don't know, really in my soul. I was not a trained musician. I was one of those "semi non-musician" musicians at the time [laughs] so I don't know how serious or forward-thinking I was then, or even am now. But I loved music and really loved playing, but once I started making films . . . There were other factors involved, like our band falling apart, so I just continued focussing on filmmaking.

c c : *So John Lurie and Tom Waits appearing in your films was a natural progression from hanging out with musicians?*

J J : Yeah, more of my friends certainly were musicians than film people and probably still are. Although, I know a lot of film people now that are close friends, like Aki Kaurismäki, Claire Denis, and Roberto Benigni. But the majority of my friends are still musicians.

c c : *What made you cast Screamin' Jay Hawkins in* Mystery Train?

J J : When I grew up in Akron, they used to play "Put a Spell on You" a lot on the AM radio stations I used to listen when I was a young teenager. This was long after it had first been released, but they still used to play it a lot. There was something about that song that was magical. I tracked Screamin' Jay down and at the time he was living in a trailer in New Jersey. I found him and met him. That was when I first used the song in *Stranger Than Paradise.* Since I knew him, I asked him a few years later if he would be in *Mystery Train.*

c c : *Did you write the part for him?*

J J : Yeah. And he agreed to do it so . . .

c c : *And how was he?*

J J : Oh, he was great. What a great character. What a wonderful man. He was living in Paris recently but I've been trying to call him and his phones are all disconnected. It happens every year. Once I find him then I lose him for two or three years, then I find him again. I don't know where he is! He was living in Japan for a while, then France.

c c : *He still takes life as it comes?*
J J : Definitely, yes. You never know where he's going to be next.

c c : *Were you able to just train the camera on him and let it run?*
J J : Well, y'know he hadn't acted before, so we talked a lot. At first he was very unused to the idea of being filmed like that. He would stop in the middle of a take while we were still rolling, turn to me and say [adopts haughty Hawkins voice], "How was that?" Finally I told him, look, this is like being in the recording studio. It's like you're laying down another track now, so you gotta go all the way through. And he said, "Oh, I understand." And he understood completely. But he was a lot of fun to work with.

c c : *This is a little off track, but there's something that runs through your films, which is the idea of travelling—going somewhere and arriving in strange, alien environments. Is this something that you've experienced?*
J J : Well, I sort of felt like an alien growing up in Akron.

c c : *Why was that?*
J J : I don't know. Everything seemed so predictable there. Everyone's father worked for the rubber company, including my own. I thought the world was very enclosed until I was a young teenager and realised, "Wow, there's a whole other world out there." When I did leave Akron, at seventeen, I went to Chicago for a while, then New York and got to go to Paris through school. I think travelling really opened up my imagination. The less one knew about a culture, or even the language spoken, the more one's imagination seemed opened. So I've always loved moving though places and cultures that I don't completely understand. And that can even be some other city in America that has things about it you are not familiar with. I'm not really sure how to analyse myself in that way, but I really love travelling. I love being in places where I don't have roots or don't know what is predictable.

c c : *You must have travelled considerably more since you started making films?*
J J : I have but there are places I haven't been to. I haven't been to Africa or India. I haven't spent much time in South America. I haven't been to Asia much, although I have been to Japan about eight times. There are a lot of places I would like to go.

cc: *Do you travel outside of work-related commitments?*
JJ: I try to. I love road trips. I love driving. I love just escaping from New York and heading for somewhere.

cc: *Do you plan those trips?*
JJ: I prefer not to. Sometimes I have a destination in mind to go visit some-one or see friends. Sometimes not though, which I really love. I need that now because I've been working on promoting *Ghost Dog* since last May [1999] when it was in Cannes. I need a road trip.

cc: *Have you ever ended up anywhere totally strange that you didn't expect to find?*
JJ: Yeah, some strange towns in the States. In Europe too, I've ended up in some small places where I didn't really know where I was. I've never been any place really foreign. Japan is the culture most difficult to comprehend. But I've been there so much that I'm starting to, on some minor level, under-stand some things about it. I think visiting somewhere like China would be interesting. But I really want to go to Africa.

cc: *Anywhere in particular?*
JJ: Well, I have a really close friend called Louis Sarno who lives with the Babenzele so-called "pygmies" in the Central African Republic and they're also in the Congo. He wrote a book about them called *Song From the Forest,* and he's just finished writing another one. He's lived with them for nine or ten years, speaks their language, and understands their culture. He's really a musicologist and records their music. I'd love to go and visit him and these Babenzele so-called "pygmies," and maybe make a film there, I'm not sure. They're really amazing musicians. It's vocal stuff with really limited instru-ments—drums and sometimes this kind of a harp. Their vocal stuff is incredi-ble. It's almost akin to yodelling—in that their voices break—but it's very elegant, complex and really particular. When Louis Sarno was first recording musicians in Africa they would tell him, our music is good but the real music is with the pygmies, you've got to hear them. So the closer and closer he got, people kept telling him the same thing. When he finally found them, he fell so in love with their music and their culture that's he's lived there for ten years.

c c : *So they're almost entirely cut off from the rest of the world?*

J J : Yeah, especially in the Congo. They've never even seen gasoline pow-ered vehicles. You have to get there partially by boat and canoes. But it's changing so much with the logging companies which is kind of sad. His books deal with that. They're the only people that really live in the rain forest. Other tribes and other people often live on the edge of the rain forest but don't know how to survive in the rain forest. And they regard the pyg-mies almost as half spirits, half humans, because for thousands and thou-sands of years they have known how to exist in the rain forests.

c c : *Did you in any way identify with the Japanese characters from* Mystery Train *that arrived in Memphis on the train? And their excitement and curiosity at arriving at this kind of holy place?*

J J : Yeah, they're kind of on a religious pilgrimage. Well, I'm sure there's parts of me in them but I don't know how to analyse it. I'm not a fanatic about pilgrimages although I certainly went to Graceland, and when I was in Japan, I went from Tokyo to Kamakura to go to the grave of the film director Ozu. So I've done a few things like that before certainly.

c c : *Did those trips have any spiritual significance for you?*

J J : Well, y'know, all things that move you become part of your spirit, so I guess there's some kind of connection. If something's important to you or has given you some gift or enlightenment on some level, whether it's Carl Perkins or whoever, then those things do have some spiritual significance, I guess.

c c : *When you were living in Ohio, what first drew you to the city?*

J J : Well, an older brother of a friend of mine, we found in his room when we were young teenagers books by William Burroughs, Rimbaud, records by the Mothers of Invention and Captain Beefheart. We were like, "Wow! There's other stuff besides what's here in Akron." Our minds were opened up so wide and so fast by these things. And we'd secretly pass around books by William Burroughs, when we were fourteen years old and didn't want our parents to know we were reading "Junkie." It really opened things up. From that point, I realised, "I don't have to live here my whole life. There's a whole world." I don't know why I got drawn to New York rather than California but I did. And I'm still there. At least for the time being. I love things about

New York, it's always changing. But I love cities in general, they're almost like different lovers you've had.

c c : *There's that clash of cultures in the city, with different smells and sounds in every neighbourhood.*
J J : Oh, for sure. Like, where I live now, if I walk outside there's Sicilian Italians, Dominicans, there's Puerto Ricans, Hasidic Jews, black, white, Chinese. In Akron, I never heard salsa music. Just never heard it, because everything is segregated and suburbanised. In New York, it's all there, concentrated. The energy is really exciting to me.

c c : *Where was Ghost Dog's neighbourhood set?*
J J : I didn't want the film to tell you where it is. It's just supposed to be an eastern urban area that's not really identifiable. We actually shot mostly in Jersey City because it looks very unrecognisable. It could be Cleveland, Philly, Baltimore, or New York somewhere, but it doesn't look like Brooklyn and not like Manhattan at all. I like that look that's hard to place.

c c : *I liked the idea that all the Italian mobsters have their nice detached houses in the suburbs but congregate in this dingy social club.*
J J : Actually, it's the back of a Chinese restaurant. Which is a joke on the fact that they don't even meet in an Italian restaurant. Things are changing so much around them that they are, in a way, an anachronism.

c c : *You still see these ethnic social clubs—like an archaic men's club—don't you?*
J J : Yeah, and there is one scene where they're in a club like that. I lived for a long time, late '70s to mid '80s, right across from the Ravenite Social Club, which was the Gambino Family social club. So I saw those guys—John Gotti, Sammy The Bull, Neil Dellacroce, before he died,—all the time on the street in my neighbourhood. In fact I had a strange encounter with them once with Tom Waits. It's sort of a long story. Tom had this big Cadillac that was being repaired, so they gave him a loan car—a little Honda Civic, which was driving Tom nuts because he likes big cars. We were on Mulberry Street and were blocked by some big Lincolns that were in front of the Ravenite Social Club. Some wiseguys were talking to a guy in one of those cars and we were behind them. Tom, who's a hothead, started honking the horn and screaming out the window, [adopts Waits growl] "Let's move along here! We got to

drive through." I was like, "Tom shut the fuck up! Let them alone. That's the Gambinos!" He's not listening to me and getting all upset. So this thousand dollar suit guy walks over to us, really slowly, leans in the car and says, "You got a problem here?" And Tom shouts, "Yeah, I got a problem! I want to drive through here. The light's been red, green, red, green, ra, ra, ra!" And I said, "It's OK, man. We're cool. Take your time." Tom blurts out, "Take your time!" The guy just looks at me, sort of smiles, and says, "I'll ask him to move." He walks back really slowly, talked for a little while longer. All the while, Tom's honking the horn. Finally we drive by and Tom gives him some gesture. And I thought, "Oh, Jesus!" It was right in my neighbourhood, but we didn't get shot or anything. Later I got it into his head, "Y'know, that's the Mafia, Tom." And he's like, "Oh, really? You should have told me!"

INDEX